Crime and Its Social Context

SUNY Series in Deviance and Social Control
Ronald A. Farrell, editor

Crime and Its Social Context

Toward an Integrated Theory
of Offenders, Victims, and Situations

Terance D. Miethe
Robert F. Meier

State University of New York Press

Published by
State University of New York Press, Albany

© 1994   State University of New York

For information, address State University of New York Press,
State University Plaza, Albany, NY, 12246

Production by Cynthia A. Lassonde
Marketing by Theresa Abad Swierzowski

Library of Congress Cataloging-in-Publication Data

Miethe, Terance D.
      Crime and its social context : toward an integrated theory of
offenders, victims, and situations / Terance D. Miethe, Robert F.
Meier.
            p.   cm. — (SUNY series in deviance and social control)
      Includes bibliographical references and indexes.
      ISBN 0–7914–1901–0 (HC : acid-free paper). — ISBN 0–7914–1902–9
(PB : acid-free paper)
      1. Criminology.   2. Criminal behavior.   3. Victims of crimes.
I. Meier, Robert F. (Robert Frank), 1944– .   II. Title.
III. Series.
HV6018.M54   1994
364—dc20   93–24503
                                                                                    CIP

10 9 8 7 6 5 4 3 2 1

To Nancy and our boys, Zachary and Alex.
T. D. M.

To Inez, who seemed to live everyone else's life
including, thankfully, mine.
R. F. M.

CONTENTS

TABLES AND FIGURES

PREFACE

Criminologists have long studied criminals but seldom their crimes. More recently, criminologists have turned their attention to crime victims but, again, not to the criminal acts that begin the victimization experience. We propose that the criminal act, not criminals or victims, is the appropriate dependent variable of criminological investigation. This is not a new idea, but it has become strangely lost in recent decades as most scholars have worked to explain aspects of offenders or victims. A social explanation of crime necessarily requires attention to offenders and to victims, but it can never be complete without a sense of the context in which criminal acts take place.

Our approach to crime recognizes the importance of both criminals and victims and the facilitating context that brings them together. This combined interest in criminals and victims represents, for lack of a better term, an integrated approach to crime.

The present work was motivated by our discovery that theories of criminality (emphasizing why offenders do what they do) and theories of victimization (emphasizing why particular persons become crime targets) have not been considered jointly in a theory of crime. Through our investigations, we noticed that neither an offender nor a victim perspective in isolation considers what the other regards as essential. Theories of offender motivation ignore how the routine activities and lifestyles of ordinary citizens create opportunities for crime, and theories of victimization ignore the social, psychological, and structural factors that generate offender motivation in the first place. The goal of the current study is to demonstrate, empirically and conceptually, the importance of integrating both sets of factors into a single perspective.

We have benefited greatly from our personal associations with collaborators and others whose thoughts on crime and social processes have, in some cognitive sense, become part of our own. We would like to thank in particular David McDowall, Michael Hughes, Mark Stafford, Gary LaFree, Colin Loftin, Kenneth Land, Gil Geis, Jim Short, Jack Gibbs, Charles Tittle and Marshall Clinard. We would also like to thank Ronald Farrell and the reviewers of this book: David Cantor, Jim Lynch, and Chris Birkbeck. Their suggestions were very helpful in revising the manuscript, although we are entirely responsible for all errors that remain.

The work reported here represents several years of research and was greatly facilitated by a grant from the National Science Foundation that enabled collection of much of the data. We appreciate the contributions of Laurie Janajreh in the data-collection phase of the research.

Finally, portions of this book were derived from previous reports of this research, as follows:

Portions of chapter 3 were derived from Robert F. Meier and Terance D. Miethe, "Understanding Theories of Criminal Victimization," *Crime and Justice: A Review of Research*, Vol. 17, 1993, edited by Michael Tonry, University of Chicago Press.

A portion of chapter 5 was reprinted from Terance D. Miethe, "Citizen-Based Crime Control Activity and Victimization Risks: An Examination of Displacement and 'Free-Rider' Effects," *Criminology*, 1991, 29(3):419–431, American Society of Criminology.

Portions of chapter 7 appeared in Terance D. Miethe, Michael Hughes, and David McDowall, "Social Change and Crime Rates: An Evaluation of Alternative Theoretical Approaches," *Social Forces*, 1991, 70(1):165–185, Southern Sociological Society.

Portions of chapter 9 are derived from Terance D. Miethe and David McDowall, "Contextual Effects in Models of Criminal Victimization," *Social Forces*, 1993, 71 (March): 741–759, Southern Sociological Society.

We gratefully acknowledge the permissions of authors and publishers to use this material here.

Introduction to
the Study of Crime

Crime has been a major social problem in the United States for decades, but an understanding of the conditions that cause or prevent it has seemingly not increased over the years. In criminology a strong historical tradition has focused on criminals and their motivation for crime, and a newer line of inquiry on victims and the conditions that expose them to risk of crime. It is now time to recognize the ways in which these perspectives enhance each other in explaining criminality. Tentative work has been done in this area with the recent concern over theoretical integration (e.g., Messner, Krohn, and Liska 1989), but that work has been limited to explorations of integration among theories of criminality, rather than integration of the larger offender and victim traditions. It is this latter topic that is the subject of this book. We attempt to explore the feasibility of integrating models of crime that involve both offender and victim variables. It is a simple approach, but sometimes the simpler ideas are the better ones. At least, that is what we argue here.

WHAT IS TO BE INTEGRATED?

This book is about crime, but to get there we need to talk about criminals, victims, and the situations that bring them together. Criminologists have studied each of these dimensions of crime, but not within an integrated framework. Theories exist for each dimension, but there is no literature that brings them all together. This is understandable, since it is unrealistic to expect a single theory to encompass all of this complexity.

The Criminal Motivation Tradition

Criminologists in the 1940s understood crime only as the activity of criminals. In order to understand crime, one had to study criminals and the social context in which they acted. Simple enough. But in the 1960s some criminologists began to understand that victims and their social context were also important. The earlier, traditional viewpoints treated the motivation of the offender as the linchpin to understanding why some persons, but not others, committed crimes. This is a line of scientific inquiry that still occupies much time and energy in contemporary criminology.

Numerous theories have been developed to account for criminal motivation and the distribution of crime. Individual-level theories emphasize how the biological composition and psychological attributes of some individuals increase their criminal propensities (see Wilson and Herrnstein 1986). Rational-choice and learning theories stress how the subjective utilities (i.e., expected rewards minus expected costs) of alternative actions determine the choice of criminal or conventional solutions to the problems of everyday life (see Cornish and Clarke 1986; Akers 1987). Social bond theory (Hirschi 1969) locates the cause of crime in the weakening of bonds to conventional institutions, and cultural deviance theories (e.g., Sutherland 1947) claim that crime is an expression of cultural conflict, normative dissension, and peer associations. Macro-structural theories of crime emphasize how high crime rates are a consequence of economic inequality, unemployment, anomie, population mobility, heterogeneity, and weak institutional control (see Merton 1938; Shaw and McKay 1942; Blau and Blau 1982). Empirical support can be found for each of these apparent sources of criminal motivation.

The Opportunity or Victimization Tradition

Regardless of what is known or speculated about crime, there is one central fact: risks of victimization are not randomly distributed across social groups. Based on data from the U.S. National Crime Survey (NCS), victimization rates for violent predatory crime (e.g., robbery, assault) are higher among persons who are male, younger (16–24 years old), black, never married or divorced, unemployed, poor, and live in central cities. For property offenses (e.g., burglary, auto theft), demographic differences in victimization risks are generally similar to those for violent crime. Various explanations for these differential risks of victimization have been proposed.

Criminologists have long been interested in the role of the victim as a contributory agent in the genesis of crime. However, it has been only in the last two decades that systematic theories of victimization have been developed. Although alternatively called a "routine activity," "lifestyle," or, more generally, "criminal opportunity" approach, each of these recent theories highlights the symbiotic relationship between conventional and criminal activities. From this perspective, routine activities of law-abiding citizens that increase their exposure to risky and dangerous situations, decrease the level of self-protection or guardianship, and enhance their perceived value or attractiveness as crime targets provide physical opportunities for criminal acts and increase individuals' risks of victimization.

A fundamental assumption underlying current victimization theories is that offenders exercise a degree of rationality when selecting crime targets. Although this "reasoning criminal" (Cornish and Clarke 1986) is constrained by the limits of time, ability, and the availability of relevant information, offenders are assumed to select particular targets that have high subjective value and low expected costs. Once offenders decide to engage in crime, a wide array of victim characteristics and situational factors are presumed to influence the process of target-selection (see, for review, Cornish and Clarke 1986). To understand the social and spatial distribution of crime, current theories of victimization place primary importance on the role of routine activities and lifestyles of potential victims in creating the physical opportunities for offenders to express their criminal intentions.

The Social Context

It is a truism that crime requires both offenders and victims (or targets) and situations or social contexts that unite them. Crime rates and individuals' risks of victimization vary widely by social context. This social context is a micro-environment that has physical and social dimensions. The importance of the social context is immediately recognized by the fact that crime is simply more common in some environments than others. Geographical areas (i.e., standard metropolitan statistical areas [SMSAs], cities, census tracts, neighborhoods, city blocks) with greater population mobility and heterogeneity and lower economic opportunities are generally associated with higher rates of criminal victimization. Within each of these aggregate units, individuals' risks of victimization may vary according to their routine activities and lifestyles, their proximity to "hot spots" for crime (see Sherman, Gartin, and Buerger 1989), and the crime-control activities of the residents and their immediate neighbors. On the other hand, several authors (e.g., Lynch 1987; Miethe, Stafford, and Long 1987; Sampson and Wooldredge 1987) suggest that the impact of various crime-enhancing factors may be dependent on the particular social context. High rates of nonhousehold activity or low levels of safety precautions, for example, may be detrimental to individuals' risks of victimization only in areas with high proximity to motivated offenders and a rich criminal opportunity structure. Alternatively, the oppressiveness of many geographical areas is so pervasive that all residents, regardless of their personal lifestyles and routine activities, may be equally vulnerable to victimization. As these examples illustrate, the social context is important for a full understanding of crime because crime does not occur in a vacuum, and this micro-environment may determine how other factors influence individuals' risks of victimization. A major purpose of the current study is to examine this basic relationship between crime and its social context.

The Union of Offender, Victim, and Context

There are several necessary conditions for the occurrence of predatory crimes (i.e., crimes that involve direct contact between a victim and offender). Lofland (1969) recognized that these criminal acts and other forms of deviance require at a minimum facilitating "places," "hardware," and "others." From this perspective, a murder is impossible without (1) the union of an offender and the crime target in time and space (place); (2) a physical weapon or other instrument of death (hardware); and (3) a victim, especially one lacking protection from bystanders who may thwart the attack (others). In contrast, the basic premise underlying a routine activity approach to victimization (Cohen and Felson 1979) is that structural changes in activity patterns influence crime rates by affecting the convergence in time and space of three elements necessary for predatory crime: motivated offenders, suitable targets, and absence of capable guardians. Although other authors may not explicitly mention these conditions, all previous studies share the basic assumption that predatory crime is impossible without an offender, a victim, and a facilitating environment.

The fact that predatory crime requires, at a minimum, the convergence of potential victims and offenders in a social context is true by definition. However, what is less obvious is that most previous research has ignored at least one of these necessary conditions. Specifically, traditional theories of criminality (e.g., strain, social bond, differential association) emphasize the sources and causes of criminal motivation, but are silent as to how the actions and characteristics of potential victims may impede or enhance the opportunity for criminal activity. On the other hand, theories of victimization (e.g., routine activity and lifestyle approaches) identify those factors that determine the selection of particular crime targets and enhance individuals' exposure to risky and vulnerable situations but pay little attention to the social forces that foster and promote criminal motivations.[1] Few studies have attempted to integrate these theories in the same model.

An integration of theories of criminality and theories of victimization is desirable for a number of reasons. First, predatory crime may be a minimal occurrence if social forces are present that decrease either criminal motivation or the availability of attractive targets. In other words, high levels of criminal motivation and an attractive opportunity structure for victimization may both be required for the maximum occurrence of crime. Second, target-selection factors and exposure to risky and vulnerable situations may explain only the differential risks of victimization for residents of geographical areas where socio-economic conditions are conducive to crime. However, the only way to evaluate such hypotheses is to include both measures of offender motivation and target-selection factors in the same empirical study. Third, as a form of model misspecification, failure to consider aspects of both criminality and target selection may dramatically alter substantive conclusions about the predictive power of each type of theory.

LINKING THEORY AND DATA

Theories of crime and victimization are usually far less precise than their counterparts in other social science disciplines (e.g., economics, psychology, geography). This lack of theoretical precision can be seen in several ways. First, even when stated as propositional inventories, criminological theories are rarely detailed enough to include the proper functional relationship among concepts or specify the relative importance of each component. According to differential association theory (Sutherland 1947), for example, are pro-crime definitions that are of longer duration more important than definitions that are more frequent or of higher intensity? Is commitment more important under social bond theory than involvement, attachment, and belief (Hirschi 1969)? Do these social bonds have linear or nonlinear effects on the likelihood of crime commission? According to current theories of victimization, are exposure and proximity to motivated offenders more influential than target attractiveness and guardianship in the selection of crime victims, and are the effects of these variables additive or multiplicative? Second, criminological theories usually do not explicitly specify their level of generality and the proper unit of analysis. For example, criminal opportunity theories of victimization do not specify whether they should equally apply to all types of predatory crime (even those involving intimates), explain both aggregate rates and individuals' risks, and account for both cross-sectional and longitudinal trends. When theories lack such fundamental details, they are basically unfalsifiable because any empirical observation can easily be construed as consistent with at least one component of the theory (see also, Garofalo 1987; Miethe, Stafford, and Long 1987).

Previous research on victimization and, to a lesser extent, criminality has been primarily descriptive rather than predictive. Much of the early American criminological research emphasized the physical mapping of crime trends across geographical units, and this tradition continues today. Over the last two decades, yearly estimates from the NCS data have been used to develop an alternative barometer of the extent and severity of the crime problem. As a result of these efforts, we are well informed about the relative risks of victimization for various social groups. The fact that persons who are young, male, nonwhite, and poor have greater vulnerability to violent crime than their counterparts is an empirical observation that is the basis for much theoretical inquiry. Unfortunately, most descriptive studies lack the strong theoretical grounding that enables the researcher to both make informed causal inferences and control for other variables that may mediate the observed relationships.

Even if theories of criminality and victimization were well specified, the limitations of available data create an enormous gap between theoretical concepts and their empirical indicators. The NCS projects, the major source of national data on victimization risks, are primarily designed to yield estimates of the prevalence of crime rather than to test criminological theories. Unfortunately, this emphasis is the fundamental reason why few measures of routine activities and lifestyles are included in the ongoing NCS series. Under such conditions, operationalization will be only marginally successful in developing indicators of each theoretical component, and demographic variables will have to be used as proxy measures for many of them.

Several major problems of inference occur when there are limited measures of theoretical concepts. First, models are misspecified by excluding relevant variables, resulting in potentially biased estimates of the net impact of the included variables. Second, the use of proxy variables in many cases leads to inconclusive findings. For example, a positive association between family income and victimization risks may represent the adverse impact of target attractiveness or greater exposure to risky environments outside the home, whereas an inverse relationship may be attributed to higher safety precautions among the more affluent or the impact of higher income on reducing individuals' criminal motivations. When there are inadequate controls for these other factors, it is impossible to attribute the net impact of family income to any particular source. Such problems continue to plague studies that rely on secondary data, both within and outside the discipline of criminology. The poor link between theory and data in most criminological studies should make our substantive inferences from empirical analyses cautious about the validity of current theories.

THE CURRENT STUDY

Crime requires both an offender and a victim, but criminological theory strangely neglects this elementary fact. The current study explores possible connections among offenders, victims, and facilitating contexts by testing an integrated model of crime that explicitly recognizes each of these elements.

The current study extends previous work by examining the predictive utility of both theories of criminality and theories of victimization in explaining aggregate rates and individuals' risks of predatory crime across different contexts. Using a variety of data sources (e.g. census data, NCS data, a city-wide telephone survey), we describe the social ecology of predatory crime within and across geographical units, identify individual-level factors associated with victimization risks, and test various hypotheses that are derived from current theories. Statistical analyses are performed to indicate the correlates of predatory crime, the inadequacies of models which ignore either aspects of criminality or victim-selection factors, and the influence of socio-economic conditions in the wider geographical area on individuals' risks of victimization.

There are four major questions underlying the current study. First, what are the major aggregate- and individual-level factors that account for variation in crime rates and individuals' risks of victimization? Second, are similar conclusions reached about the importance of target-selection factors and aspects of offender motivation across different types of predatory crime, units of analysis, and contexts? Third, does the integration of both elements of criminal motivation and target-selection factors advance our understanding of predatory crime beyond what is known from each theory treated separately? Fourth, how does the neighborhood context of routine activities and crime control influence individuals' risks of victimization? Do aspects of the wider geographical area enhance, impede, or have no impact on residents' vulnerability to crime? Answers to these questions will provide the basis for evaluating the explanatory power of criminological theories and their implications for public policy on crime prevention.

These questions will be addressed in the following chapters. Chapter 2 will describe the major theories of criminality. We focus on those macro-social theories that have been most widely used to account for variation in crime rates. Four major criminogenic factors (i.e., low socio-economic status, population mobility, ethnic heterogeneity, and single-parent families) are identified. We discuss the significance of each of these factors from various theoretical perspectives.

Recent theories of victimization and target-selection processes are summarized in chapter 3. Attention focuses on the similarities of various opportunity theories of victimization (i.e., routine activity and lifestyle approaches) and the predictive utilities of the major components underlying these theories (i.e., exposure to crime, proximity to offenders, target attractiveness, and guardianship). Chapter 4 presents an integrated perspective which unites aspects of offender motivation, victim characteristics, and the social context for crime. Chapter 5 describes the data sources that will be used to test theoretical propositions, and chapter 6 provides descriptive summaries of the social ecology of predatory crime, and the bivariate relationships among measures of theoretical concepts, crime rates, and individuals' risks of victimization. Subsequent chapters evaluate (1) the ability of criminality and victimization theories to explain crime rates in geographical areas (chapter 7), (2) the predictors of individuals' risks of victimization (chapter 8), and (3) the impact of individuals' routine activities and lifestyles on victimization risks as influenced by aspects of the wider social context (chapter 9). The final chapter discusses the implications of our study for future research on criminological theory and for social policy on crime control.

Theories of Criminality

Theories of criminality are theories of the *potential* of crime; that is, they are theories of the sufficient conditions that create potential offenders. People become offenders when, according to most theories, they are motivated to commit a crime. But there is an important conceptual difference between explaining criminality (i.e., involvement in sustained patterns of crime) and explaining crime (i.e., episodic offending or criminal events), and different theories might be required for each task (Hirschi and Gottfredson 1986). Theories of criminality have most often been concerned *not* with explaining a specific instance of crime but with explaining patterns of criminality (e.g., the current emphasis on criminal careers; Blumstein et al. 1986). Theories of victimization, on the other hand, have concentrated more on lifestyle patterns of victims to explain specific criminal acts. Put another way, most theories of criminality are not theories of crime because they do not directly link criminal motivation or inclination with the context of the criminal event. Why do specific crimes occur when and where they do? Only part of the answer can be attributed to the presence of motivated offenders. The victim's contributory role to the criminal context and the social ecology of crime is described in chapter 3. In the current chapter, we explore how aspects of criminality influence the context for crime. We look for common elements in all offender theories that could be incorporated into a larger, more integrated explanation of criminal events.

THEORETICAL LEGACIES

The search for theoretically meaningful contexts in which to explain crime must look back to the ideas of criminological ancestors and ahead to what may be new explanations that attempt to integrate theories of criminality with theories of victimization.

The Positivistic Heritage

Most theories in criminology are theories of offender behavior—primarily of the origin or restraint of criminal motivation. This viewpoint derives from positivistic approaches where the emphasis is on the isolation of factors that distinguish offenders from nonoffenders. This emphasis virtually defines positivism in criminology, although some use the term positivism to refer to a predisposition to look for "natural" causes of human behavior. Insofar as positivism is something shared by a wide array of thinkers in different disciplines examining crime, however, it cannot refer to anything but a commitment to finding in what way(s) criminals and noncriminals differ.

Most criminologists would agree that positivism does not refer to a substantive approach in the field; that is, it is not inherently psychological, sociological, or anything else. But positivism became conventional wisdom in criminology because it offered an empirical approach to studying offenders. Lombroso's lasting contribution was not to support a constitutional explanation of crime but to popularize a method of conducting criminological work that compared criminals with noncriminals to detect group differences. Once detected, Lombroso and subsequent positivists attributed causality to these factors and also identified these differences as the objects of intervention into criminal careers. Thus, if criminals were more likely to have certain physical features not found among noncriminals (stigmata), it was because of those features that they were criminals. Psychologists searched for mental differences (IQ, personality traits), psychiatrists for psychic differences (mental conflicts, early-life trauma), and sociologists for social differences (being raised in a single-parent household, peer group membership).

In this sense, even sociological theories are theories about why some individuals but not others are criminal. There are some perspectives, to be sure, that look not for individual but group differences in offending. These perspectives typically identify a correlate (e.g., economic inequality) of crime (e.g., murder) and infer causal processes from that association (Blau and Blau 1982). Such an approach, which derives strongly from the positivistic tradition, may use differences in crime or victimization rates to test hypotheses, but even in these structural approaches it is hard to resist the temptation to talk of individual offenders and their personal position in a system of economic inequality. Indeed, since crime is largely a personal kind of event that usually involves two or more people, it is virtually impossible to resist such a temptation. In the end, even structural theories imply there are individual offenders committing discrete (in time and place) acts that must ultimately be explained.

The Classical Heritage

Beccaria and Bentham, the major early proponents of a classical viewpoint of crime, believed that crime resulted from an individual computation of a hedonistic equation where behavior is oriented toward maximizing pleasure and minimizing pain. It might be assumed that the classical school of criminology was atheoretical, but that view is surely incorrect. If anything, the positivistic approach, not classicism, was atheoretical. Positivism was a method in search of content, while the classical school was content in search of a method. Because classicism has long been neglected for its theoretical content and because there appears to be a resurgence of interest in classical approaches, a few comments are in order.

The Roots of Modern Classicism Matza (1964), in a still much under-appreciated work that paved the way for what was later to be called control theory, was among the first to call attention to a central curiosity: crime required explanation, as though the rewards from crime were insufficient to account for this behavior. Sex, money, status, and revenge all seem like powerful motivators, but for Matza (1964) and Sykes and Matza (1957),[1] the trick was to look at the other side of the balance sheet to see how offenders were able to minimize the costs of crime by denying the harm or extent of illegality of their acts. In order to make such assessments, individual offenders had to engage in a conscious, deliberate exercise of weighing behavioral alternatives on the basis of their anticipated outcomes. It was on the basis of these decisions that adolescents "drifted" into delinquency, a term that denoted the temporary nature of criminal decisions. A subsequent reassessment, of course, would change the behavioral course in a more law-abiding direction. What Matza shared with positivistic writers was the concern, ultimately, to explain criminal acts by explaining offender behavior and offender motivation.

Rational choice and individual decision making. Matza's thinking was organized around the task of explaining the decision making and subsequent behavior of individual juvenile offenders. Later writers would refer to this process of weighing costs and benefits in constructing what has come to be known as the "rational choice" perspective of criminality. This perspective has been applied to various forms of crime (see Cornish and Clarke 1986), and it is not impossible to consider that virtually all crimes contain elements of rational choice. Indeed, it is the generality of the rational choice perspective that makes it so appealing. Crimes that are committed under emotional circumstances or because of physical dependency may also contain hedonistic elements (cf. Bennett 1986).

It is neither possible nor necessary to explore here the major conceptual flaws of rational choice theories, but two such flaws must at least be recognized. First, while all human action may reasonably involve elements of decision making, some persons are freer than others in the choices they make. To consider crime the single outcome of the hedonistic calculus grossly oversimplifies the nature of human decision making and makes moot what is perhaps the most interesting and important theoretical question in criminology: under what conditions do persons choose to commit crimes? Some answer this question in terms of learned criminal norms, others in terms of a lack of restraint. Still other theoretical perspectives may emphasize early childhood training, biological predisposition, or personality traits. To claim that persons in some sense decide to commit crimes does little to further our understanding of the conditions under which specific people make those specific decisions.

The second major flaw relates to the refusal or inability of rational choice theorists to define the term beyond a crude economic analogy. Even economists leave the meaning of the term vague (Gibbs 1989), so there is little use in referring to the notion of "utility." Presumably, a crime is rational if the actor perceives some benefit from the act and the benefit outweighs the consequences of getting caught and punished. But this is, at best, an obscure and conceptually unnecessary formulation since all criminals and other rule breakers, except the hopelessly mentally disordered, commit crimes out of perceived benefit and with a perception of reduced legal risk. Even kleptomaniacs, Geis (1974, 292) reminds us, seem to gain "astonishing control over their impulse when they notice a store detective about." To say that offenders commit crime for some reason that relates to their benefit does not tell us how offenders differ from nonoffenders (who also do things for their benefit) and from each other. In this sense, there is no variance to explain. Again, the really important questions are the conditions under which (1) some persons turn to crime at one time but not another and (2) some persons turn to crime while others refrain. The notion of rational choice, insofar as it refers to some anticipated level of satisfaction, fails to identify those conditions.

It is noteworthy that rational choice theories are consistent not only with their classical beginnings but also with the positivistic emphasis on offender-watching. Even the most recent versions of rational choice theory attempt to explain why persons come to want—taking into account costs and benefits—to commit crimes. Such formulations are clearly reductionistic, but any theory that has an emphasis on mental content as an antecedent to crime must necessarily be so. The contribution of rational choice perspectives is to rid the field of an implicit conception in positivistic philosophy that behavior is caused (determined) without intervening mental manipulation of the "causes." The effects of such external forces as living in a high crime area and being raised in a single-parent home must be translated, at the individual level, into illegal behavior and that requires some mental or emotional manipulation. Internal determinants, too, receive some kind of mental attention. Early childhood trauma or unresolved Oedipal conflicts, for example, must be processed somehow before being acted upon (what else does it mean that the conflicts are unresolved?). The idea that such forces are reciprocal (i.e., that crime influences the nature and extent of determinants) is consistent with individuals serving as mediating points in the causal process.

THE CRIMINAL AS A UNIFYING CONCEPT

Positivism came to dominate the criminological enterprise and classicism was relegated to the daily workings of the criminal justice system.[2] Regardless of philosophical derivative, criminological theories are united around the idea that the appropriate dependent variable of criminological inquiry is not the criminal act but the desires, or motives, of the offender. While textbooks inform us that classicism was interested in the crime, whereas positivism is interested in the criminal, even in classical theory offenders occupy a central place. It can be no other way as long as the focus is on mental states (e.g., rational choice, psychic trauma, stress from living in an anomic society, definitions favorable to violation of law, freedom from legal and social restraints) that are antecedent to crime.

There is no theory of criminality that is indifferent to the offender and most of these theories concern the offender's motivation. Control theory is sometimes thought to neglect criminal motivation, but there is perhaps more motivation (if such things can be quantified) in control theory than other theories put together; the only difference is that motivation is constant and does not vary as in other theories. In control theory, offenders are motivated to commit crimes either because of their tenuous relationship with social groups (Hirschi 1969) or their lack of "self-control" (Gottfredson and Hirschi 1990). Motivation is a central element in virtually all major sociological theories of criminality, whether they address crime from a micro- or macro-level frame of reference.

Micro-Level Theories of Criminality

Micro-level explanations of the origin or persistence of criminality explore the social processes involved in people becoming criminals. Micro-level theories attempt to trace the development of criminality in a specific person from times and places when they did not commit crimes (e.g., as a child) to times and places when he or she did (e.g., as a delinquent adolescent). Although micro-level theories may be called processual or social psychological, they are essentially offender-based theories with the task of accounting for the changes in a person; that is, micro-level theories ask: How did Joan or Joe become a criminal?

Often these theories focus on the nature of the interaction between individuals and other potential offenders or between offenders and agents of social control. Ironically, in either instance, the probability of criminality is said (for different theoretical reasons) to be increased.

Contact with Offenders   Contact with offenders, according to learning theories, increases the probability of having crime reinforced behaviorally (Akers 1987) or of acquiring criminal norms (Sutherland, Cressey, and Luckenbill 1992).[3] The relationship between delinquency and having friends who are delinquent is firmly rooted in criminological research; but the interpretation of this relationship is not agreed upon. Learning theorists attribute the relationship to the opportunity given the focal person to acquire criminal norms through a process of operant or social learning. Other criminologists have argued that the relationship suggests that delinquents—regardless of how they came to be delinquents—seek out other, like-minded persons with whom to hang out (Glueck and Glueck 1950).

A key component of learning theories involves explaining the development of criminal motivation that in turn generates criminal conduct. Those who have more contact with offenders under the right circumstances will have a greater chance of developing or enhancing criminal motivation. Sutherland's theory of differential association identifies the importance of frequency, priority, intensity, and duration as conditioners of the learning pattern (Sutherland, Cressey, and Luckenbill 1992, 89).

Evidence supporting learning theories of crime is almost compelling and much of it relates, one way or the other, to the powerful statistical effects of peers on most crimes and in most criminal careers.[4] The peer variable, in fact, may be the most powerful in the entire storehouse of criminological independent variables because it cuts across so many different types of crimes and ages of offenders. Theories that make peers central are, therefore, likely to be impossible to dismiss, even for the most individualistic crime because one can usually find peer influence earlier in that offender's life. Perspectives that do not make theoretical allowance for peers, on the other hand, must engage in considerable theoretical manipulation to either sidetrack the issue or explain away the effects.

Contact with Agencies   Another kind of micro-level theory is one that finds the context for crime not in criminal companions, but, ironically, in interactions with agents of social control. Contact with defining agencies, according to the theory of secondary deviation (Lemert 1951), is said to increase the probability that the individual will be excluded from "normal" social roles and interaction patterns, thus increasing the chances the person will find social support in deviant roles. The key is the interaction between the offender and agents of social control that results in the affirmation of criminal labels for the behavior and the attribution of a criminal social status for the offender. Unlike learning theories, criminals do not learn norms from such interactions but they do experience a forced status that places them outside the social mainstream. While crime is a status that is achieved through criminal activity within most criminological perspectives, it is an ascribed status in labeling theory; secondary deviants and criminals seem to have virtually no control over the reactions of others. In this sense, the interaction is particularly one-sided. Agents of social control are the powerful actors, criminals the passive recipients, of control definitions and decisions.

Creating Criminal Motivation   The key task for micro-level theories is to explain the development of individual criminal motivation which, in turn, generates individual criminal conduct. Those who have more contact with offenders or—depending on the theory—agents of social control will have a greater chance of developing or enhancing criminal motivation. One can presumably learn criminal motivation from others and, Sutherland excepted, perhaps from other sources, such as the mass media. The term "definition favorable to violation of law" is merely an element of the offender's motivation. The definition provides the substance of the motivation. One can also, because of the labeling process which excludes the individual from the assumption of normal social roles, become motivated as a result of being branded and regarded as an outsider. Other sources of offender motivation identified by micro-level theories include such factors as peer pressure, economic hardship, behavioral modeling, frustration, psychological disorders, thrill-seeking, "face-saving," and efforts to ward off status threats (see Cornish and Clarke 1986).

Macro-Level Theories of Criminality

Macro-level theories of criminality concentrate on structural features of aggregates or entire societies that are conducive to crime. Macro-level theories are also typically geared toward explaining group or community differences in crime rather than the behavior of individuals. While micro-level theories find the meaning of criminality in interpersonal relationships, macro-level theories seek causal antecedents in the structural features of larger aggregates, such as societies.

Most macro-level theories of criminality emphasize either crude correlates without an explanatory context (e.g., race, age) or specific causal arguments that relate antecedent variables (e.g., population density, home ownership) with criminality. Two of the most powerful structural explanations are control theory and social disorganization, and there are specific theories within each of these larger categories. Each of these perspectives is related to one another, and each treats crime as the inevitable consequence of certain structural conditions.

Social Structure as a Generator of Crime   Depending on the theory, social structure, or parts of it, either generates (Merton 1968) or restrains (Hirschi 1969) criminality. Strain theories, such as Merton's (1968) theory of anomie, assert that certain types of social structure— i.e., those in which values and norms are not well articulated and connected with one another—pressure certain groups away from conformity and toward criminality. Control theories such as Hirschi's (1969), on the other hand, assert that social structure may bond groups and individuals together to produce conforming behavior, thereby inhibiting crime.[5] In each instance, what matters is the nature of the relationship between individuals and the larger social structure of which they are a part.

These opposite predictions derive from different conceptions of socialization. Neither anomie nor control theories are "socialization" theories in the sense of learning to become criminal, but both theories begin with assumptions about socialization processes. Merton's strain theory makes sense only if persons in the anomic society are socialized to accept socially defined goals. That is, persons who do not desire (read, are not socialized) to accept society's values will not innovate to achieve those values. Likewise, Hirschi's control theory makes sense only if persons are socialized to a similar core of values. It is only after social bonds are broken or weakened that crime occurs as persons maintain their goal-directed activity. Put this way, strain and control theories sound similar. In each instance, offenders want what everyone else wants (socially defined values or goals, such as materialism). But for Merton, offenders are largely those who do not accept the culturally prescribed means to achieve those goals. For Hirschi, offenders are those who are freed from the social structural restraints that keep all people from using whatever means necessary to achieve those same goals.

These different explanations also share similar predictions about criminality. The theory of anomie predicts that criminality will be greatest among those who suffer the greatest strain, while control theory predicts that criminality will be greatest among those least well bonded with the larger society. In each case, criminality is predicted to be concentrated among the socially, economically, and politically disadvantaged—among those whose motivation for crime is presumably greatest or at least most socially understandable.

Social Structure as an Inhibitor of Crime   Control theory is usually conceived to be a social psychological perspective, but here we deal with its obvious structural features. Proponents of the theory claim that criminality is the result of social marginality—those whose bonds to conventional society are impoverished or broken are more likely to commit crimes than are those whose bonds are strong. Presumably, persons with weak bonds are those at the social periphery who have not reaped the largest rewards from the conventional social order. This idea that social structure can inhibit crime by increasing bonds to conventional society can be traced at least to the work of Durkheim. Similar ideas were expressed by Freud in *Civilizations and Its Discontents* (1930).

Theories that emphasize the inhibiting role of social structure assume that persons will naturally seek individual self-interest unless restrained by outside forces (e.g., Gottfredson and Hirschi 1990, 117). Restraint from crime is related to one's position in the social structure, but it is not related to a process of socialization whereby persons learn group norms and the sanctions for violating those norms. Rather, the impression that one gets is that offenders in these theories are unable to learn such simple dimensions of social life and therefore are unable to anticipate the consequences of lawbreaking. Such an impression, however, is mistaken if perspectives like rational choice theory (Cornish and Clarke 1986), control theory (Hirschi 1969), and self-control theory (Gottfredson and Hirschi 1990) are all essentially the same general perspective. Even if these perspectives are only in some conceptual sense compatible with one another, they each go to some length to emphasize

the ability of offenders to weigh future consequences of immediate conduct.

Social marginality can be defined in a number of ways, but we adopt
the position that social marginality is a function of occupying certain posi-
tions that place the individual at the perimeter of conventional society by
virtue of economic and social disadvantage. Marginal persons are more
likely to (1) be poor or have low income relative to others, (2) be members
of minority groups, (3) have high rates of family disruption (i.e., divorce,
children living with only one parent), and (4) possess low levels of educational attainment. Collectively, these measures appear to capture the
essence of groups of persons who have weakened bonds to conventional
society, as opposed to those with greater social and economic security.

TWO MAJOR PROBLEMS, SOME EXCEPTIONS, AND NEW DIRECTIONS

Criminologists have traditionally attempted to understand crime by
attempting to understand offenders. There are at least two dangers with
such a focus (neither of which is the subject of vigorous contemporary
debate): the first is an overemphasis on individuals and the resulting tendency toward reductionism; the second, the systematic neglect of the
larger context in which crime occurs (e.g., victims, places, and structural
influences on the availability of suitable criminal targets).

Reductionism

The positivistic tradition, from which most contemporary theoretical perspectives of crime derive, virtually dictates a strategy that demands an
understanding of offenders' biology, psychology, and social relations
because these are the "causes" of behavior. Even the classical perspective
of hedonism required an emphasis on offender-watching, although the
classicists never made the empirical link between a philosophical position
(that humans are rational, freely choosing actors) and a behavioral result
(crime). But if the classicists were contemplatively interested in offender
behavior because it generated certain legal responses—the real object of
the classical school's interest—they never approached the research commitment made by the positivists. Positivists, from Lombroso's beginning,
took offender-watching seriously and concentrated, as did the classicists,
on isolating causes of crime within the individual offender.

Sociologists later broadened the perspective to forces external to
the offender, but these external forces resulted in the same outcome as

the internal causes identified by early physicians and psychoanalysts: an individual who was in some sense determined or caused to act criminally. For example, the sociological attention on groups of offenders, such as in the early gang studies (Thrasher 1927) and community approaches (Shaw and McKay 1942), concluded that crime was not caused in individuals but that the forces were external to the individual. Indeed, for Thrasher, the cause of delinquency was natural; it grew out of common group-play experiences of youth. Similarly, Shaw and McKay examined physical dimensions of the urban space occupied by offenders. However, few sociological criminologists were able to completely counter a charge of reductionism without violating a fundamental, implicit premise of their perspective—namely, that to understand crime one must understand the individual offender. In this sense, it was the offender, not crime, that was the ultimate dependent variable in these theoretical schemes.

But if the reductionist nature of positivism was not very evident in all theories, it was inescapable in the policy inferences that flowed from them. To change gang delinquency, one needed to change gang members; to alter the pattern of biologically determined offending, one needed programs of social eugenics to breed out inadequate human stock; and to reduce burglary, one needed to reduce either the number of burglars or the causes that had produced them. Positivistic theories stress a deterministic view of offending, and such a view is largely incompatible with the dominant assumptions made in the legal system about individual responsibility. Yet, one of the main reasons that positivistic theories have been maintained so long is not that they provide concrete suggestions or technology for criminal justice change agents (e.g., probation officers), but that they direct attention to criminal individuals and make those individuals the object of public policy on crime. The legal system is simply not organized to address structural conditions and must, of necessity, limit its focus to individuals. So too do positivists, even those whose theories identify broad societal level causes of crime. In the end, the goal of most positivistic theories is to explain individual offending patterns.

Criminal Context

Crime, as all behavior, has a context. Context can be defined as a micro-environment with physical, interpersonal, and behavioral dimensions (Davidson 1989). Crime has a history of events that preceed it, a place where it occurs, a culture that defines it and conditions responses to it, and an ecology that reflects the distribution of offenses in time and among certain groups. Offenders are part of this context, but they are by no means the only part.

Criminologists have traditionally ignored the context of crime much beyond offenders. The reason for this neglect is that (1) the development of criminological theory has been associated with explaining patterns of offending, not the criminal act itself, and (2) crime, for the most part, does not seem to need much explaining. Sophisticated theories hardly seem required when one examines the content of most crime— petty thefts of nearby and convenient objects involving relatively little sophistication or planning. The neglect of rural crime can be explained in a similar manner. There doesn't appear to be much of it and criminologists are interested in where the "action" is—serious, predatory, repetitive crimes that are most often found in urban areas. To study patterns of offending (which are inherently more harmful than single, unrelated instances of crime), an explanation of the process whereby the offending continues is required. But such explanations sometimes neglect beginning points of behavior patterns, such as in the interactionist approach commonly called labeling theory. Labeling theorists are interested only in the origins of secondary deviance, the origins of primary deviance being either uninteresting or too familiar to require extensive explanation (Lemert 1982).

To date, there is no single theory of criminal context, except if one wishes to so designate perspectives on the ecology of criminality. However, even these perspectives are limited because they concentrate on the social ecology of criminals only. A more inclusive perspective would recognize that criminals are only one component of a larger equation, and that only the criminal act can unite disparate perspectives on criminals, victims, facilitating places, and structural generators and constraints.

The Crime as a Unifying Concept

There are some exceptions to the generalizations offered above, namely the now-extensive work on criminal victimization, the work done mainly in the 1970s on environmental influences and constraints affecting the occurrence of crime, and the recent concern over the importance of physical locations on crime (see Sherman, Gartin, and Buerger 1989). These latter efforts are notable because they are not easily integrated into the venerable (perhaps senescent) emphasis on explaining only offender behavior. For this reason, they remain somewhat outside the theoretical criminological mainstream. Yet, the occurrence of some behavior, like crime, requires a combination of the criminal actor and particular elements, including perhaps physical locale, certain kinds of people, equipment, and the like—what Lofland (1969) calls facilitating places, hardware, and others.

In addition to these necessary prerequisites for crime commission, the risk of crime also increases in the presence of other social, economic, and political forces. Criminologists have long been interested in various correlates of crime that place the activity in a web of larger influences, only some of which directly affect individuals. Economic pressures (Bonger 1916), a social structure that supports criminality by providing an opportunity to learn from other criminals and to reduce the risks of crime (Cloward and Ohlin 1960), a repressive political system that provides incentives for only the wealthy and otherwise powerful (Quinney 1980), and the strain of acquiring high aspirations that cannot be met in the marketplace (Merton 1968) or school system (Cohen 1955) all provide examples of structural forces that condition overall rates of criminality. The tension in such theories relates to the reductionistic comments made above; that is, the temptation to reduce structural forces to the individual offender level is virtually irresistible, even for committed Durkheimians. To explain crime sociologically is often insufficient since it is the behavior of individual offenders that must be related to the economic pressures, to the lack of legitimate opportunities, and to the debilitating effects of a middle-class dominated value system in schools.

Partly in response to these concerns, the focus on individual offenders does not characterize all theoretical efforts. Notable exceptions can be found in the recent attention given the social disorganization (e.g., Bursik 1988; Messner 1988) and anomie perspectives (Agnew 1992). The balance of this chapter focuses on a community perspective regarding crime. Subsequent chapters will provide perspectives on criminal victimization and will sketch an empirical integration of criminals, victims, and the social context of crime.

CRIME AND THE COMMUNITY

Social disorganization theory is often associated with a criminological yesteryear that attempted to explain a seemingly different criminological reality. Chicago in the 1920s and 30s is not the United States of the 1990s, and social disorganization theory has suffered severe theoretical attacks over the decades (e.g., Traub and Little 1985; Liska 1987), but the theory has remained credible (e.g., Sampson and Groves 1989). More than that, a careful assessment of the evidence suggests that a social disorganization perspective is both empirically and intuitively alive (Bursik 1988).

Communities are socially organized to the extent that members are able to achieve culturally influenced goals (Merton 1968) and common systems of values and norms are able to effectively regulate conduct

(Kornhauser 1978). These dimensions of social disorganization theory have been associated with a number of factors, such as indicators of social change (e.g., divorce rates) and physical conditions of neighborhoods (e.g., crowding, physical deterioration, vacancy rate of housing units). Unfortunately, some early investigators (e.g., Shaw and McKay 1942) also suggested that crime was an indicator of social disorganization, thus confusing a consequence of the process with an indicator of the process and leading to charges of begging the theoretical question by assuming that which was to be proved.

The approach taken here is to conceive of social disorganization as a characteristic of communities and larger geographic areas to the extent that they have experienced certain accompaniments of rapid or unintegrated social change: a high degree of population mobility, heterogeneity, crowding, family disruption, unemployment, and low income. These indicators point to the effects of rapid social change and a degree of social instability. They are also consistent both with the earlier formulations of social disorganization (Shaw and McKay 1942) and the subsequent discussions (Merton 1968) that sought a context for crime in the effects of larger social forces. At the level of the individual offender, these social forces are important because they symbolize many of the precipitating conditions (e.g., economic despair, cultural conflict, weak bonds, low supervision) that generate criminal motivations.

In their original work, it appeared that Shaw and McKay (1942) were largely struck by (1) the relationship between economic composition and rates of delinquency and (2) the distribution of these variables within the geographic boundaries of the city. They did not advance their theoretical cause beyond vague statements that social disorganization was reflected in the inability of communities to attain common values of residents (Kornhauser 1978, 63). Throughout different sections of their work, they talked favorably about the conceptual compatibility of their social disorganization perspective and theories of strain, cultural conflict, and control.

Shaw and McKay advocated, in other words, an integrated approach that sought the meaning of crime rates within community contexts. Community characteristics thought to increase social disorganization included such factors as population change and heterogeneity: these factors interfered not only with communication processes and feelings of common purpose among residents (Kornhauser 1978, 75, 78), but also with the development of primary group relationships in the community. Under these circumstances, informal structures of social control are inhibited, but learning and physical structures conducive to crime are facilitated (Cloward and Ohlin 1960).

Kornhauser (1978) implies that Shaw and McKay's position is compatible only with control theory, but this is incorrect. Sutherland (1973, 15–16) remarks in some autobiographical writing that Henry McKay complimented him on his theory in the 1934 edition of *Principles of Criminology*, a theory that Sutherland confessed he did not know he had. Upon reading the section identified by McKay, Sutherland discovered that the passage attributed crime to the conflict of cultures in communities, a term in the 1920s and 30s that referred to the same kind of processes identified in the traditional social disorganization approach (see also Sellin 1938). Sutherland's later development of the theory of differential association can best be viewed as an attempt to both specify the learning processes implicit in the social disorganization perspective and provide a sociological understanding of the fact that differences in crime rates by zone (community) persisted in Shaw and McKay's data far beyond the original residents in those areas.

The social disorganization approach is hardly indifferent to the formulation of testable hypotheses, although subsequent criticisms of the approach (which were made centrally on conceptual grounds) inhibited its development (Bursik 1988). Merton's theory is principally a theory of social disorganization (Messner 1988). Merton's notion of anomie, by which he means a lack of articulation between valued entities and nondeviant means of attaining those entities, is a theory that identifies unfulfilled, and unfulfillable, conventional aspirations as the context for most crime. Merton's innovators want to do the right thing, but they are thwarted in pursuing their goals by a social structure that fails to provide sufficient support, training, or opportunity. Similarly, the delinquents discussed by Sutherland come into contact with definitions favorable to violation of law due to forces beyond their control—living in areas with high crime rates, exposure to values from both conventional and unconventional others, and an affinity to a primary group that increases the chances of acquiring criminal norms. Sutherland would refer to this as a context of differential social organization. The imagery is one of criminal motivation being like germs in the air; Shaw and McKay, Merton, and Sutherland all portray crime as understandable only in the behavior of offenders, and the task of the criminologist is to identify the sequence that leads from the context (social disorganization, an anomic society, the conflict of cultures) to the expression of criminal motivations.

Theoretical Regularities

The community approach to crime recognizes that crime occurs in a larger social context, one dominated by cultural and social forces aside from, and in addition to, an individual's personal desires. Criminal motivation can be said to stem from these larger social conditions but it is not coterminous with them. Furthermore, if the community forces are truly influential, they will help shape the immediate circumstances of both the criminal's motivation and the victim's risk. In other words, community influences affect the entire complex of forces leading to the occurrence of crime. While the victim side of the theoretical equation will be addressed in the next chapter, we should note here that a community approach permits us to explore the impact of a number of structural influences on crime. These influences are often described as crime correlates, but they are not without theoretical substance. Rather, they are consequences of a theoretical perspective that makes such regularities meaningful.

Regardless of precise theoretical lineage, we can extract four elements that appear to be common among major theories of crime. These correlates, which make sense of crime within a community context, are (1) low socioeconomic status (SES), (2) residential mobility, (3) ethnic heterogeneity, and (4) household and family structure.

Taken individually, these correlates are not "causes" of crime.[6] They are, however, contextual influences that increase the risk of crime in those communities in which they exist. These regularities make sense regardless of whether the theoretical context is social disorganization, social learning, control, or some other specific theory of offender behavior. They are related to offender behavior because they seem to increase certain kinds of motivational states, such as relative deprivation, weak ties to traditional society, and rational responses to undesirable social, political, or economic circumstances.

Socio-Economic Status   The relationship between crime and SES is a complicated one. The social class of an individual does not appear to predict criminality in that person, and there does not appear to be any yet-studied context in which SES consistently predicts criminality. Tittle and Meier (1990) reviewed the extensive literature on the relationship between individual SES and criminality since 1978 and were unable to identify any study that found an invariant relationship. These investigators then examined a variety of social contexts in which the effects of social class might be expected to produce delinquency, but they were unable to identify any such context within the limits of their measures and data (Tittle and Meier 1991). However, the lack of a consistent association between individuals' SES and criminality does not preclude SES itself being a context in which crime occurs. Just as individuals can be characterized by a measure of SES, so too can communities. It is the aggregate indicator of SES that is associated with rates of crime and delinquency (see Sampson and Groves 1989; Bursik 1988).

Residential Mobility   Crime is associated with mobility in at least two ways. First, individual mobility may be related to crime if persons who are mobile are also those who are more likely than sedentary persons to commit crime. Second, communities in which there is greater mobility, reflected in the degree of population change, may be those who have also experienced more crime. Mobility may not be directly related to crime, but mobility, as measured by population change, may entail several social accompaniments related to crime. Tittle and Paternoster (1988) suggest that mobility is related to crime because greater mobility results in reduced moral commitment to norms that, in turn, increases the chances of law violation. Population turnover and mobility impede the construction of networks of social control that may decrease both criminal motivations and criminal opportunities. These factors also tend to hamper the ability of communities to express and realize shared values and goals.

Ethnic Heterogeneity   To the degree that a community is homogeneous, rates of crime and other forms of deviance can be expected to be lower. Population homogeneity reflects the extent to which a community is likely to subscribe to a common value system, to have a common vision of its future, and to generate bonds of attachment and commitment from residents. In contrast, there is greater opportunity for exposure to conflicting norms and values in communities with substantial heterogeneity. Greater heterogeneity also is related to such factors as population change and SES, suggesting that it might have both direct and indirect effects on crime.

Single-Parent Families   The importance of family structure, especially that in which children and both parents are present, can be sought in such nebulous notions as atmosphere (e.g., the tension or stress of divorce) or the straightforward learning of criminal norms. Regardless of the precise causal mechanism, criminologists have often considered the composition of families to be an important factor in crime. Some theories have used family composition as a direct factor in producing crime (e.g., Miller 1958), while others have suggested that parental influences are more indirect and may be related to crime via the extent of parental supervision over children (e.g, Hirschi 1969). The proportion of single-parent households in a community is related to the SES of the area as well as the degree of ethnic heterogeneity, since blacks have a much higher proportion of single-parent households than do whites. This suggests that family structure in the form of children who are living with both parents may have, as does mobility, both direct and indirect effects on the rates of crime in communities.

SOME HYPOTHESES

The four factors identified above can be associated with a variety of theoretical traditions. Shaw and McKay's writings on social disorganization made much of precisely these variables because they were most evident in the areas of the city in which the crime and delinquency rates were the highest. The development of Sutherland's theory of differential association owed much to the task of attempting to abstract from crime correlates the logical and universal mechanisms behind them. As Matsueda (1982, 279) notes about Sutherland, "He asked what blacks, males, persons from broken homes, and persons from lower classes had in common that caused them to have high rates of crime." For Sutherland, normative conflicts were rendered into rates of crime through the element of differential social organization, of which these crime correlates were an important part. Similarly, writers in the control theory tradition used the very same correlates as the starting point for their theory, but this same starting point is both a blessing and a curse. Sex, race, social class, neighborhood, mother's employment, the broken home, size of family, and so forth, are the stuff from which most empirical studies, textbooks, and theories of delinquency are constructed. " . . . The problem is not that it is difficult to account for observed relationships among these variables and delinquency; on the contrary, it is too easy" (Hirschi 1969, 65). The theory of anomie began with the same regularities. Merton was struck by the apparent relationship between crime, as reported in the initial issues of the Uniform Crime Reports, and structural correlates that drew the attention of Shaw and McKay, Sutherland, and others.

Factors such as SES, population change, heterogeneity, and family structure are among the most frequently referenced correlates of crime. When they are interpreted within a specific theoretical framework, they are widely considered among the most powerful predictors of crime.

These considerations lead us to the following hypotheses:

H1. The lower the SES, the greater the crime rate. The impact of SES on crime is not fully understood by criminologists, in part because SES may have differential effects on criminal acts. We anticipate that crime rates will be higher in low SES communities largely due to the adverse impact of the following conditions in lower-class areas: low economic resources that affect the ability to realize common goals, the amount of community control, feelings of relative deprivation, the low level of attachment and commitment to conventional institutions, and the amount of frustration that results from living in a socially and economically oppressive environment. However, higher SES in a community can also increase its attractiveness as a location for crime (e.g., because there are more and better goods to steal), thereby increasing victimization risks. Under such conditions, the overall impact of SES on crime rates may be nullified by these conflicting forces.

H2. The greater the population mobility, the greater the crime rate. Population changes are associated with greater opportunity for acquiring criminal norms, decreasing informal social control, greater anonymity in social relations, and perhaps increasing physical opportunity for crime.

H3. The greater the ethnic heterogeneity, the greater the crime rate. Ethnic heterogeneity in a community may reflect value differences and the extent to which common values are lacking. In those areas where common values are found, heterogeneity may inhibit their effective realization. Heterogeneity may also be associated with objective measures of social inequality and measures of perceived inequity that might be linked with increased criminal motivation.

H4. The greater the extent of single-parent households, the greater the crime rate. Single-parent households lack an additional adult socialization agent and may be less able to effectively supervise youthful family members (see Sampson and Groves 1989). Higher rates of children living with only one parent may also be associated with higher rates of social and economic marginality and ethnic heterogeneity, both of which are thought to be linked with higher crime rates in communities.

SUMMARY AND CONCLUSIONS

Theories of criminality are often theories of criminal motivation or the circumstances that create a potential offender. Such theories derive from either a classical or positivistic perspective. Whatever their differences, each of these approaches emphasizes a focus on the individual offender: what is important to explain, in accounting for crime, is the behavior of the offender. Subsequent versions of theories that derive from classical and positivistic roots all reflect this common theme.

We reject this view as excessively narrow and possibly reductionistic. Instead, the task of criminological theory is to account for criminal acts; this requires sensitivity to the larger context in which crime is found—a context that identifies elements of the offender, the victim, and those features of the social environment that facilitate or inhibit the expression of criminal motivation and the opportunity for crime. In this chapter, we concentrated on the context of the criminal; in the next, on the context of the victim. We think a structural-level context provides an excellent source of ideas about the relationship between community forces and individual conduct. Obviously, crime is committed by individuals, but crime is not best explained by reference to criminals only. Criminals, victims, and larger social, economic, and political forces are all elements of a grand ecology that is interdependent. Elements in this mix make sense only in reference to other elements; the isolation of just one requires that we regard it as a necessary but not sufficient explanation for crime.

In this sense, the task is to identify features of the larger context that appear to shape the other elements. Here we identify four such influences: low socioeconomic status, residential mobility, ethnic heterogeneity, and single-parent families. Each of these crime correlates leads to specific predictions that are supported by a number of specific theories of criminality. These contextual elements form part of the basis for a larger perspective on crime.

Theories of Victimization
and Criminal Opportunities

Social scientists have long recognized the contributory role of the victim in the creation of crime. The use of such expressions as "the victim-offender problem" (MacDonald 1939), "the duet frame of crime" (Von Hentig 1948), "the penal couple" (Ellenberger 1955) and, more generally, the "victim-offender relationship" (Schafer 1968; Schultz 1968; Von Hentig 1940) clearly indicate the significance of crime victims to the understanding of crime. Garofalo (1914) was one of the first to note that a victim may provoke another into attack, whereas Mendelsohn (1956) developed a victim typology that distinguishes victims who are more culpable than their offenders from those who are considered totally guiltless. Von Hentig (1948) described general classes of crime victims (e.g., the young, female, the old, the mentally defective, the depressed, the acquisitive, the lonesome and heartbroken) and some of the characteristics associated with these personal attributes that increase their vulnerability to crime.

In this chapter, we describe the historical bases for current theories of victimization and the content of these theories. Special attention is given to the lifestyle-exposure (Hindelang et al. 1978) and routine activity theories (Cohen and Felson 1979). We identify the major components of these criminal opportunity theories and review their empirical validity in accounting for individuals' risks and aggregate rates of predatory crime.

HISTORICAL FOUNDATIONS FOR
CURRENT VICTIMIZATION THEORIES

Although it is difficult to trace the origins of any theoretical perspective, two research traditions appear to be the antecedents to current theories of victimization. These include research on victim precipitation and the development of victimization surveys.

The first systematic study of victim involvement in crime was conducted in the late 1950s by Marvin Wolfgang. The term he introduced, victim precipitation, became a popular descriptor for all direct-contact predatory crime (e.g., murder, assault, forcible rape, robbery). When applied to homicide, victim precipitation is restricted to those cases in which "the victim is the first in the homicide drama to resort to physical force against the subsequent slayer" (Wolfgang 1957, 13). A similar definition is used in the case of aggravated assault, except that insinuating language or gestures are also considered provoking actions (see Curtis 1974; Miethe 1985). Victim-precipitated robbery involves cases in which the victim has acted without reasonable self-protection in the handling of money, jewelry, or other valuables (see Normandeau 1968; Curtis 1974), whereas this concept in forcible rape applies to "an episode ending in forced sexual intercourse in which the victim first agreed to sexual relations, or clearly invited them verbally or through gestures, but then retracted before the act" (see Amir 1967; Curtis 1974). Under each of these definitions there is an explicit time-ordering of events, such that victims initiate some type of action that leads to their subsequent victimization.

Previous studies using police reports suggest some level of victim involvement in a large proportion of violent crimes. The extent of victim precipitation, however, varies widely by the type of offense. Estimates of victim precipitation in homicide range from 22 percent to 38 percent, 14 percent for aggravated assault, between 4 percent and 19 percent for rape cases, and about 11 percent of armed robberies are characterized by carelessness on part of the victim (see, for review, Curtis 1974; Miethe 1985). These figures are best considered low estimates of the rate of victim involvement because of the fairly restrictive definition of victim precipitation for some crimes (i.e., murder, assault) and the large number of cases with incomplete information. The national survey of aggravated assaults reported by Curtis (1974), for example, had insufficient data for determining the presence of victim precipitation in 51 percent of the cases. Nonetheless, the importance of the notion of victim precipitation is clearly revealed by the fact that, in many cases of homicide, it is a matter of chance who becomes labelled the victim and offender (Wolfgang 1957).

There are several reasons why research on victim-precipitated crime was influential in the emergence of current theories of victimization. First, the prevalence of victim precipitation signified the importance of victims' actions in explaining violent crime, but also brought attention to the less direct ways by which citizens contribute to their victimization. These less direct forms of victim involvement include such acts as getting involved in risky or vulnerable situations, not exercising good judgment when in public places, leaving property unprotected, and interacting on a regular basis with potential offenders. Second, the notion of victim precipitation, by definition, attributes some of the blame for crime on the actions of its victims. The fact that victim precipitation researchers had to deal directly with such an unpopular public and political stance may have made it easier for subsequent scholars to examine how the routine activities and lifestyles of citizens provide opportunities for crime. Thus, current theories of victimization may have benefited greatly from the prior work on victim precipitation.

The second major contributor to the emergence of current victimization theories is the development of large-scale victimization surveys. Prior to the advent of victimization surveys in the late 1960s and early 1970s, official reports on crimes known to the police and self-reports of offending were the only available documents on criminal activities. However, neither of these sources gave any systematic information about the actions and characteristics of crime victims. Although it is possible to understand crime without directly surveying its victims (e.g., by interviewing offenders about their choice of crime sites, doing observation studies in areas with high rates of crime), victim surveys provide information about aspects of the criminal event that is not routinely collected from other sources. The largest of these projects, the National Crime Surveys (NCS), involves yearly reports from between 59,000 and 72,000 United States households, in which questions are asked that enable researchers to identify personal attributes of crime victims and characteristics of the offense.

Even in their earlier stages of development, victimization surveys addressed fundamental questions about crime. As is widely known, victim surveys represent an alternative barometer of the extent and distribution of crime, identify factors associated with reporting crime to the authorities, and yield detailed information about the consequences of crime for the victim. For present purposes, however, the major contribution of victimization surveys is that they provide detailed information about the ecology of crime (e.g., where it occurred, type of injury, victim-offender relationship) and the demographic characteristics of victims. It is the distribution of crime and the characteristics of victims identified in victimization surveys that are the social facts to be explained by current theories of victimization.

THE LIFESTYLE-EXPOSURE THEORY OF VICTIMIZATION

One of the first systematic theories of criminal victimization was the lifestyle-exposure approach developed by Hindelang, Gottfredson, and Garofalo (1978). This theory was originally proposed to account for differences in the risks of violent victimization across different social groups, but has been extended to include property crime, and forms the basis for more elaborate theories of target-selection processes (see Hough 1987; Miethe and Meier 1990).

   The basic premise underlying the lifestyle-exposure theory is that demographic differences in the likelihood of victimization are attributed to differences in lifestyles. Variations in lifestyles are important because they are related to the differential exposure to dangerous places, times, and others—i.e., situations in which there are high risks of victimization. A graphic representation of this theoretical perspective is presented in Figure 3.1.

   From this perspective, an individual's lifestyle is the critical factor that determines risks of criminal victimization. Lifestyle is defined in this context as "routine daily activities, both vocational activities (work, school, keeping house, etc.) and leisure activities" (Hindelang et al. 1978, 241). Differences in lifestyles are socially determined by individuals' collective responses or adaptations to various role expectations and structural constraints (see Figure 3.1). Under this theoretical model, both ascribed and achieved status characteristics (e.g., age, gender, race, income, marital status, education, occupation) are important correlates of predatory crime because these status attributes carry with them shared expectations about appropriate behavior and structural obstacles that both enable and constrain one's behavioral choices. Adherence to these cultural and structural expectations leads to the establishment of routine activity patterns and associations with others similarly situated. These lifestyles and associations are expected to enhance one's exposure to risky or vulnerable situations that, in turn, increase an individual's chances of victimization. Several examples will clarify the basic logic underlying this lifestyle-exposure model.

   Despite major efforts to promote greater gender equality in American society, there remain fundamental differences in role expectations and structural opportunities for men and women. Gender stereotyping results in gender differences in such basic activities as where and with whom time is spent, the degree of supervision in daily activities, the likelihood of con-

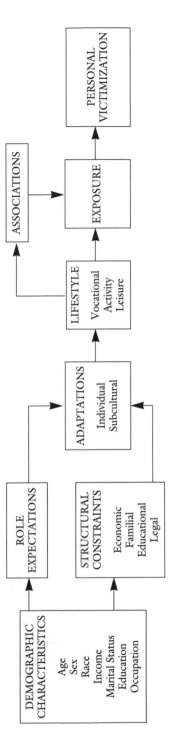

Source: Hindelang, Michael, Michael Gottfredson, and James Garofalo. 1978. *Victims of Personal Crime.* Cambridge, MA: Ballinger. Reproduced with permission from Michael Gottfredson.

Figure 3.1   Hindelang et al.'s (1978) Lifestyle-Exposure Model

tact with strangers, and the exposure to risky and dangerous public places. For example, females spend a greater proportion of their time inside the home because as adolescents they are more closely supervised than males, and as adults they are more likely to assume housekeeping and child-rearing responsibilities (Hindelang et al. 1978). Greater familial responsibilities and the systematic denial of educational and economic opportunities may severely impede women's participation in public life. Furthermore, even when engaged in public activity, women's routine activities are more likely than men's to take place in the presence of friends and intimate others, rather than in isolation. These role expectations and structural impediments are assumed to increase private domestic activities among women, increase supervision of their public behavior, decrease their exposure to high risk persons and places, and subsequently decrease their relative risks of criminal victimization. Men, on the other hand, are traditionally socialized to be active in the public domain, assertive and aggressive in social situations, have fewer restrictions on their daily lives, and spend more time away from a protective home environment. Accordingly, gender differences in traditional lifestyles are said to explain the higher victimization risks of men.

Other strong determinants of lifestyle and exposure to crime are economic resources and family income. As a fundamental aspect of stratification, income determines whether structural conditions either enable or constrain various aspects of social life. For persons who are economically disadvantaged, low income severely restricts choices with regard to housing, transportation, associations with others, and leisure activities. Individuals' abilities to move out of crime-prone environments, live in apartments or homes with elaborate security measures (e.g., security guards, video surveillance, burglar alarms), avoid contact with potential offenders, and undertake leisure activities in safer areas are limited when living under conditions of economic despair. As family income increases, there is greater flexibility to adjust one's lifestyle to select the area in which to live, the mode of transportation for daily activities, the amount of time spent in private versus public places, and the type of leisure activities (Hindelang et al. 1978). The greater choices afforded persons with higher economic resources allow them to more easily avoid risky and vulnerable situations. Thus, by patterning the nature of social life, income is a lifestyle characteristic that is expected to lead to differential risks of victimization.

From a lifestyle-exposure perspective, differences in risks of violent victimization by gender, income, and other status characteristics are attributed to differences in lifestyles that increase individuals' exposure to risky and vulnerable situations. Given that victimization risks are not uniformly distributed across time and space, lifestyles are assumed to affect the probability of victimization because different lifestyles are associated with differential risks of being in particular places, at particular times, under particular circumstances, and interacting with particular kinds of people. Accordingly, persons who are between 18 and 30 years old, male, not married, low income and black should have higher risks of violent victimization than their counterparts because each group is thought to engage in more public activity (especially at night), spend less time with family members, and/or associate more frequently with persons who have offender characteristics. Under this theoretical model, individuals' risks of property theft from their dwelling should also be higher among those social groups (e.g., young, male, single persons) who spend more time engaged in public activity because such persons would be less able to protect their property from crime.

If a lifestyle-exposure theory is an adequate explanation for differential risks of predatory victimization, several outcomes would be expected. First, if demographic differences in victimization risks are due to differences in lifestyles and routine activities, the impact of each demographic variable (e.g., age, gender, race, social class) should decrease in importance once separate measures of lifestyles and routine activities are included as control variables. Second, persons with the configuration of status characteristics commonly recognized as having the most vulnerable lifestyles (i.e., young, single, low income, black males) should have a greater risk of victimization than any other configuration, and their exact opposites (i.e., older, married, high income, white, females) should have the lowest relative risks. Third, given increases in efforts to promote gender and racial equality in all institutional domains over the last two decades, differences in victimization risks by these factors should decrease over time. In other words, smaller differences in victimization risks by gender and race would be expected over time if there were fewer group-specific role expectations and fewer structural obstacles that impede the daily activities of persons within each of these groups.

THE ROUTINE ACTIVITY THEORY

The routine activity perspective, developed by Cohen and Felson (1979), has many similarities with the lifestyle-exposure theory. Both emphasize how patterns of routine activities or lifestyles in conventional society provide an opportunity structure for crime. Each theory also downplays the importance of offender motivation and other aspects of criminality in understanding individuals' risks of victimization and the social ecology of crime. These theories are also representative of a wider "criminal opportunity" perspective because they stress how the availability of criminal opportunities is determined, in large part, by the routine activity patterns of everyday life (see Cohen 1981; Cohen and Land 1987). The fundamental differences between these theories are in terminology and in the fact that routine activity theory was originally developed to account for changes in crime rates over time, whereas lifestyle-exposure theory was proposed to account for differences in victimization risks across social groups. Over the past decade, however, each theory has been applied across units of analysis and in both cross-sectional and longitudinal designs.

According to Cohen and Felson (1979: 589), structural changes in routine activity patterns influence crime rates by affecting the convergence in time and space of three minimal elements of direct-contact predatory crimes: (1) motivated offenders, (2) suitable targets, and (3) the absence of capable guardians against a violation. As necessary elements, the lack of any of these conditions is sufficient to thwart criminal activity. Furthermore, Cohen and Felson (1979) note that large increases in crime rates could occur without any increase in the structural conditions that motivate offenders to engage in crime as long as there has been an increase in the supply of attractive and unguarded targets for victimization. Their argument about how crime rates can increase, even if offender motivation remains constant, is important because it allows them to account for the apparent contradiction underlying most theories of criminality: that crime rates continued to rise throughout the 1960s and 1970s in the United States even though conditions that foster criminality (e.g., unemployment, racial segregation, economic inequality) were decreasing.

From this perspective, routine activities are defined as "any recurrent and prevalent activities which provide for basic population and individual needs" (Cohen and Felson 1979: 593). Similar to the notion of lifestyle, these routine activities include formalized work, leisure, and the ways by which humans acquire food, shelter, and other basic needs or desires (e.g., companionship, sexual expression). Drawing from work in human ecology (e.g., Hawley 1950), Cohen and Felson (1979) argue that humans are located in an ecological niche with a particular tempo, pace, and rhythm in which predatory crime is a way of securing these basic needs or desires at the expense of others. Potential victims, in this environment, are likely to alter their daily habits and take evasive actions which may persuade offenders to seek alternative targets. It is under such predatory conditions that the routine activities of potential victims are said to both enhance and restrict opportunities for crime.

The basic premise underlying routine activity theory is that various social changes in conventional society increase criminal opportunities. For example, given the assorted costs for stealing items with great weight (e.g., their theft requires more physical energy, they are harder to conceal), it is not surprising that burglars are most attracted to items that are easily portable and have high resale value (e.g., cash, jewelry, electronic equipment). Accordingly, any changes in manufacturing or production activities that decrease the size or increase the demand for expensive durable goods (e.g., televisions, tape decks, VCRs, home computers, compact disk players) are expected to increase the attractiveness of these goods for victimization. Similarly, increases over time in the level of safety precautions taken by the public would apparently decrease crime rates by reducing the accessibility of potential crime targets to would-be offenders.

With regard to the various social changes in routine activities that have occurred over the last four decades, Cohen, Felson, and their colleagues have placed primary importance on changes in sustenance and leisure activities away from domestic life and family-based living arrangements. In fact, a basic proposition underlying this theory is that any decrease in the concentration of activities within family-based households would increase crime rates (see Cohen and Land 1987). There are several ways by which such social changes are assumed to increase criminal opportunities. First, a rise in single-person households or households consisting of unrelated persons requires a greater supply of durable consumer goods and other merchandise which is considered attractive property to steal. Such a duplication of consumer goods is unnecessary in family-like living arrangements. Second, increases in non-familial activities and households decrease the level of personal guardianship over others. The mere presence of a spouse, child, or other relative in a household provides greater protection over the individual and their property than is true of persons who live alone, and living with other relatives also increases the likelihood that public activities will be undertaken in a group situation. Third, increases in non-family households alter the location of routine activities from a private domain to a public domain, thereby also increasing one's exposure to risky and vulnerable situations. Thus, changes in domestic activities and living arrangements may increase the supply of attractive crime targets, decrease the level of guardianship, and consequently increase criminal opportunities.

Although applicable to various social science disciplines, there are several reasons why the routine activity theory is especially attractive to sociologists. First, this theoretical approach clearly highlights the symbiotic relationship between conventional and illegal activity patterns. In fact, illegal activities are presumed to "feed upon" the routine activities of everyday life (Felson and Cohen 1980; Messner and Blau 1987). Second, this theory identifies a fundamental irony between constructive social change and crime rates. Specifically, many social changes that have improved both the quality and equality of social life in the United States (e.g., increased labor-force participation and educational attainment among women, increases in out-of-home leisure activities) are the same factors predicted to increase rates of predatory crime. Third, both routine activity and lifestyle-exposure theory attempt to explain crime not in the actions or numbers of motivated offenders, but in the activities and lifestyles of potential victims. Given this emphasis, both perspectives have more relevance to a wider range of sociologists than most theories of criminality because they ignore the sources of criminal motivation and other major topics in traditional criminology (i.e., you don't have to be a criminologist to understand these theories!!) and direct attention to how the habits, lifestyles, and behavioral patterns of ordinary citizens, in their daily lives, create an environment for predatory crime.

Over the last decade, routine activity theory has been used to explain aggregate rates and individuals' risks of victimization, changes in crime rates over time, and the social ecology of crime (see, for review, Cohen and Land 1987; Miethe and Meier 1990). Each of these applications focus on how the nature of non-household activity influences one's exposure to crime. For example, Cohen and Felson (1979) examine the relationship between crime rates and the "household activity ratio" (i.e., the sum of the number of married female labor force participants and the number of non-husband-wife households divided by the total number of households). Felson and Cohen (1980) investigate the impact of increases in the rate of primary households on increasing burglary rates over time. Arguing that high rates of unemployment lead to decreases in non-household activity, Cohen, Felson and Land (1980) also apply this approach to study how unemployment rates and the household activity ratio influence temporal changes in rates of robbery, burglary, and automobile theft. Messner and Blau (1987) examine the relationship between crime rates for SMSAs in the United States and measures of the volume of household activity (i.e., size of television viewing audience) and non-household activity (i.e., the supply of sport and entertainment establishments). Miethe, Hughes and McDowall (1991) use this perspective to examine how measures of guardianship, non-household activity, and target attractiveness influence offense-specific crime rates and changes in crime rates in 584 U.S. cities from 1960 to 1980. Finally, Messner and Tardiff (1985) apply routine activity theory to examine the social ecology of urban homicide.

Most previous studies using the individual or household as the unit of analysis can be interpreted as tests of both routine activity and lifestyle-exposure theories. Cohen and Cantor (1980, 1981), for example, examine how characteristics of individuals and their lifestyles (e.g., income, age, race, major daily activity, household size) influence risks of residential burglary and personal larceny. Miethe et al. (1987) assessed the net and conditional effects of major daytime activity (i.e., work/school versus "other" activities) and the frequency of nighttime activity outside the home on individuals' risks of victimization by violent and property crime. Cohen, Kluegel, and Land (1981) evaluate whether measures of exposure, guardianship, proximity to motivated offenders, and target attractiveness mediate the impact of income, race, and age on individuals' risks of predatory victimization. The impact of measures of non-household activity, target suitability, and guardianship on individuals' risks of victimization has also been examined in other studies (e.g., Clarke et al. 1985; Lynch 1987; Maxfield 1987; Sampson and Wooldredge 1987; Massey, Krohn and Bonati 1989; Kennedy and Forde 1990; Miethe and Meier 1990). In the only study that uses longitudinal data on individuals, Miethe, Stafford and Sloane (1990) explore the interrelationships among changes in the level of non-household activity, guardianship patterns, and temporal changes in individuals' risks of violent and property victimization.

Although studies vary widely in terms of their units of analysis and measurement of key concepts, the predictive validity of routine activity theory ultimately rests on the empirical observation of three outcomes. First, routine activity patterns that indicate greater levels of non-household activity should increase victimization risks by increasing one's visibility and accessibility as a crime target. Second, routine activity patterns that indicate higher levels of self-protection or guardianship should decrease individuals' risks and aggregate rates of predatory crime. Third, persons and property with higher subjective or material value to offenders should have higher risks of victimization than less attractive crime targets. Taken together, a routine activity approach predicts the greatest risks for predatory crime when potential victims have high target suitability (i.e., high visibility, accessibility, and attractiveness) and low levels of guardianship.

ALTERNATIVE THEORETICAL MODELS

Lifestyle-exposure and routine activity theories have been the most widely applied perspectives in accounting for individuals' risks and aggregate rates of criminal victimization. However, other studies have attempted to integrate these perspectives more directly, to derive a clearer conceptual framework for explaining the process of target selection, and to examine the context-specific effects of routine activities and lifestyles on risks of criminal victimization. Each of these developments is summarized below.

A Structural-Choice Model of Victimization

Miethe and Meier (1990) examined the feasibility of integrating routine activity and lifestyle-exposure theories into what is called a "structural-choice" theory of victimization. Consistent with other work (see Cohen et al. 1981), we argued that current theories of victimization highlight the importance of physical proximity to motivated offenders, exposure to high-risk environments, target attractiveness, and the absence of guardianship as necessary conditions for predatory crime. Furthermore, two central propositions are said to derive from current theories. First, routine activity patterns and lifestyles create a criminal opportunity structure by enhancing contact between potential offenders and victims. Second, the subjective value of a person or object and its level of guardianship determine the choice of the particular crime target. In combination, these propositions imply that "routine activities may predispose some persons and their property to greater risks, but the selection of a particular crime victim within a socio-spatial context is determined by the expected utility of one target over another" (Miethe and Meier 1990: 245). Under this revised theoretical model, proximity and exposure are considered "structural" features (because they pattern the nature of social interaction and predispose individuals to riskier situations), whereas attractiveness and guardianship represent the "choice" component (because they determine the selection of the particular crime target within a socio-spatial context).

There are several reasons why we think that this structural-choice model is a useful integration of current victimization theories. First, this revised model emphasizes both macro-dynamic forces that contribute to a criminal opportunity structure (as identified by routine activity theory) and micro-level processes that determine the selection of particular crime victims (as implied by lifestyle-exposure theory). Second, it retains the view that exposure, proximity, attractiveness, and guardianship are necessary conditions for victimization, meaning that the absence of any of these factors is sufficient to eliminate predatory crime. Third, a structural-choice model closely follows the distinction between predisposing and precipitating factors (see Miethe et al. 1987). Specifically, both characterizations assume that living in particular environments increases one's exposure and proximity to dangerous situations, but whether or not a person becomes a crime victim depends on his or her presumed subjective utility over alternative targets. Fourth, the structural-choice perspective emphasizes the context-specific effects of routine activities and lifestyles on risks of predatory crime. For example, target attractiveness and guardianship may have little impact on victimization risks for residents of areas with a low criminal opportunity structure because, by definition, such environments are not conducive to predatory crime. Alternatively, geographical areas with a high concentration of offenders may have such a high criminal opportunity structure that all residents, regardless of their perceived attractiveness or level of guardianship, are equally susceptible to criminal victimization. Thus, for these reasons, we think this revised theoretical model has much to offer as an integration of current theories of victimization.

Conceptualizing Target-Selection Processes

Both routine activity and lifestyle-exposure theories attempt to explain crime rates and clarify why particular groups of individuals have higher risks of victimization than others. Differences in victimization risks for different demographic groups (e.g., males, young persons, non-whites, low income) are attributed to differences in lifestyles and routine activities that enhance individuals' exposure to risky times, places, and potential offenders. However, neither approach develops an adequate micro-level theory to account for the selection of particular crime targets within a particular socio-spatial context. This is the case because both theories pay little attention to factors associated with criminality and offender motivation. Offender motivation, in these theories, is either assumed to be constant or there is no explicit reference to what motivates people to commit crime (see Cohen and Land 1987).

A closer examination of these theories, however, reveals two specific images of criminality. First, an implicit assumption underlying criminal opportunity theories is that offender motivation is at least partially caused by the lack of external physical restraints. Criminal intentions are translated into actions when there is a suitable person or object for victimization, and "an absence of ordinary physical restraints such as the presence of other people or objects that inhibit, or are perceived to inhibit, the successful completion of direct contact predatory crime" (Cohen and Land 1987: 51). Second, offenders are assumed to make choices, no matter how rudimentary, in the selection of targets for victimization. In fact, it is this rational conception of criminal behavior underlying current victimization theories which offers the most promise in explaining target-selection processes.

From the perspective of a "reasoning criminal" (Cornish and Clarke 1986), offenders seek to benefit themselves by their criminal behavior and select victims who offer a high payoff with little effort or risk of detection. The decision to get involved in crime, and the subsequent choice of particular crime victims, are influenced by the constraints of time, ability, energy, limited information, and the availability of alternatives. Nonetheless, offenders are assumed to engage in some level of planning and fore-sight, and adapt their behavior to account for situational contingencies (Cornish and Clarke 1986). Through selective filtering and processing of information, the rational offender is believed to select from a pool of potential victims those targets thought to offer the greatest net rewards.

Interviews with convicted offenders reveal that many personal and situational factors are considered in the selection of crime targets. Bur-glars, for example, report that the risks of detection (i.e., the likelihood of getting caught), the potential yield or reward, and the relative ease at which the home can be entered are the critical factors in selecting targets for victimization (see Bennett and Wright 1984). Similar aspects of the physical environment and victim characteristics are considered by other offenders (e.g., robbers, muggers) when selecting crime targets (see Cornish and Clarke 1986).

Hough (1987) has developed a conceptual framework to explain target selection which clarifies the importance of routine activities and lifestyles in this process. According to Hough (1987: 359), this concep-tual scheme considers it axiomatic that if members of one group are selected as crime targets more frequently than another, they must meet at least one of three conditions: (a) exposed more frequently to motivated offenders (proximity), (b) more attractive as targets in that they afford a better "yield" to the offender (reward), or (c) more attractive in that they are more accessible or less defended against victimization (absence of capable guardians). This theoretical approach is graphically represented in Figure 3.2. The value of this perspective for understanding criminal vic-timization is that it clearly states that differences in proximity, attractive-ness, or guardianship can account for differences in individuals' risks of victimization, and that persons who possess each of these characteristics are especially vulnerable to crime. Consistent with both routine activity and lifestyle-exposure theory, these differences in target-selection factors are determined by individuals' routine activities and lifestyles.

Although this revised model clarifies the role of routine activities and lifestyles in target-selection processes, it is still limited in several respects. First, victimization most likely occurs under conditions of prox-imity, reward and no guardianship, but the model does not specify which factor is most important. Second, while interviews with convicted offend-ers suggest that target-selection factors may vary widely for different types of predatory crime (see Bennett and Wright 1984; Carroll and Weaver 1986; Cornish and Clarke 1986; Feeney 1986; Walsh 1986), this theo-retical perspective does not capture these crime-specific differences. Third, even within particular types of crime (e.g., muggings), there appear to be major differences in factors associated with target selection

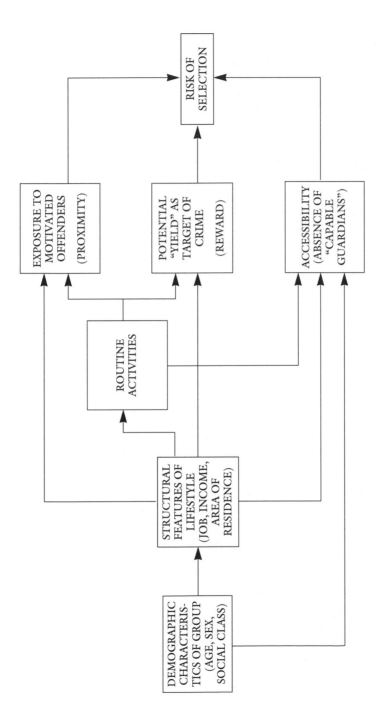

Source: Hough, Michael. 1987. "Offenders' Choice of Targets: Findings from Victim Surveys." *Journal of Quantitative Criminology,* 3: 355–369. Reproduced with permission from Plenum Press.

Figure 3.2   Hough's Framework for Explaining Target Selection

between novice and seasoned offenders (Cornish and Clarke 1986). These within-crime differences are also not directly incorporated in the model. Nonetheless, the conceptual framework outlined by Hough (1987) is a major improvement over the original formulations of routine activity and lifestyle-exposure theories.

CONTEXTUAL EFFECTS IN MODELS OF VICTIMIZATION

A fundamental aspect of predatory crime is that it occurs in a social context where there exists a convergence of victims and offenders in time and space. Given this characteristic of predatory crime, it is surprising that little research has incorporated aspects of the social context directly into theories of victimization. To their credit, routine activity and lifestyle-exposure theories acknowledge the importance of exposure and proximity to risky or vulnerable situations as necessary conditions for predatory crime. However, what is absent is a clear specification of how aspects of the wider social context influence risks of victimization. There are several ways in which the social context can both facilitate and constrain the occurrence of crime.

A major contribution of macro-sociological theories of criminality is the identification of the structural conditions associated with crime. For example, population heterogeneity and density, residential mobility, and low economic opportunity are identified as criminogenic forces because they either increase cultural conflict, decrease economic resources, or hamper the development of effective mechanisms of social control (Kornhauser 1978; Bursik 1988; Sampson and Groves 1989). One primary way in which these social forces generate a facilitating context for crime is by increasing the pool of potential offenders. The greater one's proximity to these criminogenic areas, the greater one's risks of victimization.

According to current theories of victimization, an alternative way in which the social context influences predatory crime is by increasing the supply of criminal opportunities. Because routine activities of everyday life are said to create criminal opportunities, geographical areas with high levels of public activity, expensive and portable consumer goods, and lower levels of physical guardianship are presumed to have higher rates of crime. In fact, regardless of their own routine activities and lifestyles, some persons may be more vulnerable to crime than others simply by living in these "attractive" areas. The composition and structure of neighborhoods may influence individuals' victimization risks because these characteristics give off cues to would-be offenders about the potential yield and costs for engaging in crime in those geographical areas.

Previous research on the crime-reduction benefits of safety precautions is a good example of how elements of the wider social context influence individuals' risks of victimization. As a form of guardianship, it is widely assumed that taking safety precautions (e.g., locking doors, installing alarms, owning dogs) reduces one's risks of predatory crime. However, what is less clear is how a person's chances of victimization are influenced by the safety precautions taken by others in their immediate neighborhood. In fact, the safety precautions of others may either enhance or reduce an individual's risks of victimization. According to the arguments regarding crime displacement (see Gabor 1981, 1990; Cornish and Clarke 1987; Miethe 1991), persons are negatively affected by the protective actions of others in their neighborhood because these actions are assumed to deflect crime to less protective others. Alternatively, a "free rider" effect suggests that persons benefit from the social control activities of their immediate neighbors because these actions convey to would-be offenders an image that this area, in general, is a risky place to commit crime. Regardless of whether the safety precautions of others inhibit or enhance victimization risks, the major point is that the community context of crime control, in both cases, is said to determine the availability of criminal opportunities and individuals' risks of victimization.

An implicit assumption underlying a contextual analysis is that victimization risk and its predictors vary by characteristics of the wider social context. These contextual effects can take various forms. First, living near "hot spots" for crime (see Sherman et al. 1989) may be especially harmful because of one's proximity to areas with high concentrations of offenders. Second, routine activities and lifestyles may have context-specific effects on victimization risks. For example, the crime-enhancing effects of exposure and proximity to motivated offenders may be important only in neighborhoods with low levels of informal and formal social control. When there are high levels of social integration and safety precautions in an area, these social control mechanisms may be of sufficient strength to deter crime and overwhelm the adverse effects of exposure and proximity to crime. Alternatively, the supply of expensive consumer goods in the immediate environment may influence the risks of property victimization even for residents who lack these possessions. As indicated by the conflicting predictions about displacement and free-rider effects, it may be unclear in other cases whether the same contextual factor impedes or enhances an individuals' risks of victimization. However, regardless of the particular type of contextual effect, what is important about multi-level models and contextual analysis is that victimization risks are seen as a function of both the routine activities of residents and the composition and structure of the wider geographical area.

There are several basic reasons why it is important to include both measures of individuals' lifestyles and contextual variables in studies of victimization. First, a major premise of sociological theory is that social conditions enable and constrain human activity. Although not denying that individuals' lifestyles influence their vulnerability to crime, most sociological theories assume that the community context has a direct impact on victimization risks independent of individual characteristics. Second, it is possible that many of the presumed individual-level effects are actually reflective of community dynamics. For example, the strong impact of being young or unmarried on victimization risks is commonly attributed to the lifestyles of such persons (see Hindelang et al. 1978; Miethe et al. 1987). Yet, the influence of these factors may stem from the fact that both single persons and young adults are more likely to live in transitional neighborhoods with more potential offenders, lower internal social control, and high rates of public activity (see also Smith and Jarjoura 1989). Under these conditions, failing to include measures of the community context would misspecify the true relationship between individuals' characteristics and victimization risks.

The importance of contextual factors has been empirically documented in several recent studies. Using a sample of individuals in political districts in Great Britain, Sampson and Wooldredge (1987) found that personal risks of burglary were influenced by the level of family disruption, single-person households, and density of ownership of portable consumer goods (i.e., VCR's) in the wider community. Smith and Jarjoura (1989) found that risks of burglary for residents in 57 neighborhoods were influenced by several neighborhood factors (e.g., racial heterogeneity, population instability, median income). Measures of community composition and structure have been included in several additional studies of individuals' risks of victimization (e.g., Cohen et al. 1981; Simcha-Fagan and Schwartz 1986; Sampson and Lauritsen 1990). The research by Lynch (1987) on victimization at work and Davidson (1989) on the micro-environments for violence are other studies that highlight the importance of the social context in understanding predatory crime.

MAJOR CONCEPTS IN VICTIMIZATION THEORIES

Although the terminology differs across studies, the central concepts underlying criminal opportunity theories of victimization are proximity to crime, exposure, target attractiveness, and guardianship. The measurement of these concepts and their empirical validity in previous studies are outlined below.

Proximity to Crime

One major factor that is presumed to increase the likelihood of victimization is physical proximity to high-crime areas. Following Cohen et al. (1981: 507), proximity is best represented as the physical distance between areas where potential targets of crime reside and areas where relatively large populations of potential offenders are found. Living in a high-crime area increases the likelihood of frequent contact with offenders, and thus increases one's risks of victimization. The fact that persons spend a majority of their time around the home, and that offenders tend to select targets in close proximity to their residence (see Hindelang et al. 1978) further indicates the adverse consequences of living in a high-crime area.

Both theories of criminality and research in the spatial ecology of crime identify characteristics of high-crime areas. Macro-sociological theories of criminality (e.g., social disorganization, anomie, differential social organization) suggest that high-crime geographical areas have high levels of population turnover, ethnic heterogeneity, and low socio-economic status. However, the work on deviant places and "hot spots" (Stark 1987; Sherman et al. 1989) indicates that even within a large geographical area with a high crime rate (e.g., neighborhood, subdivision, a side of town) there is enormous variation in the amount of crime. From this perspective, some places (e.g., bars, convenience stores, adult bookstores, apartment complexes) are more dangerous than others because they attract deviant and crime-prone people, provide more targets for victimization, and have a diminished capacity for social control. Living near major transportation arteries, fast-food restaurants, bus stops, schools, and other places which attract a larger number of strangers would also increase one's vulnerability to crime for similar reasons.

Common measures of physical proximity used in previous research include place of residence (e.g., rural or urban resident), socio-economic characteristics of the area (e.g., income level, unemployment rate, racial composition) and the perceived safety of the immediate neighborhood (see Cohen et al. 1981; Hough 1987; Lynch 1987; Sampson and Wooldredge 1987; Miethe and Meier 1990). The average rate of offending in an individual's immediate neighborhood is probably the best single indicator of proximity, but self-report and official measures of offending are rarely available at the neighborhood level. Studies using the British Crime Survey (Sampson and Wooldredge 1987; Miethe and Meier 1990) are the exception to this rule. The absence of multi-level research designs has been a major impediment to the development of measures of offending rates in models of victimization risks.

Previous empirical studies generally find that measures of proximity are associated with increased risks of victimization. For example, we found in our study of British residents (Miethe and Meier 1990) that persons who lived in inner city areas, perceived their neighborhood to be unsafe at night, and lived in areas with higher levels of offending had higher risks of burglary, personal theft, and assault victimization. Using a seven-category variable based on the income of neighborhoods and the size of the population, Cohen et al. (1981) found that persons who lived in central cities and low-income areas had higher risks of assault, burglary, and personal larceny than persons who lived in other types of areas. Given the high levels of residential segregation in the United States based on status characteristics, the observed association between particular demographic factors (e.g., low income, being single, non-white, high residential mobility) and individuals' risks of victimization may also be attributed to the proximity of these social groups to pools of motivated offenders (see Hindelang et al. 1978; Miethe et al. 1987; Smith and Jarjoura 1989). However, as will be discussed shortly, it is important to note that such findings are also consistent with other major components of victimization theories (i.e., exposure, target attractiveness, and low guardianship).

Exposure to Crime

Contrary to proximity, which reflects the physical distance between large numbers of offenders and victims, "exposure to crime" is indicative of one's visibility and accessibility to crime (Cohen et al. 1981; Miethe and Meier 1990). Accordingly, a building or dwelling has higher exposure to burglary if it is detached from other units, has multiple points of entry, and is located on a corner lot. Persons are exposed to higher risks of personal theft and assault when their routine activities and lifestyles place them in risky or vulnerable situations at particular times, under particular circumstances, and with particular kinds of persons. For example, risks of personal victimization are assumed to be directly related to the amount of time spent in public places (e.g., streets, parks) and, especially, public places at night (Hindelang et al. 1978: 251). Furthermore, the research on "hot spots" suggests that frequent contact with drinking establishments, bus depots, public transit, convenience stores, shopping malls, and other dangerous public places would also increase one's exposure to crime (Sherman et al. 1989).

The primary means by which exposure has been measured in past studies involves the level and nature of non-household activity. Several authors have used the individual's primary daily activity as a measure of exposure (e.g., Cohen and Cantor 1980, 1981; Cohen et al. 1981; Miethe et al. 1987), arguing that persons who are employed or in school have greater exposure to crime because such persons spend more time away from home. More detailed indicators of this concept include the average number of evenings per week spent outside the home for leisure activities, and the average number of hours per week the dwelling is unoccupied during the day or night (see Sampson and Wooldredge 1987; Massey et al. 1989; Miethe and Meier 1990). When applied to the study of crime rates, measures of exposure have included the household activity ratio (see Cohen and Felson 1979), aggregate rates of television viewing, the supply of entertainment establishments (e.g., commercial cinemas, profit-making sport activities, opera and symphony orchestra companies), public transportation, female labor force participation, and retail sales from eating and drinking establishments (see Messner and Blau 1987; Miethe, Hughes and McDowall 1991).

Previous studies yield mixed results about the impact of exposure on individuals' risks and aggregate rates of victimization. Increases in non-household activity are associated with higher crime rates in some studies (e.g., Cohen and Felson 1979; Cohen et al. 1980; Felson and Cohen 1980) but not in others (Miethe et al. 1991). Increases over time in individuals' levels of daytime and nighttime activity outside the home do not necessarily lead to increased risks of violent or property victimization (Miethe, Stafford, and Sloane 1990), whereas cross-sectional analyses generally reveal that victimization risks are higher for persons who have higher levels of activity outside the home (Hough 1987; Sampson and Wooldredge 1987; Massey et al. 1989; Kennedy and Forde 1990; Miethe and Meier 1990). Studies of the physical characteristics of burgled households and interviews with known offenders also suggest that the visibility and accessibility of targets influence risks of victimization (see Reppetto 1974; Waller and Okihiro 1978; Walsh 1980; Bennett and Wright 1984; Hough 1987). Unfortunately, little research has examined how active participation in particular types of routine activities (e.g., bar visits, visiting places where teenagers "hang out") influences risks of violent victimization.

Target Attractiveness

A central assumption underlying current victimization theories is that particular targets are selected because they have symbolic or economic value to the offender. However, crime targets are also attractive to offenders when they are smaller in size (i.e., more portable) and offer less physical resistance against attack or illegal removal (see Cohen et al. 1981). Under a structural-choice model of victimization (Miethe and Meier 1990), it is the differential value or subjective utility associated with crime targets that determines the source of victimization within a social context.

A variety of indicators of target attractiveness have been used in past research. In the original work on routine activity theory, Cohen and Felson (1979) compared the theft rate for portable and movable durables (e.g., electronic components, television sets, radios, automobiles and their accessories) with their overall circulation rate. The decreased size of these durable goods from the early 1960s through the mid 1970s also corresponds with increases in official crime rates in the United States. However, the supply of many of these portable durable goods (e.g., televisions, radios, car tape players, phonograph cartridges) may not be a good indicator of target attractiveness for studies of crime rates over time when one considers that the reduced costs and increased availability of many of these items may lead to their devaluation as "attractive" crime targets. As a general proxy for purchasing power and the supply of expensive goods, median family income and the gross national product are aggregate measures of target attractiveness that are not susceptible to such a devaluation over time.

The major measures of target attractiveness at the individual-level of analysis have been the ownership of expensive and portable consumer goods (e.g., video-cassette recorders, color television sets, bicycles, motorcycles), the possession of cash and jewelry in public, family income and social class (see Sampson and Wooldredge 1987; Miethe and Meier 1990). As a measure of economic attractiveness, family income should be a good indicator of this concept because it can be recognized immediately by offenders in most cases (e.g., through the geographical location of a dwelling within a city, its exterior condition, or the general appearance of the individual). However, in the case of expressive acts of interpersonal violence, it is difficult to think of an unambiguous measure of target attractiveness.

The results of previous research provide mixed support for the importance of target attractiveness in explaining individuals' risks and aggregate rates of victimization. Greater risks of victimization for persons with higher income are observed in some studies but not in others (see Cohen and Cantor 1980, 1981; Cohen et al. 1981; Hough 1987; Miethe and Meier 1990; Miethe, Stafford, and Sloane 1990). Persons who carry larger sums of money while in public places have a greater net risk of assault victimization, but ownership of a video-cassette recorder was found to either decrease or have no significant impact on individuals' risks of burglary (Sampson and Wooldredge 1987; Miethe and Meier 1990). Studies of crime rates for geographical areas also yield inconsistent results about the relationship between economic conditions and crime rates (see

Cohen et al. 1980; Cohen 1981; Stahura and Sloan 1988; Miethe, Hughes, and McDowall 1991).

Capable Guardianship

The final major component of current victimization theories involves the ability of persons or objects to prevent the occurrence of crime. Guardianship is usually conceptualized as having both social (interpersonal) and physical dimensions. Social guardianship includes the number of household members, the density of friendship networks in the neighborhood, and having neighbors watch property or a dwelling when the home is unoccupied. The availability of others (e.g., friends, neighbors, pedestrians, law enforcement officers) may prevent crime by their presence alone or through the offering of assistance to ward off an attack. Physical guardianship involves target-hardening activities (e.g., door/window locks, window bars, burglar alarms, guard dogs, ownership of firearms), other physical impediments to household theft (e.g., street lighting, guarded public entrances), and participation in collective activities (e.g., Neighborhood Watch programs, home security surveys). Regardless of its particular form, the availability of capable guardianship is important because it indicates increased "costs" to would-be offenders (e.g., greater effort, greater risk of detection and apprehension), and thus decreases the opportunity for victimization.

A review of previous research on guardianship activities reveals several general trends. First, target-hardening efforts are widespread in the United States. The majority of urban residents take routine precautions against crime, including locking doors and windows, using exterior lighting and having neighbors watch their property (Dubow 1979; Skogan and Maxfield 1981; Miethe 1991). Collective crime prevention activities (e.g., property marking projects, Neighborhood Watch) have also been organized throughout the country (see Rosenbaum 1987, 1990). Second, the success of guardianship activities has been mixed. Physical and social guardianship is associated with lower rates of victimization in several studies but not in others (see Scarr 1973; Reppetto 1974; Skogan and Maxfield 1981; Lavrakas et al. 1981; Winchester and Jackson 1982; Yin 1986; Rosenbaum 1987, 1990; Miethe and Meier 1990). However, several authors (Mayhew 1984; Miethe 1991) argue that the use of cross-sectional designs and the lack of a clear temporal ordering among variables have contributed to these inconsistent results due to the "victimization effect" (i.e., the tendency for persons to take precautions as a consequence of being victimized). Third, few studies of guardianship have exercised sufficient controls for other factors influencing victimization risks. Under such conditions, it is impossible to ascertain whether differences between protected and unprotected residents are due to the deterrent effect of protective actions or to other factors (e.g., lifestyles, target attractiveness, proximity to high-crime areas) which also alter the likelihood of victimization (see Miethe 1991).

PROBLEMS WITH PREVIOUS EVALUATIONS OF VICTIMIZATION THEORIES

Although criminal opportunity theories of victimization have been widely applied in previous research, there are several basic limitations of past studies which cast doubt on substantive inferences about the predictive utility of the overall perspective and its specific components. These problems involve inadequate measures of key concepts, the lack of sufficient statistical controls, and the failure to examine multi-level and context-specific models of victimization.

Inadequate Measures of Key Concepts

The development of empirical indicators of key theoretical concepts has been a major problem in social science research, and previous research in victimization is no exception. Clear and concise theories of human behavior become muddled when one begins to operationalize and measure concepts. Questions about the validity and reliability of these indicators are commonly raised, making it difficult to determine whether it is bad theory, bad measures, or a combination of both which form the basis for disconfirming evidence. The inherent fallibility in collecting and coding data, demand characteristics in the evaluation setting (e.g., response sets, yea-saying, acquiescence), and enormous individual differences among humans are contributory factors to the greater imprecision of measurement in the social sciences. The major impediments to primary data collection (e.g., the economic, legal, and/or ethical constraints) and the subsequent reliance upon secondary data sources also have been primary causes of the relatively poor quality of empirical indicators of key concepts. Given these problems with measurement, it is easy to be critical of much social science research.

    The reliance upon secondary data sources is one of the basic causes of measurement problems in previous studies of victimization. Given that victimization is such a rare event (only about 25 percent of United States households are "touched" by any crime each year), it is not surprising that the enormous economic costs of obtaining a large sample of particular types of crime victims and non-victims prohibit many researchers from collecting their own data. However, the largest data source on individuals' victimization experiences, the yearly National Crime Survey (NCS) series, was designed primarily to provide alternative estimates of the rate of crime rather than to test theories of victimization. Similarly, census data is the primary data source for studies of crime rates in geographical areas. Unfortunately, census data is collected primarily for political and administrative reasons. Thus, although both NCS data and census reports for various aggregate units are widely available, neither of these sources provide complete and unequivocal measures of the key concepts underlying victimization theories.

The major limitation of using secondary sources has been the necessary reliance upon proxy measures of key theoretical concepts. This can be demonstrated for each of the major components underlying victimization theories.

Proximity to motivated offenders is generally considered to be the physical distance between pools of offenders and victims, but it is usually measured by the degree of population concentration (e.g., living in an urban versus rural area) and the socio-economic characteristics of the geographical area. From this perspective, living in a large urban area and a low socio-economic neighborhood are widely used as proxy measures of proximity (see Cohen et al. 1981; Hough 1987; Miethe and Meier 1990). However, it is easy to see that these variables are equally indicative of a breakdown in social control, population heterogeneity, low economic opportunity, and other factors underlying traditional theories of criminality. Thus, higher victimization risks for persons who live in urban areas or low income neighborhoods would not empirically distinguish theories of victimization from theories of criminality.

As mentioned previously, exposure to crime is usually indicated by the level of non-household activity (see Miethe et al. 1987). Accordingly, persons who are employed outside the home or attending school are assumed to be more exposed to crime than persons whose daily activities are more likely to take place around the home (e.g., unemployed, homemakers, retired, disabled). Yet, such non-household activities may actually be associated with "low exposure," because both work and school occur in a confined environment with a relatively high level of guardianship and supervision. However, only in the cases of the Victim-Risk Supplement of the NCS and the British Crime Survey (BCS) are activities in particular public places (e.g., going to bars/taverns, taking public transit) included as variables that can be used to develop better measures of exposure to risky and vulnerable situations.

When examining crime rates and social trends, Cohen and Felson

(1979) used the "household activity ratio" as a measure of exposure. This ratio is a composite index of the number of married women in the labor force and the number of non-husband/wife households. Cohen and Felson (1979) assume that this ratio measures both the dispersion of the population away from households and the supply of durable goods susceptible to theft, but it is equally indicative of the prevalence of non-traditional families and reductions in social integration. Under such conditions, the positive association between crime rates and non-household activity could be due as much to social disorganization processes (e.g., problems of norm transmission and community control) or a breakdown of bonds to mainstream society (i.e., lower attachment, commitment, involvement and/or belief in conventional activity) as to increases in the supply of criminal opportunities from greater exposure and lower guardianship. If findings fit both sets of theories equally, then opportunity-based theories, while plausible, do not tell us anything unique about the social ecology of crime (see Miethe, Hughes, and McDowall 1991).

Target attractiveness is defined both in terms of its material and symbolic value to offenders (Cohen et al. 1981). However, measures of individual ownership and the circulation of small, but expensive durable goods (e.g., jewelry, audio-visual equipment) are not routinely available in the NCS yearly data or census reports. Thus, target attractiveness is usually measured by general economic conditions (e.g., family income, unemployment rate), even though such indicators are also representative of lower criminal motivation (because higher income and lower unemployment indicates greater legitimate economic opportunities) and greater exposure to crime (because higher income affords greater leisure activity outside the home).

The only available measure of guardianship in the NCS series and census data is the number of members in the household. Neither source provides measures of safety precautions and other types of guardianship. In the case of property crimes against the dwelling (e.g., burglary, vandalism, theft of property around the home), larger households should have lower victimization risks because the dwelling would be less likely to be unoccupied. As a measure of guardianship for violent crime, it must be assumed that the greater the household size, the less likely a person will be alone in a public place. However, household size may also have a crime-enhancing effect due to the impact of household size on household crowding and, in turn, the adverse consequences of crowding on criminal motivation (see Miethe, Hughes, and McDowall 1991).

What is clearly revealed in these examples is that the reliance upon secondary data has contributed to the use of inadequate measures of proximity, exposure, attractiveness, and guardianship. The proxy measures used in past studies do not tap each dimension of the underlying concepts and have ambiguous meanings. Substantive inferences about the predictive utility of victimization theories are questionable under such conditions.

Statistical Control

It is widely known that statistical control for other variables is a crucial requirement for causal inference in non-experimental designs. Statistical control allows for an assessment of the net impact of one variable on another, once adjustments are made for the variation shared between the primary independent variable and other predictor variables. However, previous empirical studies have rarely included measures of each major component underlying victimization theories, even though proximity, exposure, attractiveness, and lack of guardianship are considered necessary conditions for predatory crime (see Miethe, Hughes, and McDowall 1991). The failure to include adequate statistical controls for all relevant variables may seriously distort our inferences about the substantive impact of each of these factors on victimization risks.

When measures of a particular concept have multiple meanings, statistical controls are one method of disentangling and isolating the unique effects of each theoretical component. Given the pervasiveness of ambiguous measures of key concepts underlying theories of victimization, statistical control is especially pertinent here. In fact, most measures of theoretical concepts used in previous studies of victimization have ambiguous meanings. These include: female labor-force participation (indicating either wider exposure, decreased guardianship, increased target attractiveness, or reduced criminal motivations due to rising economic resources), income (indicating attractiveness, higher exposure from non-household activity, or reduced criminal motivations), unemployment (may indicate criminogenic conditions, reduced circulation of money, and reduced levels of non-household leisure activities [Cohen et al. 1980; Cohen 1981; Cohen and Land 1987; Land, McCall, and Cohen 1990]), and household size (indicating higher guardianship or increases in criminogenic conditions due to the adverse impact of household crowding). Obviously, a proper examination of how each theoretical component influences crime rates and individuals' risks of victimization requires adequate controls for these competing elements and other relevant variables. Nonetheless, previous evaluations of criminal opportunity theories have not exercised sufficient statistical controls to isolate the unique impact of each theoretical component (see Miethe, Hughes, and McDowall 1991).

Multi-Level Analysis and Contextual Effects

Previous evaluations of theories of criminality and victimization have relied upon what is called a "main effects" or "additive model." Under such a specification, the impact of a variable is assumed to be identical across levels of another variable. When applied to theories of victimization, the additive specification assumes that the impact of target attractiveness, for example, is the same for persons who vary in their exposure to crime and have different levels of guardianship. The impact of guardianship is likewise presumed to be the same across various social contexts. Regardless of where one lives and his or her particular routine activities and lifestyles, increases in household size or the number of safety precautions is assumed to decrease one's risks of predatory crime. However, the failure to examine whether variables have different effects across different contexts is a type of model misspecification that may dramatically alter substantive conclusions about the predictive validity of current theories.

As mentioned earlier in this chapter, there are various ways in which contextual effects can occur in models of victimization. However, what is important here is that available data is limited in terms of its ability to either examine multi-level relationships or perform contextual analyses. This is the case because most large data sources are restricted to one level of analysis (e.g., individual, census tract, city, SMSA) and do not contain measures of contextual variables. The opportunity to perform contextual analyses is important because it may more clearly specify the conditions under which proximity, exposure, target attractiveness, and guardianship alter individuals' risks and aggregate rates of predatory crime. The results of the few previous studies using this approach also suggest its utility as a research tool for testing theories of victimization (see Sampson and Wooldredge 1987; Smith and Jarjoura 1989; Miethe and McDowall 1991).

SUMMARY AND RESEARCH HYPOTHESES

Current theories of victimization highlight the symbiotic relationship between conventional and illegal activities. Regardless of their particular terminology, routine activities and lifestyle-exposure theories emphasize how criminal opportunities develop out of the routine activities of everyday life. Routine activity patterns that increase proximity to motivated offenders, increase exposure to risky and dangerous situations, enhance the expected utility or attractiveness of potential crime targets, and reduce the level of guardianship are assumed to increase aggregate rates and individuals' risks of predatory crime. These criminal opportunity theories have been used to account for changes in crime rates in the United States over time, the level of crime in aggregate units (e.g., cities, SMSAs), differences in victimization risks for different social groups (e.g., males, single persons, younger people), and individuals' risks of victimization.

The results of previous studies give some indication of the explanatory power of criminal opportunity theories. There is some evidence to support each of the major components underlying these theories (i.e., proximity, exposure, attractiveness, and guardianship). However, this supporting evidence is less impressive when one considers the major limitations of previous work. The fact that previous research has generally used inadequate proxy measures of key concepts, includes few statistical controls, and has not examined rigorously multi-level models and contextual effects casts some doubt on the substantive conclusions from these studies.

Our review of the literature on theories of victimization reveals seven major research hypotheses. Finding empirical support for each of them across different levels of analysis and research designs would clearly document the importance of an opportunity perspective in understanding predatory crime. Using various sources of data, the following research hypotheses will be addressed in the current study:

H1. Demographic differences (e.g., age, gender, race, income, marital status, education) in victimization risks should decrease in magnitude once controls are introduced for routine activities and lifestyles. This hypothesis is based on the assumption that demographic differences in victimization risks are due to differences in routine activities and lifestyles (Hindelang et al. 1978; Miethe et al. 1987).

H2. Persons with the configuration of status characteristics commonly recognized as having the most vulnerable lifestyles (i.e., young males, low-income young males) should have a greater risk of victimization than any other status configuration. These differences in victimization risks should also be explained by differences in the level of non-household activity for each group.

H3. Differences in victimization risks by status characteristics should dissipate over time. Such an outcome would be expected if role expectations and structural constraints based on status attributes have weakened in the United States over the last three decades. Given the specific efforts to promote gender and racial equality in all institutional domains, differences in victimization risks by either gender or race should exhibit the greatest decrease in magnitude over time.

H4. The greater the proximity to motivated offenders, the higher the risks of victimization. This expected positive relationship should hold true with and without controls for other variables that influence criminality and victimization risks.

H5. The greater the exposure to risky and vulnerable situations, the higher the risks of victimization. This expected positive relationship should hold true with and without controls for other variables that influence criminality and victimization risks.

H6. The greater the attractiveness of the crime target, the higher the risks of victimization. This relationship should hold true with and without controls for other variables that influence criminality and victimization risks.

H7. The greater the level of guardianship, the lower the risks of victimization. This relationship should hold true with and without controls for other variables that influence criminality and victimization risks.

In addition to these basic relationships, we will also examine whether criminal opportunity theories are better able to predict victimization risks for some types of crimes than others, and whether the impact of each theoretical component varies across different social contexts.

An Integrated Perspective

There are at least three necessary conditions for crime: (1) a motivated offender, (2) a vulnerable victim or target, and (3) a facilitating social context. These conditions identify basic elements in a social explanation of crime. For this reason, these are the building blocks on which most sociological theories of crime are based, including offender-based theories, victim theories, and opportunity theories.

However, necessary conditions are not sufficient conditions, and a complete explanation of crime requires attention to the conditions under which both offender and victim characteristics combine. Unfortunately, the field of criminology is not yet ready to make a theoretical statement about both necessary and sufficient conditions for crime. One stumbling block, as we have noted, is that theories of criminal behavior and theories of victim behavior have not been informed by one another. A second obstacle is the relatively primitive state of both types of theories. One could argue that theoretical development in criminology will not progress until discursive theories (i.e., those stated in language, such as English) are dropped in favor of formal theories (i.e., those stated in mathematical relationships) (Gibbs 1985). Even if mathematical theories are beyond the present grasp of most criminologists, attempts to incorporate offender and victim factors into a discursive framework would still advance the cause.

While many criminologists agree that such a strategy is not only warranted but preferred, there is disagreement about how to go about the task of theoretical integration. There is even disagreement over how theories of criminality and theories of victimization can be combined.

COMPATIBILITY OF THEORIES OF CRIMINALITY AND VICTIMIZATION

Over the last two decades, much has been written about theoretical integration in the study of crime (see Elliott 1985; Hirschi 1986; Farrell 1989; Messner et al. 1989). Proponents of integration often emphasize the gains in explanatory power over single-variable models and how integration highlights the commonalities in theories (see Elliott 1985; Akers 1989; Thornberry 1989). As long as the separate formulations are logically compatible, a theoretical integration may also offer a more comprehensive and accurate model of crime. Integration is nothing new in criminology. In fact, each of the major theoretical perspectives in this area is, to some extent, an integration and consolidation of previous orientations (see Farrell 1989). However, a comprehensive integration of theories of criminality and victimization has not yet been undertaken even though, as shown below, such a union is easily defensible.

We have characterized most theories of criminality as being deterministic theories of offender motivation. From this perspective, crime is produced by particular biological, social, economic, and/or environmental conditions. Social disorganization theory, for example, considers population heterogeneity, poverty, mobility, and family disruption to be criminogenic forces that increase offenders' motivation by decreasing the availability of economic resources for subsistence activities and reducing the level of collective supervision and social control over young persons. According to Hirschi's (1969) control theory, these same social factors are said to enable individuals to follow their natural criminal proclivities by weakening their bonds to conventional society. Population mobility, heterogeneity, and family disruption are also salient criminogenic forces in Sutherland's theory of differential association, because these factors are suggestive of cultural conflict and the relative presence of pro- and anti-crime definitions. While the particular explanation for the observed effects varies according to perspective, these major sociological theories of criminality share a common set of social correlates thought to account for both the onset of individuals' criminal activity and rates of crime in geographical areas.

It is important to note that none of these theories of criminality view the ability to engage in criminal behavior as problematic. Once a person has the desire or motivation to commit crime, crime is more or less assumed to occur. Such an image is reasonable when one considers that there are only a few basic prerequisites for the commission of most predatory crimes (e.g., there must be a victim or target, a facilitating context, some skill or physical ability, and perhaps hardware to commit the act). However, this perspective fails to recognize that the actions of potential crime victims help to determine the supply of criminal opportunities. When there is a rich abundance of criminal opportunities in a geographical area, these opportunities may be the only motivations necessary for crime. In fact, current efforts in designing crime-free environments and situational crime prevention measures (see Clarke 1983) virtually ignore criminal motivation due to the assumption that criminal desires may be held in check by eliminating environments that facilitate crime. A fundamental weakness of current theories of criminality is the failure to consider how these criminal opportunities, created by the routine activities and lifestyles of potential crime victims, both enable and constrain the expression of criminal motivation.

Theories of victimization directly address the opportunity structure for crime and the factors associated with the selection of targets for victimization. As previously mentioned, criminal opportunity theories indicate how the nature of routine activities and lifestyles facilitate predatory crime by increasing the proximity and exposure of potential victims to would-be offenders. While exposure and proximity to risky and vulnerable locales may predispose individuals to higher risks of victimization, whether a person becomes a victim in this particular environment depends on the attractiveness of the crime target and its level of guardianship (Miethe and Meier 1990). From this perspective, offenders are rational actors who select targets for victimization that offer the greatest payoff with the least costs. However, the social forces that produce criminal motivation or weaken social restraints, the mainstays of theories of criminality, are largely ignored in theories of victimization.

The Process of Crime

The integration of theories of criminality and theories of victimization recognizes that crime involves a two-step process: (1) the decision to engage in crime (crime commission) and (2) the selection of a particular source for victimization (target-selection). Both of these decisions need to be considered for a full understanding of crime. Criminal intentions without the availability of a suitable crime target and a facilitating context will go unfulfilled.[1] Any theory of crime that ignores its social context and the actions of either offenders or potential victims is, therefore, incomplete.

In theories of victimization, the image of criminals as rational decision-makers is contrary to the deterministic conception of crime causation underlying most theories of criminality. These images are not incompatible, however, when one considers that crime commission and target-selection are two separate processes in the etiology of crime (see also Cornish and Clarke 1986). External forces, or the lack of internal social control, may drive an individual to seek criminal solutions for his or her problems (see Gottfredson and Hirschi 1990), but the actor has enormous latitude (i.e., choice) in terms of the type of crime to commit and the selection of the particular target for victimization. Under this formulation, there is obviously room for both rational-choice and deterministic components in a comprehensive theory of crime.

Integration Strategies

There are several defensible strategies for integrating theories of criminal motivation and victimization. First, as an example of theoretical elaboration (see Thornberry 1989), we can simply supplement each of the two distinct traditions by consolidating elements into a more general model. Analytically, this entails the estimation of models which include elements from both theories of criminality and theories of victimization. This strategy allows for the evaluation of (1) the relative improvement of a combined model to explain crime, which extends beyond the scope accounted for by each separate perspective and (2) how the inclusion of both perspectives modifies the importance attributed to any particular element. We may find, for example, that some aggregate indicators of exposure due to non-household activity (e.g., public transportation, female labor force participation) may continue to have a strong net impact on crime rates even after controlling for aspects of criminal motivation.

A second type of integration of theories of criminality and victimization involves cross-level integration (see Messner et al. 1989). Here, we could include neighborhood-level correlates of crime rates (e.g., the level of economic decline in the community, population mobility and diversity) in models of individuals' risks of victimization. Independent of individuals' own actions or personal attributes, the mere fact of living in a geographical area with signs of social disorganization (e.g., high levels of poverty, population mobility, ethnic heterogeneity, and/or family disruption) may dramatically increase one's risks of predatory crime. In fact, the crime-enhancing effect of the wider neighborhood context may be so powerful that it essentially nullifies any personal advantage particular residents in these areas (e.g., more "protected" residents, those who spend less time away from home or have fewer valuables to steal) may have in reducing their victimization risks. Under this form of theoretical integration, the wider social context may have both a direct effect on victimization risks and mediate the impact of individuals' routine activities and lifestyles on these risks.

While the decisions to commit crime and target selection are cognitively independent events, the use of empirical indicators of theoretical concepts with multiple meanings in previous studies makes it difficult to evaluate theories underlying these decisions. This indeterminacy of empirical indicators is especially common in aggregate-level studies of crime rates using secondary data (see Miethe, Hughes, and McDowall 1991). The major consequence of this problem is an inability to distinguish the predictive validity of competing theories when different perspectives yield the same empirical predictions. Several standard measures of theoretical concepts illustrate this problem. For example, household size can be considered a measure of both "guardianship" in opportunity theories (e.g., representing the level of protection for persons or property) and "social integration" in theories of criminality (e.g., "living alone" implies weaker bonds or lower social integration). The empirical discovery of a negative relationship between household size and crime rates would therefore provide no discriminatory evidence for either theoretical approach in explaining the onset of crime or the selection of particular targets for victimization. Similarly, the fact that greater levels of public activity increase individuals' risks and aggregate rates of predatory crime may be due to either higher levels of exposure to risky and vulnerable situations (according to opportunity theory), decreased guardianship (also according to opportunity theory), or lower levels of social integration and weakening social bonds (according to theories of criminality). The same arguments can be made for nearly all empirical indicators of major concepts underlying theories of criminality and victimization.[2]

A HEURISTIC MODEL

A complete explanation of criminal events requires attention to offenders, victims, and the social context that brings them together. Most of criminological theory has dealt with offender characteristics, and recent literature has explored victim behavior and characteristics. The social context, which includes elements of both the interpersonal and physical environment, is where criminal intentions and attractive victim characteristics are translated into action. Figure 4.1 shows a graphic representation of the relationships between offender motivation, victim characteristics that enhance criminal opportunities, and the social context of criminal events. Using the language of path analysis,[3] presumed direct causal relationships are represented in this diagram as solid arrows. A dashed stem is used to convey residual causal relationships. These residual paths are defined as direct relationships that are of a smaller absolute magnitude, because the primary influence of a variable is being transmitted through another variable in a causal chain. A curved double-headed arrow indicates a correlation.

This general model assumes a particular causal ordering between each component. Offender motivation and criminal opportunities provided by victim characteristics are related to one another, but the direction of this relationship is unclear. Specifically, motivated offenders may seek out suitable crime targets (i.e., victims who are in proximity to offenders, involved in risky or vulnerable situations, economically or physically attractive, and lack guardianship) or, alternatively, these characteristics of potential victims may generate criminal intentions. However, the presence of criminal intentions and "attractive" victim characteristics will not necessarily result in a criminal act unless the wider social context is also conducive to crime. The centrality of the social context in understanding crime is indicated in Figure 4.1 by its assumed direct causal path to criminal events and the manner in which the primary impact of both offender motivation and victim characteristics on crime is transmitted through it.

As indicated by the residual paths (i.e., the dashed arrows), our model allows for the occurrence of criminal events even when the nexus of offender motivation, victim characteristics, and the social context is not ideal or optimal. For example, criminal motivation may be so strong (e.g., because of immediate financial problems, peer pressure, or inflamed passions) that offenders do not exercise sound judgment in selecting the most attractive location, time, and target for victimization. Many violent crimes that occur in the "heat of passion" and various kinds of "thrill-seeking" offenses by juveniles to gain peer approval occur under these less than ideal conditions. Similarly, a facilitating social context and the opportunities provided by attractive, accessible, and unprotected crime targets may be too good to pass up, even among persons who do not have prior motivations and the stressful life events that commonly trigger criminal acts. Thus, the convergence of motivated offenders, criminal opportunities, and a facilitating social context dramatically increases the likelihood of crime events under our theoretical model. However, crime is possible even when only one of these components is present.[4]

Sources of Offender Motivation

The particular sources of offender motivation have been identified in previous studies of criminality. They include factors as diverse as economic disadvantage, weak social bonds, pro-crime values, psychological or biological attributes, generalized needs (e.g., money, sex, friendship, excitement), and the availability of non-criminal alternatives. Our empirical

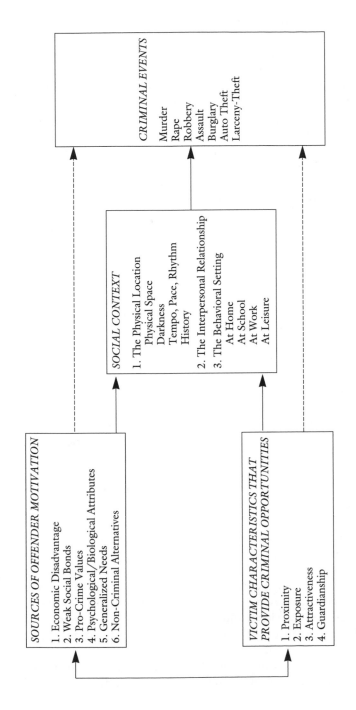

Figure 4.1 Heuristic Model of Criminal Events

analyses focus on the impact of population mobility, low socio-economic status, ethnic heterogeneity, and single-parent families for three major reasons. First, these factors are the most widely recognized correlates of crime rates in previous research. Second, it is widely assumed that an individual's decision to engage in crime is influenced by these factors because they are ultimately indicative of the social forces that trigger criminal motivation (e.g., economic despair, weak bonds to traditional society, cultural conflict). Third, the observed effects of these factors can be explained by a variety of theoretical perspectives on criminality. The importance of these factors was more fully discussed in chapter 2.

Criminal Opportunities Provided by Victims

Routine activity and lifestyle-exposure theories of victimization identify fundamental characteristics of victims that create criminal opportunities. These major factors include measures of proximity to offenders, exposure to high-crime situations, target attractiveness, and the absence of guardianship. While the presence of these factors helps define a social context as conducive for crime, these victim characteristics are also assumed in our model to have an independent impact on the probability of crime events regardless of the particular social context. The causal significance of victim characteristics in generating criminal opportunities was discussed in chapter 3.

The Social Context of Crime

Factors that enhance offender motivation and factors that increase victim risk do not exist in a vacuum. Rather, each operates in a social context that brings them together and enhances their effects. Among the key components underlying an integrated theory of crime, however, the social context has been least investigated in previous research. The scant attention paid to the social context has lead several authors to advocate greater research on the "neglected situation" (LaFree and Birkbeck 1991) and the micro-environments of crime (Davidson 1989).

While rarely defined in past research, we maintain that the social context consists of several major dimensions. Beyond simply the characteristics of motivated offenders and crime victims, the social context is a micro-environment that involves (1) a physical location, (2) the interpersonal relationship between the victim and offender, and (3) a behavioral setting that establishes the activities of the victim at the time of the offense.

The Physical Location One obvious characteristic of the social context is its physical location or setting. Whether referred to as "hot spots" for crime (e.g., Sherman et al. 1989), the ecology of deviant places (Stark 1987), or "facilitating places" (Lofland 1969), dangerous places appear to vary by the type of crime and have specific characteristics and histories. Many residents are keenly aware of the most dangerous areas in their cities and towns that are to be avoided at all costs.

Concerning differences by the type of offense, previous research on the physical location for crime indicates that inside shopping malls, for example, may be considered "hot spots" for shoplifting but not personal assault. Parking lots surrounding shopping malls, however, are not uncommon locations for personal assaults, abductions, and drive-by purse snatchings, even though bars, adult bookstores, and shelters for the homeless are more frequent sites for violent crimes (see Sherman et al. 1989). The high rate of violent crime during nighttime hours, and on streets near drinking establishments, gives some additional indication of the "hot spots" for these offenses (see Hindelang et al. 1978; Roncek and Maier 1991). Previous research on burglaries and other property offenses (see Reppetto 1974; Waller and Okihiro 1978; Bennett and Wright 1984) suggests that these offenses more commonly occur in geographical locales characterized by physical signs of low income and incivilities (e.g., abandoned buildings, multi-unit dwellings, garbage and trash on streets).

The particular physical attributes that underlie "dangerous places" involve basic properties of the setting that may influence what happens during a criminal event. For example, the amount of physical space in a setting becomes important in explaining the likelihood of criminal events because closed and confined spaces may (1) impede the ability of potential victims to flee from a threatening situation, (2) reduce offenders' motivation because it limits escape options, and (3) increase criminal desires because excessive crowding may fuel tension, anxiety, and frustration. The amount of lighting in a physical setting also seems to be a characteristic of dangerous places. While darkness is a major factor underlying people's evaluations of dangerous places (see Warr 1990), poor lighting may facilitate the occurrence of crime by providing greater anonymity and cover for offenders. Physical locales within geographical areas also have their distinct "tempo," "pace," and "rhythm" (Hawley 1950), which further define them as dangerous places. Urban locations that serve as major arteries for foot traffic and are crowded with strangers have a particular ambience that make them prime spots for pick-pocketing offenses (see LaFree and Birkbeck 1991).

Similar to individual offenders, it is important to note that physical environments also have "histories" of criminal activity. The early Chicago ecologists (Park, Burgess, Shaw, McKay) were the first to recognize that there are "natural areas" for crime that persist over time. In fact, one of the lasting contributions of this tradition was the empirical observation that particular areas retain high levels of criminal activity even after their composition and structure had changed over time. More recent work on the criminal "careers" of neighborhoods (see Schuerman and Kobrin 1986) reinforces these findings. From a social disorganization perspective, these high-crime areas are said to be characterized by higher rates of population mobility, ethnic diversity, socio-economic deterioration, and disruptive family relations. It is safe to say that every U.S. city has a particular physical area that is designed as the "bad part" of town, where high rates of crime and fear have a long history.

Current efforts at crime control through environmental design are clearly indicative of public policy that attempts to modify the physical location of crime. These programs are based on the assumption that changes in the physical environment (e.g., improved lighting, rerouting traffic patterns, modifying housing designs) can reduce the opportunities for crime, thereby decreasing the likelihood of criminal events. Reductions in the volume of crime are expected under these programs, even when the level of offender motivation and other victim characteristics in this environment have not been altered.

The Interpersonal Relationship   This aspect of the social context involves the particular association between the victim and the offender. Criminal acts involving victims and offenders who are known to each other (e.g., family members, relatives, co-workers, friends, acquaintances) and those involving strangers are distinct in terms of their physical ecology and underlying motivation. In the case of crimes involving "known" offenders, it makes little sense to place any great causal significance on the victim's proximity and exposure to risky and dangerous physical environments, because such offenses are motivated primarily by a particular grievance between the parties that can be resolved in any physical location, at any time, and under the most idiosyncratic conditions. Strangers, on the other hand, are motivated by different concerns (e.g., sexual conquest, money, thrill-seeking), have less accessibility to particular crime targets, and consequently must wait for victims to be exposed to risky and vulnerable situations. The likelihood of bystander intervention, the chances that a criminal attack will be completed, and the response from social control agencies is also likely to vary widely by this contextual factor. As a result of these differences, criminal opportunity theories of victimization and theories of criminality that emphasize economic marginality as a motivator for crime (e.g., strain, social bond, social disorganization) would seem less relevant in explaining the likelihood and distribution of predatory crimes involving known offenders.

The Behavioral Setting   The last dimension of the social context is concerned with the functional properties of micro-environments that indicate why a potential victim is at a particular setting (see Davidson 1989). The most common behavioral settings or "domains" for crime (see Lynch 1987) include the (1) home environment, (2) school environment, (3) work environment, and (4) leisure environment. These behavioral contexts are important because crimes that occur in these particular domains may have a different frequency, a different *modus operandi*, involve different motivations, and be explained by different predisposing and precipitating factors. The empirical discovery of such domain-specific models would severely question the utility of general theories of criminal events that are assumed to apply across these contexts.

Crimes that occur in or near the home of the victim have a general ecology that is quite different from other behavioral contexts, in several respects. First, there is no other setting with which a person is more familiar than the area in and around one's dwelling. This familiarity gives potential victims of "home" assaults an enormous advantage over potential victims in other settings in warding off a stranger attack, establishing an escape route, and summoning outside assistance. Second, because they occur in a non-public location and are viewed as "private" matters, crimes among intimates that happen in the home are unlikely to involve external intervention (by neighbors or police) until well after the completion of the criminal act. Third, the probability of a property or violent offense occurring in a home is influenced, to a large degree, by the characteristics of the wider physical environment. For example, regardless of the particular characteristics of a dwelling (e.g., its accessibility, visibility, attractiveness, guardianship), persons who live in geographical areas that exhibit signs of social disorganization may have greater risks of victimization, in or near their home, than residents of more affluent neighborhoods. Thus, the likelihood of victimization in this context is expected to vary widely depending upon the particular victim-offender relationship and the characteristics of the wider physical environment.

Over the last decade, increased attention has been given to crimes that occur within schools. At first glance, one might expect the structural environment and the level of supervision in schools to make this behavioral setting an unlikely site for criminal activity. However, schools have particular characteristics that enhance their attractiveness as criminogenic environments. The concentration of persons and property in such settings, for example, provides ample opportunities for crime commission. Peer pressures, petty jealousies, status threats, failed romances, and the general volatility of the adolescent years offer rather unique motivations for crime in this behavioral context. Inner city public high schools are especially prone to attenuated social control and other characteristics (e.g., economic inequality, cultural conflict) that fuel motivated offenders and enhance the risks of predatory offenses.

The work environment shares some of the characteristics of schools (e.g., a structured setting), but has other attributes that contribute to its appeal as a location for criminal events. Some occupational groups (e.g., police officers, prison guards, bartenders, bank cashiers, checkers in convenience stores) are routinely exposed to motivated offenders and risky situations in their daily work activities. Similarly, some work settings (e.g., banks, convenience stores) are attractive crime sites because they provide the money or merchandise wanted by offenders. Some corporate businesses may actually contribute to violence among co-workers by overemphasizing internal competition and reward structures. In similarity to other domains for crime, there can be major differences between work environments in terms of their proximity to high-crime areas, their exposure to risky situations, their attractiveness as crime targets, and their level of protection or guardianship. Persons in particular occupations may run a greater risk of victimization due to the specific work they do and the characteristics of the wider environment in which this activity takes place. Whether the work takes place in a public or private setting also contributes to its appraisal as an attractive crime environment.

The last behavioral setting involves the leisure domain. Leisure activities may take place in settings that vary widely in terms of the criminal opportunities that they provide. Some leisure activities (e.g., going to movies, out to dinner, sporting events, music concerts) are especially dangerous because they occur in public places, at nighttime, increase the chances of physical contact with strangers, and may involve the consumption of alcohol which can impede one's judgment and abilities. The relative risks of other leisure activities, like shopping or jogging, depends in a large part on when, where, and with whom these activities take place.

Each of these behavioral domains serves as its own micro-environment for what Lofland (1969) refers to as "facilitating places, hardware, and others." The physical space surrounding each domain facilitates crime by providing multiple escape routes, sufficient cover (e.g., trees, shrubs, dark corners) to conceal the presence and identity of offenders, and has a predictable rhythm and pace which allows offenders to more easily "size up" potential victims. Home, school, work, and leisure settings that are located in physical areas characterized by low social control, high population density and turnover, and a concentration of young persons would seem especially prone to predatory offenses. Similarly, each domain provides an assortment of rudimentary hardware (e.g., rocks and boards to break windows, tools to pick locks, knives to threaten and assault victims) that is required for the commission of offenses. The absence of such hardware in a particular setting may be sufficient to deter the novice or opportunistic offender from criminal activity. Finally, the availability of "facilitating" others in each domain may either impede or enhance the likelihood of a criminal event. An offender's perception of the likelihood of bystander intervention may be sufficient to discourage a criminal act. However, the presence of bystanders in some situations may also promote crime by encouraging offended persons to "save face" and stand up to abuse from others (see Luckenbill 1977). In either case, the presence of others becomes an important situational determinant of the likelihood of criminal events.

The Importance of the Social Context

As we have just described, the social context is a micro-environment that has physical, interpersonal, and behavioral dimensions. Some social contexts are more receptive to criminal events than others. Our theoretical model assumes that much of the impact of offender motivation and victim characteristics on the likelihood of criminal events is transmitted directly through this social context. Furthermore, criminal intentions and the presence of attractive crime targets may not be sufficient to generate crime when the wider social context is not conducive to it. Economically motivated offenders, for example, may be able to reap their greatest rewards by pulling off a bank robbery, but the structural features of this work context (e.g., armed security, electronic monitoring) are probably sufficient to deter all but the most desperate offenders. Under a displacement hypothesis (see Gabor 1990), these economically motivated offenders, deterred by the bank security, would be expected to seek out another context for crime (e.g., a convenience store) which may offer less payoff, but involves considerably lower risks of detection and apprehension.

Using a variety of data sources, several analyses will be conducted in the current study to assess the importance of the social context in explaining predatory crime. First, police reports and victimization data will be used to describe the social ecology of different types of predatory offenses (e.g., where, when, and with whom it occurs). These analyses will reveal, for example, the prevalence of crimes involving strangers, the temporal patterning of criminal activity, and its distribution over various physical contexts (e.g., at home, in streets, in public buildings). Second, models of individuals' risks of various types of victimization will be estimated to examine how well these victimization risks are accounted for by differences in individuals' routine activities and lifestyles. Aspects of the wider social context (e.g., the level of public activity in the neighborhood, the average income of the neighborhood) will be added to these models to indicate how these contextual factors influence victimization risks and modify the impact of individual-level attributes. Combined, these analyses will empirically evaluate the social contexts in which crime occurs and how knowledge of the micro-environment can improve our understanding of the correlates of criminal events.

SUMMARY

Any adequate explanation for crime must recognize its basic structural features. The features of predatory crime are that crime involves offenders, victims, and a social context.

The task of criminological theory is to identify the sources of offender motivation and criminal opportunities which make crime a likely outcome in a particular social context. Factors such as population mobility, low socio-economic status, ethnic heterogeneity, and family structure are key factors underlying offender motivation in theories of criminality. They are also central physical aspects of a micro-environment for criminal events. Opportunity theories of victimization identify proximity to offenders, exposure to high-risk situations, target attractiveness, and guardianship as key elements for understanding target-selection decisions. However, our heuristic model assumes that it is the social context that ultimately determines the conditions under which crime occurs, and whether aspects of offender motivation and target-selection factors enhance, impede, or have no impact on the likelihood of victimization. Measures of each of these concepts and their explanatory power in accounting for crime rates and individuals' risks of victimization are described in the remaining chapters.

Data Sources for Evaluating Criminological Theories

Different types of data have been used to evaluate the predictive utility of theories of criminality and victimization. Our knowledge about crime and victimization is based primarily on police reports, self-report studies, field observations, case studies, and victimization surveys. As a basis for identifying the extent, causes, and the social distribution of predatory crime, each of these data sources has well-known strengths and limitations. When interpreted with some caution, these sources can be used to describe the social and spatial distribution of crime and to construct general profiles of offenders and victims.

This chapter describes three data sources used in the current study: (1) the F.B.I.'s Uniform Crime Reports (UCR) and data collected by the U.S. Bureau of the Census, (2) victimization data from the National Crime Survey (NCS), and (3) a 1990 telephone survey of 5,302 Seattle residents. UCR data and census reports will be analyzed later to examine the distribution and predictors of official crime rates over time and various aggregate units (i.e, census tracts, cities, SMSAs). UCR data also provides a demographic profile of arrested offenders for various types of predatory crime. NCS data, from the last two decades, are used to identify the social characteristics of crime victims and the ecology of predatory crime (e.g., when and where it occurs). Data from the Seattle telephone survey are analyzed to evaluate criminal opportunity theories of victimization. This chapter also describes the operationalization and measurement of the key concepts underlying theories of criminality (i.e., low socio-economic condition, population mobility, ethnic heterogeneity, family disruption) and theories of victimization (i.e., proximity, exposure, target attractiveness, guardianship). The data analytic procedures used to test hypotheses are outlined in the final part of the chapter.

UCR DATA AND CENSUS REPORTS

The primary source of data on crime in the United States is the Federal Bureau of Investigation's *Uniform Crime Reports* (UCR). Derived from monthly reports of local law enforcement agencies, and covering over 90 percent of the total national population, the annual UCR data provides information on various topics, including the number of offenses known to the police, crime and arrest trends over time, and offense-specific arrest rates by age, gender, race, and size of community. UCR data are used in the current study to provide official rates of homicide, rape, robbery, aggravated assault, burglary, and motor vehicle theft for various aggregate units (i.e., census tracts within a city, cities, SMSAs). However, as a major source for evaluating theories of criminality and victimization, UCR data have both strengths and limitations.

The major advantage of UCR data over other sources on offending (e.g., self-report studies) involves the longitudinal nature of the data collection and the extensive coverage across various geographical units. One research question underlying the current study is the relationship between changes in social conditions and crime rates over the last three decades (1960-1980). Police reports are the only available longitudinal crime data, representing various geographical units, for examining the correlates of crime rates and changes in crime rates over time. The fact that uniform definitions of most of the index crimes (except larceny-theft) have been used over time also enhances the utility of UCR data for longitudinal analysis. The comprehensive coverage and the longitudinal nature of police reports contribute to the unique value of UCR data in examining aggregate crime rates within and across time periods.

The limitations of UCR data are so well known that it is unnecessary to repeat them here (see, for review, Gove, Hughes, and Geerken 1985). However, there are two basic shortcomings of this data that require some attention, since they cast the most doubt on the utility of police reports for evaluating criminological theories. These limitations involve the magnitude of reporting bias and problems with aggregating different offenses into the same crime categories.

It has been long recognized that police reports about crime are sensitive to fluctuations in reporting behavior by citizens. The vast majority of crimes become "known" to the police in response to a citizen complaint. If citizens do not perceive the crime to be serious enough to warrant official action, feel that "nothing can be done," "it was a private matter," or any of a number of other reasons for not calling the police, the act will not be officially designated as a crime. Furthermore, even if a crime is observed by the police or reported to them, there is no guarantee that it will be so recorded. Of the various factors that influence reporting decisions, the seriousness of the offense is a major determinant. The fact that most serious offenses are reported by citizens and police has lead Gove et al. (1985) to conclude that the UCRs are a valid measure of the extent of serious crime.

Given the arguments by Gove et al. (1985), and our interest in the index crimes, the level of reporting bias in the current study should be less dramatic than would be the case for a study of less serious offenses. Nonetheless, the fact that over 50 percent of all burglaries and robberies go unreported to the police indicates that under-reporting remains a problem even with "serious" offenses. When one also considers the possibility that reporting behavior varies by the size of the community (i.e., there may be more reporting in smaller cities than in large, urban areas), this selective reporting across units raises doubt about the validity of police data for evaluating inter-city differences in crime rates.

Certain assumptions can be made about the nature and consequences of reporting bias on our substantive conclusions. First, some types of crime (e.g., murder) will be less susceptible to reporting bias than other offenses (e.g., rape). In fact, given the changing public attitudes and greater sensitivity to victims of rape and domestic assault over the last thirty years, changes in official crime rates for these offenses should be especially inflated by changes in reporting over time (see LaFree 1989). We have no compelling reason to believe that a similar situation characterizes the reporting of other index crimes. However, data from national victimization surveys for the years 1976 and 1988 indicate that reporting rates for rape actually decreased over time (53 percent reported in 1976 versus 45 percent in 1988), whereas reporting rates for assault changed very little over this same time period (48 percent versus 46 percent). In contrast, reporting rates for robbery increased from 53 percent to 57 percent, and increased from 48 percent to 51 percent for residential burglary. The general conclusion from these comparisons is that there has been only a modest change in crime reporting over time. Second, if reporting does vary by population size (e.g., highest in small cities, lowest in large, urban centers), this differential reporting will result in error variance in models of crime rates across geographical areas. Third, when examining longitudinal models of changing crime rates over time, our working assumption is that temporal changes in reporting should be fairly uniform across cities. If changes in reporting over time are uniform across cities, longitudinal models of crime rates will be less susceptible to correlated measurement error.

A second fundamental problem with analyses based on UCR data is that different types of offenses are collapsed into the same crime category. For example, both residential and non-residential burglary are included in the same UCR category (i.e., burglary), and a similar situation applies to personal and institutional robbery (i.e., robbery). Although over half of all reported robberies are street/highway holdups of individuals, and two-thirds of the burglaries against residents (UCR 1980), the mixing of crimes with different physical structures within the same category is a source of error variance which will typically decrease the explanatory power of our estimated models.

When attention focuses on the determinants of aggregate rates of predatory crime, the major predictor variables will be derived from various census reports. The *County and City Data Book* (CCD) distributed by the U.S. Census Bureau is the primary source for this information. The consolidated CCD files and reports for specific years between 1947 and 1987 are available through the Inter-University Consortium for Political and Social Research (ICPSR). Other secondary sources (e.g., State Census Volumes, State and Metropolitan Area Book) were used to supplement observations with missing data. Using the CCD files and supplements, we were able to construct a longitudinal panel of 584 U.S. cities with populations over 25,000 for the years 1960, 1970, and 1980. Census data for the 148 largest SMSAs in the United States for 1970 was recorded from the 1972 CCD files and a book entitled *Quality of Life Indicators in U.S. Metropolitan Areas* (Liu 1976). The original sources for SMSA data include various supplemental census reports (e.g., census of housing, retail sales, population characteristics), climatological reports, and a survey of Chamber of Commerce officials in metropolitan areas.

There are several basic issues that arise when using census data as the major source to derive measures of key concepts underlying theories of criminality and victimization. First, data collected for primarily administrative purposes is usually not of the specificity or scope required for scientific inquiry. Basic demographic variables that represent major elements of theories of criminality (e.g., ethnic heterogeneity, population mobility, low SES, and family disruption) are provided in census data for various aggregate units and over time periods, but measures of the important causal processes that distinguish between these theories (e.g., level of attachment to formal institutions, the amount of supervision of youth) are not contained in these data. Unequivocal indicators of the major components underlying theories of victimization (i.e., proximity, exposure, target attractiveness and guardianship) are also not available from census reports, requiring the use, in many cases, of gross proxy measures of these concepts. Second, supplemental census data is not collected on a continuous yearly basis. One immediate implication of this fact is that the only available measures of key concepts in some cases involve data that refers to social conditions present several years prior to the year used for the analysis of crime rates. However, for purposes of temporal ordering, this situation is preferable to one in which the dependent variables precede the independent variables in time.

Although both UCR data and census reports have limitations as a basis for examining the predictors of crime rates, they remain the only available longitudinal data that are collected across different geographical units. Consequently, these data will be the primary source for the aggregate analysis in the current study. These data will be used for three different units of analysis: (1) 148 SMSAs for the year 1970, (2) a panel study of 584 U.S. cities with populations over 25,000 for the years 1960, 1970, and 1980, and (3) 114 census tracts in the city of Seattle, Washington for the years 1960, 1970, and 1980.[1]

There are several reasons why it is important to use multiple units of analysis and different time periods in a study of crime rates. First, the analysis of crime rates for different times and aggregate units provides a means to cross validate research findings and to evaluate their robustness over various conditions. From this perspective, each subsample, by unit and time, serves as a possible replication of the theoretical model. Second, of the aggregate units, we expect our results to be most consistent with theoretical predictions utilizing the census tract as the unit of analysis, and least consistent when based on the SMSA. This is anticipated because census tracts are well-defined geographical areas that tend to minimize within-group variation (due to the presumed similarity of persons within a census tract), and maximize between-group variation (due to the presumed differences in the persons that live across these different geographical areas). An opposite situation seems to characterize the SMSA as an aggregate unit. Third, theories of criminality and victimization have been applied both to explaining the social organization of crime and how it changes over time (see Miethe et al. 1991). We have no reason to expect analyses based on cross-sectional models to be any more predictive of theoretically expected relationships than those based on longitudinal data.

NATIONAL CRIME SURVEYS

The growth of victimization surveys, since the early 1960s, stems largely from their use as an alternative measure of the extent and distribution of crime. By eliciting reasons for not reporting offenses to the authorities, victimization surveys also are used to identify the nature of bias in official crime reports. Furthermore, no other data source provides as much information on the location of crime, characteristics of the criminal episode, and the consequences of crime than do victimization surveys.

By far, the most comprehensive data source on crime victims is the National Crime Survey (NCS) annual series, sponsored by the Bureau of Justice Statistics and administered by the U.S. Bureau of the Census. Its purposes are to measure the extent of crime in the United States and to provide a data base for understanding the causes and consequences of crime from the victim's perspective (Cantor 1989: 26). Initiated in 1973, the NCS series uses a rotated panel design in which sampling units are reinterviewed every six months, for a total of seven complete interviews.[2] About 72,000 households were included in the NCS series until 1984 when the sample size was reduced to 59,000 housing units. All persons in the household over 12 years old are interviewed, and in some cases, proxies are used for those absent at the time of the interview. Persons who move out of a household are not followed to their new address, but if a new person or entire family moves into one of the sampled housing units between panel waves, this person or family is interviewed as part of the series. The ICPSR User's Manual for the NCS data provides a detailed description of the sampling design and technical issues about the structure of the data.

As noted by Cantor (1989), the NCS annual series is a longitudinal survey covering almost every analytic level of interest to criminologists. This observation is supported in several ways. First, at the national level, the NCS series is a repeated cross-section that has accumulated, at present, an 18-year time series. Second, the NCS sample design clusters observations according to address segments (i.e., groups of four households in an enumeration district), which allows for analysis of these smaller units over time. Third, the NCS collects data at the level of the individual housing unit. Although there is major attrition across successive waves, changes in individuals' risks of victimization over time can also be examined with NCS data (see, for application, Miethe et al. 1990).

The national sampling design makes the NCS data a good source for trend studies. For researchers with an interest in individuals or households, the multi-wave panel design permits the analysis of both short-term (i.e., six months) and long-term (i.e., up to three years) changes in victimization experiences over time. If the criminal act is the focus of investigation, the fact that the NCS data are fairly rich in details about the nature of the crime (e.g., where it occurs, degree of injury/loss, victim-offender relationship, number of offenders, demographic attributes of offenders) allows one to examine changes in crime characteristics over time. The coding and classification of some response categories has changed over time (e.g., location of crime), but great effort has been taken to maintain the continuity of the NCS series over time. The NCS panel design also minimizes the problems associated with asking retrospective questions, and the use of a bounding interview reduces telescoping and other recall problems (see, also, Cantor 1989).

As a primary source for social scientific inquiry and policy analysis, however, the NCS data are limited in several respects. These data suffer many of the same problems that plague other longitudinal designs (e.g., panel attrition, respondent conditioning), but the major limitation involves the type of information collected in the survey.

Information from the NCS series is heavily skewed toward basic demographic attributes of the household member (e.g., age, sex, race, income) and details about the criminal event. Aside from these questions, however, little information is collected on the characteristics of the resident's neighborhood, routine work and leisure activities, or safety precautions undertaken by the respondents. General attitude and perceptual questions (e.g., fear of crime, perceived vulnerability to crime) are also given scant attention in the NCS series. Consequently, NCS data do not provide the type of information necessary to evaluate current theories of victimization. The exception to this pattern is the NCS "victim-risk supplement," conducted on one rotation panel in February 1984. Although measures of each major concept underlying victimization theories can be developed from this NCS supplement, these data are still less amenable to theory testing than other victimization data. Data from the NCS series will be used, in the current study, to describe the social ecology of victimization (e.g., where and when it occurs, the victim-offender relationship) and changes in the characteristics of predatory crime over time. Bivariate relationships between demographic variables and risks of various types of victimization will also be reported on the basis of the most current year of the NCS data (i.e., 1989). These NCS analyses will be performed primarily to cross-validate research findings from a victimization survey in Seattle, Washington.

SEATTLE TELEPHONE SURVEY

The primary data source used in this study to evaluate theories of victimization involves a telephone survey of 5,302 residents of Seattle, Washington. The interviews were conducted from February to May of 1990. The telephone survey was part of a larger study of crime in Seattle over the last three decades, and was funded by a grant from the National Science Foundation. Three research questions underlie this larger project: (1) Do the major components of criminal opportunity theories of victimization (i.e., proximity, exposure, target attractiveness, guardianship) adequately account for individuals' risks and neighborhood rates of violent crime and property victimization?, (2) Do socio-economic changes in geographical areas explain the changes in their crime rates over time?, and (3) How does the target-hardening efforts of residents and their immediate neighbors influence individuals' risks of victimization?

To evaluate how the wider social context of crime control activities influences individuals' risks of victimization, a complex sampling design was used to select immediate neighbors and bordering city blocks. The final sample involves 5,302 residents who live on 600 city blocks in 100 of the 121 census tracts in Seattle. Stratifying the sample by both census tract and city blocks within tracts insured a sufficient number of respondents for each of these aggregate units. The 100 census tracts used here represent a random subsample of the 114 census tracts which had not changed their geographical boundaries since 1960.

After selecting census tracts, the next stage of sampling involved identifying three pairs of city blocks per census tract.[3] One block per pair contained a street address in which a burglary was reported to the police during 1989, whereas the other block per pair involved a street segment which was bordering the street on which the burglary occurred. The selection of a city block with a known burglary was made to increase the number of victimized households in the sample. Once these 300 blocks with known burglaries were identified, a detailed city map was used to select, at random, one of the four adjoining city blocks for each pair. This aspect of the sampling design was important in the original study because it allowed for an assessment of how the wider social context of safety precautions influences victimization risks across adjoining city blocks.

A reverse telephone directory (organized sequentially by street address) was used to select adjacent housing units on each city block. A maximum of eighteen households were initially selected per block, however additional households were also chosen when large rates of "disconnects," "no answers," or "wrong addresses" were observed on a block.[4] Replacement sampling was done to insure a sufficient number of respondents for deriving aggregate rates for each block. For each household in the sampling frame, a maximum of five call-backs were made to contact respondents. Special efforts were made to interview a particular person (the one listed in the directory), but another adult in the same household was interviewed when the primary person was not available. No interviews were completed when an adult was not present or when an adult did not feel qualified to answer questions about the household. Identical procedures were used to select respondents on blocks with and without known burglaries.

Overall, there were 12,303 phone numbers dialed by the interviewers which resulted in contact with 9,250 residential households. Noncontact phone numbers included "no answer" (n = 1,548), "disconnects" (n = 1,355), and businesses (n = 150). The sample size was reduced further because the primary respondent or another knowledgeable adult in the household was not available (n = 742), changed addresses (n = 940), or the respondent was hearing impaired or did not speak English (n = 409). Of the remaining 7,159 eligible households, 5,302 interviews were completed, resulting in a response rate of 74.1 percent. The number of complete interviews per city block ranged from four to twelve, with 99.2 percent (595/600) having six or more respondents per block. The number of completed interviews per pair of city blocks ranged from thirteen to twenty-one, and from forty-five to fifty-seven respondents per census tract.

Detailed field observations were also made on each housing unit in order to evaluate the proximity of the sample units on a city block and the validity of collapsing observations to form neighborhood rates. Information was recorded on the characteristics of each city block (e.g., its length, number of cross-streets, traffic flow) and each housing unit (e.g., security equipment on premises, the dwelling's physical condition, visibility of front yard, its location on the block). Although a vacant lot or another dwelling not included in the sample separated housing units in many cases, the field observations clearly confirmed the physical proximity of neighbors, and supported the aggregation of individual responses to derive rates per block and rates per census tract.

Several additional comments about the sampling design are worth noting. First, telephone directories are limited because they do not include persons with unlisted phone numbers (about 28 percent in Seattle households) and are particularly unrepresentative of recent movers. Only 7.3 percent of our sample respondents had moved in the last year, compared to a national rate of about 18 percent. Nonetheless, telephone directories were used because they are the best available source for drawing a comprehensive sample of immediate neighbors and adjoining blocks across an entire city. Second, the sampling design and the survey results limit generalizations that can be made about the entire city of Seattle. This is the case due to the use of the telephone directories, the sampling of only "stable" census tracts (i.e., those that had not changed their boundaries since 1960), the deliberate oversampling of 300 city blocks with known burglaries, a 9 percent higher response rate for street addresses with known burglaries over housing units in which it was unknown, in advance, whether a burglary had occurred, and the relatively high rates of home ownership (65 percent) and college education (71 percent had at least "some college") in the survey sample. When the Seattle respondents are compared with the household respondents in the 1989 NCS data (see Table 5.1), it is easy to see that the Seattle sample is older, more educated, less transient (i.e., less frequent movers, higher rates of home ownership), and more evenly distributed with regard to gender than the NCS sample.

If our interest was in generating city-wide estimates of demographic characteristics and victimization rates, the sampling limitations of the Seattle survey would severely question the validity of these inferences. The differential composition of the Seattle and NCS samples also hampers comparisons of bivariate relationships across samples. When samples have different characteristics, it cannot be easily determined whether differences in substantive findings are due to unreliable results or differences in sample composition. On the other hand, comparisons of the relative risks of victimization within categories of demographic attributes (e.g., gender, race, or age differences) are less affected than city-wide estimates by the problems with the sampling design. Given that our primary interest is to examine how relative differences in routine activity patterns and lifestyles alter individuals' risks of victimization, the sampling bias against lower income, transient, and young persons in the Seattle data is less bothersome than would be true in other studies.

The multi-level sampling design, and the type of information collected in the Seattle survey, contribute to its uniqueness as a data source for testing theories of victimization. Specifically, each of the potential aggregate units (e.g., city block, pairs of city blocks, census tracts) is physically well defined and contains a sufficient number of respondents to provide stable estimates of aggregate parameters. In contrast to other data sources for multi-level and contextual analyses (e.g., the NCS files, the British Crime Surveys), the independent confirmation, through field observations of the physical proximity of residents on city blocks and within census tracts, provides unique validation for the merits of these aggregate units.[5] Given that the primary goal of the Seattle study was to evaluate theories of victimization, the survey was also designed to collect a rich array of measures on the routine activities and lifestyles of the respondents. As described in the next section, these measures provide multiple indicators of each of the major concepts underlying theories of victimization.

Table 5.1 Sample Characteristics for Seattle Survey and 1989 NCS Data

Demographic Variable	Seattle Survey	NCS Survey
Age Category		
16–29 yrs. old	13.9%	23.2%
30–59 yrs. old	55.3%	54.8%
60 and older	30.8%	22.0%
Gender		
Female	49.8%	37.5%
Male	50.2%	62.5%
Ethnicity		
White	84.9%	86.0%
Black	6.5%	11.5%
Other	8.6%	2.5%
Median Family Income		
Low (<$10k)	8.6%	22.7%
Medium ($10–$30k)	44.2%	42.3%
High (>$30k)	47.2%	35.0%
Marital Status		
Married	54.5%	51.1%
Widowed	10.5%	10.3%
Separated/Divorced	11.4%	18.7%
Never Married	23.6%	19.9%
Educational Attainment		
< HS Graduate	6.2%	19.6%
HS Graduate	23.1%	34.3%
> HS Graduate	70.7%	46.1%
Times Moved in Last 5 yrs.		
0 moves	57.4%	47.9%
1 move	18.1%	19.7%
2 or more moves	24.4%	32.4%
Housing Unit		
Single-unit Dwelling	79.1%	65.1%
Multi-unit Dwelling	20.9%	34.9%
Home Tenure		
Renter	35.0%	43.4%
Owner/Buying	65.0%	56.6%
Household Size*		
Live Alone	28.0%	31.1%
2 Persons	53.0%	46.1%
3 or more Persons	19.0%	22.8%

Note:

*The total number of persons in the household is used in NCS sample, whereas the number of persons 16 years or older is used in the Seattle sample.

MEASURES OF MAJOR CONCEPTS

Several major concepts underlie theories of criminality and theories of victimization. As described in chapter 2, the major correlates of crime in theories of criminality involve low socio-economic conditions, population mobility, ethnic heterogeneity, and family disruption. As described in chapter 3, the major components in current theories of victimization are proximity, exposure, target attractiveness, and guardianship. How each of these concepts will be measured from information in census data and the Seattle telephone survey is described below. Appendix I provides a detailed summary of descriptive statistics and the coding for each of these variables.

Low Socio-Economic Conditions

In Shaw and McKay's theory of community social disorganization (1942), the socio-economic condition of the community is the primary correlate of crime rates. Other theoretical perspectives (e.g., anomie, social bond theories) also recognize the salience of low socio-economic status on criminality. Low socio-economic status is assumed to increase crime rates by decreasing the ability of persons to acquire basic human necessities, and limiting the resources that communities have to achieve common goals and to generate effective systems of institutional control.

Two measures of low socio-economic status are used here: median family income and the unemployment rate. Both of these measures are available for all three decades and for different aggregate units. For analyses of change in crime rates over time, median family income will be transformed into constant 1980 dollars. Each of these measures of socio-economic status has been widely used in previous studies of predatory crime (see Sampson and Groves 1989; Miethe et al. 1991).

Population Mobility

The adverse impact of population mobility is also widely recognized in theories of criminality. Population mobility is said to increase crime rates in geographical areas by increasing exposure to conflicting values, weakening ties to conventional society, reducing community cohesion and integration, and decreasing the collective level of supervision over others in the community.

The measure of population mobility used here is the percent of the population that has moved in the previous five years. This variable is available for census tracts in Seattle and the 584 cities for each decade from 1960 to 1980, but is missing when the SMSA is the aggregate unit.

Other measures of population mobility (e.g., the number of times persons have changed residences over the previous five years) are not available in census data on a regular basis.

Ethnic Heterogeneity

From various theories of criminality, population heterogeneity is widely identified as a major correlate of crime rates. Heterogeneity is assumed to increase crime because it generates conflict in values, impedes the realization of common goals, and weakens bonds to traditional society.

The measure of population heterogeneity most commonly used and discussed in previous research is ethnic heterogeneity (see Bursik 1988; Sampson and Groves 1989; Miethe, Hughes and McDowall 1991). Accordingly, this will be the measure of population heterogeneity used in the current study. Ethnic heterogeneity is computed as the product of the percent black and non-black in the particular census tract, city, or SMSA. Based on this measure, ethnic heterogeneity is highest at the value of 0.25, which indicates that 50 percent of the population is black and 50 percent is non-black. This measure of ethnic heterogeneity can be derived for each aggregate unit (e.g., city block, census tract, city, SMSA) and over each decade since 1960. However, census data for 1960 includes only the percent of the population that was non-white, whereas percent black is used in other decades. Given that the majority of the non-white population in the United States is black, the differences in the measurement of these variables over time should have a minimal effect on the obtained results.

Family Disruption and Single-Parent Families

Much has been written on the criminogenic impact of disruptive family relations and marital instability. The Chicago ecologists and others have long been interested in the relationship between measures of family disruption (e.g., divorce rates, rate of children living with one parent) and crime rates. While this factor also tends to be associated with low socioeconomic status and population mobility, family disruption is assumed to increase crime rates by weakening bonds to traditional institutions and lowering levels of both parental and community supervision of youth.

The measure of family disruption used here involves the percent of children under 18 years old that live with both parents. Higher values on this variable represent lower levels of "family disruption." This measure is available over time and for each aggregate unit. An advantage of this variable over other measures (e.g., divorce rates) is that it covers what seems to be the major criminogenic effect of divorce—that is, the reduction in the possible number of potential adults available to exert control over youth. Divorce rates are not included as an alternative measure of family disruption because this data is only sporadically contained in census files across aggregate units and time periods.

Proximity to High Crime Areas

According to current theories of victimization, being in physical proximity to high crime areas or pools of offenders increases one's risks of predatory crime. Measures of proximity used in previous studies include place of residence (e.g., city versus rural area), the perceived safety of one's neighborhood, and living in areas with high rates of offending.

Physical proximity to high crime areas is most difficult to measure when the unit of analysis is the city or SMSA. Census data on aggregate units do not provide measures of the physical distance between pools of motivated offenders and victims (see Cohen et al. 1981; Miethe and Meier 1990) or subjective ratings of the perceived safety of the environment. In fact, as a characteristic of individuals' immediate environment (rather than an attribute of an entire city or SMSA), proximity is not relevant for most aggregate-level analyses of crime rates, and cannot be adequately measured from census data, even if it was appropriate.[6] Accordingly, our models of crime rates for aggregate units (e.g., census tracts, cities, SMSAs) will not include a direct measure of proximity to high crime areas.

When attention shifts to explaining individuals' risks of victimization and victimization rates for pairs of city blocks, several measures of proximity to high crime areas are available in the Seattle survey. These include: (1) the rate of property victimization and violent victimization in the resident's neighborhood, (2) the average rating of the perceived safety of the resident's immediate neighborhood, and (3) a composite measure of the average number of signs of social and economic deterioration within three blocks of the resident's home. Average scores were computed for each of these variables by aggregating individual responses within pairs of city blocks and, when appropriate, within each census tract. Higher values on each variable are assumed to indicate greater proximity to motivated offenders and high crime areas. The composite measure of neighborhood deterioration represents the average number of the following problems within three blocks of each resident's home: (a) groups of teenagers "hanging out" on the street, (b) litter and garbage on the street, (c) abandoned houses and run-down buildings, (d) poor street lighting, and (e) vandalism—such as broken windows and graffiti. The importance of this composite variable is that it indicates the level of community supervision and informal social control in the neighborhood, conditions that are likely to be associated with rates of predatory crime. Collectively, these three measures tap aspects of the residents' immediate environment that are thought to increase one's proximity to high crime areas.

Exposure to Motivated Offenders

Contrary to proximity, which reflects the physical distance between where a potential target resides and where offenders are concentrated (see Cohen et al. 1981: 507), "exposure to crime" is more indicative of one's overall visibility and accessibility to crime. From this perspective, a dwelling has high exposure to burglary if it is unoccupied, detached from other units, has multiple points of entry, or is located on a corner lot, whereas persons have high exposure to violent crime when they undertake public activities in risky and vulnerable places. Exposure is traditionally measured, in past research, by the level of non-household primary activity (see Cohen and Felson 1979; van Dijk and Steinmetz 1984; Messner and Blau 1987; Miethe et al. 1987; Miethe and Meier 1990).

Multiple measures of exposure are contained in both census data and the Seattle survey. Unfortunately, the same measures are not available across all levels of analysis. For aggregate-level analyses of crime rates for the 584 U.S. cities from 1960 to 1980, three measures of exposure to crime are included: (1) the percent of the civilian labor force that is female, (2) the percent of employees who use public transportation, and (3) the average retail sales from eating and drinking establishments per population member. Each of these measures represents an aspect of non-household activity, but they differ on other dimensions and are only weakly interrelated (correlations range from 0.10 to 0.30), which questions the development of a composite index. For example, both rates of public transportation and female labor force participation involve public activities performed in settings removed from intimate familial relations, whereas the consumption of food or drink in public establishments is an activity that takes place with close friends and relatives (i.e., persons who will offer some protection if a dangerous situation arises). For violent crimes, the rate of public transportation is most indicative of an activity that occurs in dangerous places (as will be shown in chapter 6), and involves direct contact with potential offenders. In contrast, for residential burglary and other offenses against the dwelling, each measure of non-household activity is more representative of both increases in accessibility and decreases in guardianship than simply higher exposure per se. Assuming that total sales are strongly related to public demand for these services, the average sales from eating and drinking establishments is a good indicator of exposure due to public leisure activities, whereas the other variables are restricted to the work domain. Finally, we think that each item adequately represents exposure due to different types of non-household activity, but female labor force participation is the only indicator of this concept that has been widely used in previous research (see Miethe et al. 1991). Each variable is coded so that larger values indicate greater exposure to crime.

For the sample of 148 SMSAs in 1970, two of these measures of exposure were available from secondary sources: (1) the rate of public transportation by workers and (2) the percent of total retail sales from eating and drinking establishments in 1967. For Seattle census tracts from 1960 to 1980, the rates of female labor force participation and public transportation are included as measures of exposure.

The Seattle survey provides more direct measures of individuals' exposure to risky and vulnerable situations. These five different indicators include: (1) the number of nights, in the previous week, spent outside the home for work, leisure, and/or social activities, (2) the number of evenings, in the previous week, that the home was unoccupied for some time at night, (3) a three-item composite index of the number of different types of dangerous public activities undertaken by the respondent (i.e., going to bars, being in places where teenagers "hang out," and taking public transit), (4) an eight-item scale of the number of places within three blocks of the resident's home that attract strangers (i.e., schools, convenience stores or gas stations, bars or nightclubs, fast food restaurants, banks or office buildings, parks or playgrounds, shopping centers or malls, and hotels/motels), and (5) the number of times, in the previous month, that the respondent felt at danger of a physical attack by a stranger. For predicting individuals' risks and aggregate rates of property victimization, the level of home unoccupancy and its location near busy public places are used as measures of exposure. For violent crime, exposure is measured by the level of nighttime activity outside the home, participation in "dangerous" public activity, living near busy public places, and the frequency of situations in which the resident felt in danger of a physical attack. Each variable is coded so that higher values represent greater exposure to crime. As was true of the indicators of exposure in the aggregate-level data, each item in the Seattle survey is sufficiently different to thwart any attempt to develop one composite index of this concept.

Target Attractiveness

Another major aspect of current theories of victimization is target attractiveness. A structural-choice theory of victimization (see Miethe and

Meier 1990) presumes that it is the differential value or subjective utility associated with particular crime targets that determines the source of victimization within a socio-spatial context. Targets are attractive to offenders because they have some material or symbolic value and offer little resistance against attack or illegal removal. From an offender's perspective, particular items (e.g., cash, jewelry, electronic gadgets) are especially attractive targets because they are small in size, easily concealed, and have high monetary or resale value. Most of the measures of target attractiveness available in the current study differ across data sources.

Based on their economic value, measures of the density of portable consumer goods in a geographical area may best represent target attractiveness (see Cohen 1981; Cook 1986; Miethe and Meier 1990), however data on such consumer products are not routinely available for cities and SMSAs at any given time period, or over time. Data limitations, therefore, restrict our attention to median family income as the only aggregate-level indicator of target attractiveness. The lack of direct measures of particular purchasing activities, however, is not necessarily problematic when one considers that the reduced costs and increased availability of many "valued" consumer goods over time (e.g., color T.V.'s, cameras, calculators) may actually lead to their devaluation as attractive crime targets (see Miethe and Meier 1990). Median family income serves as a general proxy for purchasing power and the supply of expensive goods that is not susceptible to such a devaluation over time.

When attention shifts to the predictors of individuals' risks of predatory crime, there are other potential measures of target attractiveness in addition to family income. These alternative measures include: (1) a five-item composite index of the number of expensive consumer goods owned by the resident (i.e., portable color T.V., videocassette recorder [VCR], 35mm camera, home computer, and bicycle/motorcycle) and (2) the number of times, in the previous month, that the resident either carried $50 in cash or wore jewelry worth $100 when in a public place. Both family income and ownership of expensive consumer goods are measures of target attractiveness in models of property victimization. Family income and carrying valuables in public are indicators of this concept in analyses of violent crime. By acting overly cautious when in public places, it is assumed that persons who carry large amounts of cash or jewelry give off visual cues about their attractiveness as crime targets in a manner similar to how "signs of wealth" in the immediate area surrounding a dwelling give an indication, to offenders, of the potential yield inside the home. All variables are coded so that higher values indicate greater target attractiveness.

Guardianship

Guardianship refers to the ability of persons or objects to prevent the occurrence of crime (see Cohen et al. 1981; Miethe and Meier 1990). There are both social (i.e., interpersonal) and physical dimensions of this concept. Social guardianship, in past research, has been measured by the number of household members, the density of friendship networks in the immediate neighborhood, marital status, and having neighbors watch one's home or property when the dwelling is unoccupied. The availability of others may prevent crime by their presence alone or through offering assistance to ward off an attack. Physical guardianship includes various types of target-hardening activities (e.g., door/window locks, burglar alarms, guard dogs), other physical impediments to household theft (e.g., street lighting, guarded public entrances), and participation in collective activities (e.g., Neighborhood Watch programs). As with the other major concepts underlying theories of victimization, our measures of guardianship differ across aggregate and individual levels of analysis.

The only measure of guardianship in the aggregate data is the average number of persons per occupied dwelling. This measure of household size is similar to that used in previous studies (see Miethe and Meier 1990), and was computed by dividing the population size by the number of occupied dwellings. Unfortunately, this measure of guardianship, in and of itself, has multiple meanings. In cases of violent crime, household size may indicate guardianship or increases in criminogenic conditions due to the adverse effect of crowding in the household on criminal motivation (see Miethe et al. 1991). When household size is included in multivariate models, we will also include a measure of household crowding (i.e., the percent of occupied units with more than 1.01 persons per room) to more properly specify and isolate the net impact of guardianship on crime rates.

The Seattle survey includes measures of both social and physical guardianship. Social guardianship is represented by: (1) the number of persons in the household over 16 years old, (2) whether the respondent has any good friends or relatives who live on his or her block, and (3) a five-item composite index of the activities performed with neighbors which indicate social integration and informal social control (i.e., watching neighbor's property, borrowing tools or small food items, having dinner or lunch with a neighbor, helping neighbors with a problem, participating in a block activity). Physical guardianship is measured by (1) an eight-item composite index of the number of safety precautions taken by the resident (i.e., lock doors, leave lights on, install extra locks, belong to a crime prevention program, have burglar alarms, dog ownership, have neighbors watch home, and have a weapon in the dwelling) and (2) whether residents perceive that they are capable of defending themselves from an attack by another. The items in the composite scale for protective actions refer to behavior that took place two years ago, rather than current precautions.[7] This was done to eliminate the artificial positive correlation between current safety precautions and victimization experiences due to persons taking protective actions as a consequence of being victimized by crime (see Mayhew 1984; Miethe 1991). Each measure of this concept is coded so that higher values indicate greater guardianship.

Measures of Crime Rates and Types of Victimization

This study focuses on the social characteristics and determinants of predatory crime. As developed by Glaser (1971: 4), predatory crimes are illegal acts in which "someone definitely and intentionally takes or damages the person or property of another." Our attention is restricted to those predatory offenses that involve direct physical contact between at least one offender and at least one person or property victim. We will examine both violent crimes and property offenses. The particular crimes included under these general categories vary somewhat by data sources and the unit of analysis.

When attention focuses on predicting crime rates for various aggregate units (i.e., census tracts, cities, SMSAs), UCR data will be used to examine rates of murder, rape, aggravated assault, robbery, burglary, and motor vehicle theft. Larceny-theft is excluded because it covers a wide assortment of different crimes against persons and property which have quite different offense characteristics (e.g., pocket-picking, purse snatching, shoplifting, theft of auto accessories, bicycle theft). Arson is also excluded because of its relative rarity and recency as an index crime. For the other offenses, it is important to note that both completed acts and attempts are included in the same category. As mentioned previously, crimes that vary in terms of victim characteristics (e.g., residential versus non-residential burglary, personal versus institutional robbery) are also included in the same generic categories in the UCR data used in the current study.

For analyses based on the NCS data, most of the crimes are similar to the UCR categories. The NCS offenses examined here involve both attempted and completed victimizations from personal robbery (i.e., muggings and other thefts from the person including purse snatching and pocket picking), assaults (both aggravated and simple assaults), residential burglary, household larceny (i.e., the theft of property or cash from a residence by a person who has the right to be there, or theft from the immediate vicinity of the home), and motor vehicle theft (including automobiles and motorcycles). NCS data on attempted and completed rapes are not rigorously investigated in the current study because of the small number of these offenses in any given year of the survey. Each of the screener questions about victimization experiences in the NCS data use a six-month reference period. Although published UCR data is not disaggregated by the victim-offender relationship, we are able to restrict the NCS data on violent victimizations to crimes committed by strangers.[8]

The type and definition of offenses in the Seattle victimization survey are generally similar to those in the NCS classification, but differ in several important respects. First, the reference period is two years rather than six months, which will result in higher rates of victimization for each offense in the Seattle data. Second, household larceny in the Seattle survey is restricted to completed thefts outside the dwelling and in its immediate vicinity (e.g., thefts from the yard or porch). Third, questions on victimization by a violent crime (i.e., assaults and robberies) are restricted to completed offenses and threats committed by strangers. The Seattle survey did not collect data on domestic assaults or other violent crimes by non-strangers. Fourth, motor vehicle theft includes both thefts and illegal entry into the motor vehicle. Obviously, these differences in reference period and crime definitions are sufficiently large to question the validity of comparing rates of victimization across these surveys. However, these differences in survey items do not preclude basic comparisons of the correlates of victimization across surveys. In fact, our results will be all the more robust if similar findings are found across surveys that vary in their sample characteristics and the specific wording of the questionnaire items.

Although several types of crime will be investigated in this study, we will place primary importance on assault, robbery, burglary, and motor vehicle theft because these offenses fit traditional categories of violent and property crimes, are included in each data source, cover a full range of motivations for offending, and have somewhat different opportunity structures. However, we also expect some differences by the particular type of predatory offense. For example, if the motivations for violent offending are more diverse (e.g., revenge, jealousy, frustration, status threats, economic marginality) than for property crimes, theories of victimization which adopt a rational conception of criminal behavior, and emphasize only the economic motivations for crime, should be most predictive of property offending. We have no clear predictions about which particular types of predatory crime are best accounted for by macro-level theories of criminality.

ANALYTIC PROCEDURES

Several different analytic strategies will be used to examine the research hypotheses underlying the current study. The particular statistical procedures vary by the coding of the dependent variable. Multiple regression and logistic regression will be the primary analytic tools to model crime rates and individuals' risks of victimization.

A pooled cross-sectional and panel design is used in the analysis of crime rates and changes in crime rates over time for 584 U.S. cities and 114 census tracts. Ordinary least squares regression is used in the analysis of crime rates for 148 SMSAs in 1970. When we pool the data over cities and census tracts for the years 1960, 1970, and 1980, the number of observations for the cross-sectional analyses is 1,752 (i.e., 584 x 3) and 342 (i.e., 114 x 3), respectively. Models with lagged variables and change scores are estimated when attention shifts to predicting changes in crime rates over the two successive ten-year periods from 1960 to 1980. Such a specification allows for an assessment of how the initial levels and changes in the exogenous variables over time influence change and stability in crime rates over time.

Both the cross-sectional and change models for cities and census tracts are estimated using a variety of statistical procedures, including ordinary least squares, generalized least squares allowing for autoregressive and heteroscedastic errors, and generalized least squares allowing for random variance components (see, for review, Dielman 1989; Stimson 1985). Each method yielded similar substantive inferences about the effects of the exogenous variables. Following Hannan and associates (Hannan and Young 1977; Tuma and Hannan 1984), we present the results from the variance components estimation, because simulation studies show that this procedure is slightly superior to other methods for estimating change models with short panels of data. The variance components estimates adjust for random variation across cities and time periods, as well as for cross-sectional and time-wise autocorrelation. These models are estimated using the algorithm developed by Fuller and Battese (1974).

Logistic regression analysis is used to examine the predictors of individuals' risks of victimization. Logit models are preferred over ordinary least squares when the dependent variable is a categorical variable (as with victimization, which can only take on two values). We pay particular attention to the magnitude of the net effects of the variables and the relative improvement of fit in the likelihood ratio chi-square (LRX2) over a baseline model. For example, such a procedure is used in chapter 9 to determine whether the inclusion of contextual factors (e.g., the socio-economic status of the resident's neighborhood) improves our ability to predict victimization risks over and above a model which includes only the individual-level measures of theoretical concepts. Bivariate associations and descriptive statistics for analyses of crime rates and individuals' risks of victimization will also be presented.

Given that the appropriateness of any statistical procedure depends on the assumptions underlying the estimated models, we performed several supplemental analyses to evaluate the validity of the model assumptions and the robustness of the obtained findings. For example, a fundamental assumption underlying pooled cross-sectional models is that the hypothesized structural relationships are invariant over the selected time periods (see Stimson 1985; Hannan and Young 1977). Preliminary analyses were, therefore, performed using ordinary least squares to determine if decade-specific models would produce different substantive conclusions than would the analysis based on all observations. We found some decade-specific effects (i.e., variables being significant at one time period but not another), but our substantive inferences are similar across the pooled and decade-specific models. Consequently, we can report the results from the pooled models for purposes of parsimony and without loss of generality. Similarly, each model was assessed for multicollinearity. We observed some limited problems with collinearity in analyses based on the SMSA and census tract (involving ethnic heterogeneity and single-parent households), but estimates of the unique net effects of these variables were not affected by this problem in the city sample. Overall, these supplemental analyses and others (e.g., examining non-linear functional forms) revealed that the results presented in the remaining chapters are quite robust across alternative analytic procedures. Neither pooling cross-sectional data, multicollinearity, or an additive specification of the functional form limited the generalizability of the observed findings.

SUMMARY AND CONCLUSIONS

This chapter has presented the characteristics of the data sources and measures of variables that will be used to evaluate theories of criminality and victimization. UCR data, census data, national victimization surveys, and a local survey of Seattle residents will be analyzed to evaluate the research questions underlying this study. The fact that we have multiple measures of most theoretical concepts, various units of analysis (e.g., individuals, city blocks, census tracts, cities, and SMSAs), and both cross-sectional and longitudinal data provides an unique opportunity to evaluate the predictive utility of current theories of criminality and victimization. If findings are similar across different units of analysis and measures of concepts, there will be a strong empirical foundation for substantive conclusions about the causes and social distribution of predatory crime. How well current theories explain predatory crime is addressed in the next four chapters.

ତ୍ୟୁ

MEASURES OF CONCEPTS AND DESCRIPTIVE STATISTICS

Low Socio-Economic Condition

1. Median Family Income:
   Census Tracts [mean = $22,536.1; sd = 6,145.4]
   Cities [mean = $21,041.6; sd = 5,221.6]
   SMSA [mean = $10,021.7; sd = 1,322.4]
2. Unemployment Rate:
   Census Tracts [mean = 7.4 percent; sd = 4.6]
   Cities [mean = 5.5 percent; sd = 2.4]
   SMSA [mean = 4.3 percent; sd = 1.4 percent]

Population Mobility

Measured as the percent of the population that has moved in the previous five years. This variable is not available for SMSAs. Census tract [mean = 51.8 percent; sd = 10.9]. City [mean = 49.4 percent; sd = 9.8].

Ethnic Heterogeneity

Computed as the product of the percent black and non-black in the particular census tract, city, or SMSA. For each aggregate unit, the descriptive statistics on this variable are: (a) census tract [mean = 0.048; sd = 0.072], (b) city [mean = 0.083; sd = 0.080], and (c) SMSA [mean = 0.083; sd = 0.061].

Single-Parent Families

Measured as the percent of the children under 18 years old that live with both parents. Census tract [mean = 78.5 percent; sd = 14.6]. City [mean = 79.4 percent; sd = 10.3]. SMSA [mean = 82.9 percent; sd = 4.1].

Proximity to High Crime Areas

1. Property Victimization Rate: The average victimization rate for property offenses (i.e., burglary, household theft, and motor

vehicle theft within four blocks of home) from 1988 to 1990. Pairs of city blocks [mean = 33.1 percent; sd = 14.5]. Census Tracts [mean = 33.1 percent; sd = 10.6].

2. Violent Victimization Rate: The average victimization rate for violent offenses (i.e., stranger assault, robbery) within four blocks of the resident's home from 1988 to 1990. Pairs of city blocks [mean = 2.8 percent; sd = 5.3]. Census Tracts [mean = 2.8 percent; sd = 4.2].

3. Perceived Safety of Neighborhood: Average rating of individual scores (1 = very safe; 2 = somewhat safe; 3 = somewhat unsafe; 4 = very unsafe). Pairs of city blocks [mean = 2.11; sd = 0.38]. Census Tracts [mean = 2.11; sd = 0.33].

4. Neighborhood Decay/Deterioration: Five-item scale representing the average number of different signs of incivility within three blocks of each resident's home. Calculated by averaging individual scores. Items include: (a) groups of teenagers "hanging around" the street, (b) litter/garbage/trash on the street, (c) abandoned houses and run-down buildings, (d) poor street lighting, and (e) vandalism—like broken windows or writing on walls. Scale values range from 0 to 5. Pairs of city blocks [mean = 1.34; sd = 0.71]. Census Tracts [mean = 1.34; sd = 0.60].

Exposure to Risky and Dangerous Situations

1. Female Labor Force Rate: The percent of the civilian labor force that is female. Available for U.S. cities and Seattle census tracts from 1960 to 1980. Census Tracts [mean = 38.0 percent; sd = 7.1]. U.S. Cities [mean = 40.1 percent; sd = 5.0].

2. Public Transportation Rate: The percent of workers who use public transportation. Available for U.S. cities and Seattle census tracts from 1960 to 1980, and SMSAs for 1970. Seattle Census Tracts [mean = 18.8 percent; sd = 8.0]. Cities [mean = 8.1 percent; sd = 8.3]. SMSAs [mean = 6.1 percent; sd = 6.1].

3. Sales from Eating/Drinking Establishments: The average retail sales from eating and drinking establishments per population member. U.S. cities from 1960 to 1980 [mean = $433.04; sd = 204.4]. For SMSAs, the item represents the percent of total retail sales from eating and drinking establishments. SMSAs [mean = 7.5 percent; sd = 1.4].

4. Nights Out: The number of nights, in the previous week, that the respondent was outside the home for work, leisure, and social activities. Values range from "0" to "7" nights. Available for individuals in the Seattle survey and can also be aggregated by pairs of city blocks and census tracts. Individuals [mean = 2.43; sd = 2.0].

5. Home Unoccupied at Night: The number of evenings, in the previous week, that the home was unoccupied for some time at night. Values range from "0" to "7" nights. Available for individuals in the Seattle survey and can also be aggregated by pairs of city blocks and census tracts. Individuals [mean = 1.78; sd = 1.97].

6. Dangerous Activities: Three-item scale of the number of different types of dangerous public activities undertaken by the respondents. Items include: (a) going to bars or night-clubs that serve alcohol, during the previous week, (b) being in a public place, in the previous week, where groups of teenagers or young adults were "hanging out" on the street, and (c) taking a city bus or other types of public transportation. Scale ranges from "0" to "3" activities. Available for individuals in the Seattle survey and can also be aggregated by pairs of city blocks and census tracts. Individuals [mean = 0.88; sd = 0.81].

7. Busy Public Places: Eight-item scale of the number of different types of public places, within three blocks of the resident's home, that attract strangers. Items include: (a) high schools or junior high schools, (b) convenience stores or gas stations, (c) bar or nightclub that serves alcohol, (d) fast food restaurant, (e) bank or office building, (f) park or playground, (g) shopping center or mall, and (h) hotel or motel. Scale ranges from "0" to "8" places. Available for individuals in the Seattle survey and can also be aggregated by pairs of city blocks and census tracts. Individuals [mean = 2.51; sd = 1.8].

8. Times Felt in Danger: The number of times, in the previous month, that the respondent felt at danger of a physical attack by a stranger. Values range from "0" to "5" (5 or more times). Available for individuals in the Seattle survey and can also be aggregated by pairs of city blocks and census tracts. Individuals [mean = 0.20; sd = 0.76]. 89.8 percent of the respondents said "0 times."

Target Attractiveness

1. Median Family Income: Census Tracts [mean = $22,536.1; sd = 6145.4]. Cities [mean = $21,041.6; sd = 5,221.6]. SMSA [mean = $10,021.7; sd = 1,322.4].

2. Family Income: Categories of total family income before taxes in 1989. Values included "1" (less than $10,000), "2" ($10,000 to $20,000), "3" ($20,000 to $30,000), "4" ($30,000 to $50,000), "5" ($50,000 to $75,000), "6" ($75,000 to $100,000), and "7" (over $100,000). Available for individuals in the Seattle survey and can also be aggregated by pairs of city blocks and census tracts. Individuals [mean = 3.37; sd = 1.36].

3. Expensive Consumer Goods: Five-item scale of the number of different types of expensive consumer goods owned by the resident. Items include: (a) portable color T.V., (b) videocassette recorder, (c) 35mm camera, (d) home computer, and (e) bicycle or motorcycle. Values range from "0" to "5" items. Available for individuals in the Seattle survey and can also be aggregated by pairs of city blocks and census tract. Individuals [mean = 2.53; sd = 1.41].

4. Carry Valuables in Public: The number of times, in the previous month, the respondent either carried at least $50 in cash or wore jewelry worth over $100 when in a public place. Values range from "0" to "8" (8 or more) times. Available for individuals in the Seattle survey and can also be aggregated by pairs of city blocks and census tract. Individuals [mean = 3.24; sd = 2.63].

Guardianship

1. Average Household Size: The number of persons per occupied housing unit. Available for U.S. cities and census tracts in Seattle from 1960 to 1980, and SMSAs for 1970. Census Tracts [mean = 2.56; sd = 0.57]. Cities [mean = 3.03; sd = 0.37]. SMSA [mean = 3.26; sd = 0.19].

1a. Household Crowding: The percent of occupied units with more than 1.01 persons per room. Available for U.S. cities and census tracts from 1960 to 1980, and SMSAs for 1970. Used as a control variable to isolate the net effects of household size due to guardianship from the adverse impact of crowding on criminality. Census Tracts [mean = 3.6 percent; sd = 2.8]. Cities [mean = 7.0 percent; sd = 4.4]. SMSAs [mean = 7.6 percent; sd = 2.7].

2. Persons over 16 years old: The number of persons in the household over 16 years old. Values range from "0" (live alone) to "3" (3 or more persons). Available for individuals in the Seattle survey and can also be aggregated by pairs of city blocks and census tract. Individuals [mean = 2.00; sd = 0.89].

3. Friends/Relatives Live Nearby: Whether or not the resident has any good friends or relatives who live on their city block. Values range from "0" (no) to "1" (yes). Available for individuals in the Seattle survey and can also be aggregated by pairs of city blocks and census tract. Individuals [mean = 0.61; sd = 0.49].

4. Social Integration: Five-item composite index of the number of different activities performed with neighbors which indicate neighborhood integration and informal social control. Items include: (a) watching the neighbor's property when they are out of town, (b) borrowing tools or small food items, (c) had dinner or lunch with a neighbor, (d) helped a neighbor with a problem, and (e) participated in an organized block activity or neighborhood association. Scale values range from "0" to "5." Available for individuals in the Seattle survey and can also be aggregated by pairs of city blocks and census tract. Individuals [mean = 2.79; sd = 1.57].

5. Safety Precautions: Eight-item composite index of the number of different types of safety precautions taken by the respondent "two years ago." Items include: (a) locking doors, (b) leaving lights on, (c) belonging to a community crime prevention program [e.g., Neighborhood/Block Watch], (d) installing extra locks, (e) having a burglar alarm or other electronic security devise, (f) owning a dog, (g) having neighbors watch the home when the owner is out of town, and (h) having a weapon in the home for protection. Scale values range from "0" to "8" precautions. Available for individuals in the Seattle survey and can also be aggregated by pairs of city blocks and census tract. Individuals [mean = 3.91; sd = 1.47].

6. Defending Self from Others : Self-rating of the perceived ability to physically defend self or ward off an attack from another person. Values ranged from "0" (no, don't know) to "1" (yes). Available for individuals in the Seattle survey and can also be aggregated by pairs of city blocks and census tract. Individuals [mean = 0.47; sd = 0.50].

Types of Predatory Crime and Victimization

1. Violent Crimes: UCR data provides rates of homicide, rape, aggravated assault, and robbery for U.S. cities and Seattle census tracts from 1960 to 1980 and for SMSAs in 1970. Individuals' risks and aggregate rates of violent victimization for pairs of city blocks are derived from the Seattle telephone survey. Violent crimes in the Seattle victimization survey include stranger assault and personal robbery (i.e., street mugging, purse snatching, pocket picking).

2. Property Crimes: UCR data provides rates of burglary and motor vehicle theft for U.S. cities and Seattle census tracts from 1960 to 1980 and for SMSAs in 1970. Individuals' risks and aggregate rates of property victimization for pairs of city blocks are derived from the Seattle telephone survey. Property crimes in the victimization survey include residential burglary, household theft (i.e., theft of property from outside the dwelling, in the yard, or on a porch), and motor vehicle theft (i.e., theft of vehicle, illegal entry).

The Empirical Distribution of Crime and Victimization

A primary task of criminological theory is to account for the social and spatial distribution of predatory crime. All theories of criminality and victimization assume that crime is not a random event, but rather is more common at particular times, particular places, particular circumstances, and among particular types of persons. This distribution or social ecology of crime constitutes the "facts a theory must explain" (Cohen 1955). The data sources identified in the previous chapter are used here to describe the physical, interpersonal, and behavioral aspects of the social context for various types of predatory crime.

VICTIM-OFFENDER RELATIONSHIP

One important aspect of predatory crime is the victim-offender relationship. Persons can be victimized by others who are strangers or non-strangers (e.g., relatives, acquaintances). The empirical nature of this victim-offender relationship sets immediate limits on the applicability of current victimization theories. Specifically, routine activity and lifestyle theories assume that non-household activity increases the likelihood of predatory crime by enhancing the exposure of persons and property to risky and dangerous situations. However, offenses among non-strangers (especially those by family members) are not easily explainable by these theories because one's exposure and proximity to crime is largely determined by the particular characteristics of his or her immediate relatives and friends, rather than the physical location and nature of public activity. Criminal opportunity theories would only predict temporal increases in public activities to be associated with increases in rates of stranger violence over time. At any given time period, the greater the rate of predatory crime involving non-strangers, the less applicable would be a criminal opportunity theory.

An examination of police reports and NCS data reveal several general trends about the victim-offender relationship.[1] First, rates of stranger violence vary widely by the type of crime. Analysis of NCS data for 1989 indicates that 78 percent of the robberies, 58 percent of the rapes, and 52 percent of the assaults are committed by strangers. UCR data for 1989 reveals that only 20 percent of the homicides, in which information was available on the victim-offender relationship, involve strangers. Second, changes in rates of stranger violence over time also differ by type of crime. The rate of stranger assaults varies from 60 percent in 1973-1975, 56 percent in 1980–1982 and 51 percent in 1987–1989. Robberies by strangers are more stable over these time periods (82 percent, 82 percent, and 79 percent, respectively), but rapes by strangers show a dramatic decrease over time (70 percent, 62 percent, 50 percent). Homicides involving strangers have remained fairly stable over time, ranging from 21 percent in 1976-78, 24 percent in 1980-82, and 19 percent in 1987-89. Third, a clear majority of violent crimes involving non-strangers are committed by acquaintances rather than relatives. According to a report from the Bureau of Justice Statistics (*BJS* January 1987), about 18 percent of homicides are committed by relatives compared to rape (4 percent), robbery (4 percent) and assaults (8 percent). However, most of these estimates of violence by relatives are probably far lower than the actual rates, due to the well-known fact that victimization surveys undercount crimes among non-strangers.

Although changes in victims' willingness to report crimes to survey interviewers may cast doubt on comparisons of trends over time, these results, nonetheless, provide no indication of an increase in stranger violence, as would be predicted from criminal opportunity theories of victimization. Given that over 80 percent of murders and about 50 percent of the assaults and rapes involve non-strangers, a majority of these violent crimes would be largely unaffected by increases in public activity and the subsequent contact with greater pools of potential offenders.[2] Alternatively, personal robbery is the only violent crime in which increasing levels of non-household activity could dramatically increase victimization risks. Other aspects of criminal opportunity theory (e.g., proximity to pools of motivated offenders, target attractiveness, guardianship) would also seem less relevant to violent crimes by non-strangers, largely because crimes involving known parties are more likely to be motivated by a grievance with a particular person. When there is a dispute between individuals (i.e., an expressive rather than instrumental crime), the particular grievance is what determines victim selection, not the relative attractiveness or guardianship of alternative crime targets. Overall, these observations on the victim-offender relationship suggest that current victimization theories have the greatest potential in explaining aggregate rates and individuals' risks of personal robbery and property crime. These theories will be applicable to a smaller proportion of murders, rapes, and assaults.

PHYSICAL LOCATION OF CRIME

One of the lasting contributions of the early Chicago ecological school and current research on "hot spots" is the recognition that some physical settings are more attractive micro-environments for crime than others. According to theories of victimization, there should be a direct association between exposure to these dangerous places and risks of predatory crime.

The Location of Violent Crime

The spatial distribution of violent crime depends on the type of crime and the victim-offender relationship. UCR data and census reports can be analyzed to provide information on the conditions, in wider geographical areas (e.g., census tracts, cities, SMSAs), that are most conducive to crime, whereas NCS data allows one to identify the particular types of locations or places where violent crimes are most likely to occur.

According to traditional theories of criminality, geographical areas with high levels of population mobility, ethnic heterogeneity, family disruption, and low economic opportunity are believed to have higher rates of violent crime. These social factors are linked to higher crime rates because they are associated with lower levels of internal social control, weakened bonds to traditional society, and fewer resources to allow for the realization and achievement of collective goals. Table 6.1 provides offense-specific rates of violent crime for areas with varying levels (i.e., low, medium, and high) of several presumed crime-producing factors for census tracts in Seattle (in 1980), U.S. cities with a population greater than 25,000 (in 1980), and U.S. standard metropolitan statistical areas (SMSAs) with over 200,000 residents in (1970). Each of these variables is collapsed into ordinal categories by dividing their empirical distribution into thirds.

Table 6.1 Violent Crime Rates per 100,000 by Categories of Theoretically Relevant Variables and Aggregate Units

Predictor Variable	HOMICIDE			RAPE		
	Tract	City	SMSA	Tract	City	SMSA
Overall Mean Rate	14.2	9.9	7.8	103.2	44.4	19.0
Ethnic Heterogeneity						
Low	3.7	3.6	3.9	34.1	24.9	15.2
Medium	8.0	8.2	6.9	62.8	41.2	19.3
High	30.8	18.1	12.6	212.7	67.2	22.3
Population Mobility						
Low	6.1	8.8	—	36.1	31.3	—
Medium	10.8	11.0	—	89.8	48.4	—
High	25.6	9.9	—	183.6	53.3	—
Median Family Income						
Low	30.9	15.0	10.2	208.2	56.8	21.0
Medium	7.9	9.2	6.9	69.4	44.6	17.5
High	3.7	5.5	6.4	32.0	31.7	18.5
Unemployment Rate						
Low	3.6	7.1	9.3	30.2	37.3	18.9
Medium	8.2	9.6	7.7	65.5	40.8	17.4
High	30.7	13.1	6.5	213.9	55.1	20.9
Children in Two-Parent Homes						
Low	24.2	17.9	11.7	164.7	70.1	23.4
Medium	7.5	8.4	8.2	71.1	40.3	21.8
High	11.2	3.5	3.5	76.1	22.9	11.8

	ROBBERY			ASSAULT		
	Tract	City	SMSA	Tract	City	SMSA
Overall Mean Rate	614.3	284.2	139.1	608.8	359.5	161.4
Ethnic Heterogeneity						
Low	156.9	120.4	78.6	194.3	205.8	108.8
Medium	296.3	246.4	136.9	314.8	321.8	147.7
High	1389.8	486.9	200.5	1317.4	551.9	226.3
Population Mobility						
Low	185.6	240.9	—	234.4	293.0	—
Medium	427.5	310.7	—	516.5	413.1	—
High	1229.9	300.1	—	1075.5	370.7	—
Median Family Income						
Low	1359.3	412.1	114.7	1277.8	497.1	202.6
Medium	360.8	232.9	127.3	393.5	356.1	142.4
High	122.9	207.2	175.5	155.1	224.6	139.6
Unemployment Rate						
Low	128.1	211.8	150.5	147.9	272.5	173.8
Medium	306.8	265.7	133.0	359.2	371.8	154.2
High	1408.1	375.4	133.9	1319.3	434.0	156.4
Children in Two-Parent Homes						
Low	948.5	511.9	167.5	1002.6	573.9	230.7
Medium	315.3	235.4	164.1	364.8	318.4	157.8
High	588.7	106.5	86.6	473.0	187.3	95.5

An examination of UCR data on violent crimes, for these geographical units, supports the characterization of criminal areas derived from theories of criminality. Regardless of the unit of analysis or type of violent offense, areas with higher levels of ethnic heterogeneity, lower family income, higher unemployment, and lower rates of children under 18 living with both parents generally have higher rates of violent crime (see Table 6.1). The exception to this general trend involves how measures of economic status (i.e., family income, unemployment rates) influence rates of homicide, robbery, and assault in SMSAs. Census tracts with higher levels of residential mobility have higher rates of each type of violent crime, whereas areas with moderate levels of residential mobility generally have the highest rates of violence when the city is the unit of analysis. Furthermore, differences in violent crime rates by these demographic attributes are most pronounced in analyses based on the census tract. In fact, as the unit of aggregation increases (from tracts, to cities, to SMSAs), demographic differences in violent crime rates become progressively smaller.[3]

The results in Table 6.1 illustrate the substantial differences in rates of violence within categories of traditional criminological variables. For example, violent crime rates for each offense are at least six times higher in census tracts with high levels of ethnic heterogeneity or high rates of unemployment compared to their respective "low" categories. Offense-specific crime rates, in census tracts, are also at least six times higher for low (versus high) income areas, four times larger based on the level of residential mobility, and at least twice as large, in most cases, for census tracts with low rather than high rates of children living with both parents. Differences in violent crime rates across categories of the demographic variables were usually of a smaller magnitude (i.e., only from two to four times larger) when the city was the unit of analysis. In contrast, differences in violent crime rates for SMSAs across particular categories were rarely greater than a factor of two, occurring only five times in sixteen comparisons. Collectively, these findings are important because they emphasize that any adequate theory of criminality or victimization must account for this unequal distribution of crime across geographical areas. However, they also indicate the importance of the unit of analysis for substantive conclusions about crime rates. Both the magnitude and direction of demographic differences in violent crime rates are most divergent across comparisons when the SMSA is the unit of analysis. Analyses based on the census tract and city yield similar results.

The Seattle victimization survey provides information about the geographical area around a person's home, which may also enhance risks of violent crime. For example, analysis of these data reveals that about 11 percent of the persons living near places that attract high levels of public activity (e.g., schools, fast food restaurants, shopping centers, convenience stores/gas stations, bus stops) were victims of stranger assault in their neighborhood, compared with only 3 percent of the residents of less busy areas. Residents of areas with greater signs of neighborhood decay and disintegration (i.e., litter/garbage on streets, abandoned and run-down buildings, vandalism, groups of teenagers "hanging around" the street) also had greater risks of stranger assault in their neighborhood (13 percent) than those who live in less deteriorated areas (3 percent). Similar patterns were observed for personal robbery, but the differences were smaller across categories. These findings give further indication of the types of physical contexts with the highest rates of violent crime.

The NCS data include a somewhat detailed measure of the place of occurrence for violent offenses. For violent crimes involving strangers, the most common location is on a street (31.6 percent in 1987–1989), whereas the victim's home is the modal category for violent offenses among non-strangers (25.4 percent for 1987–1989). Table 6.2 summarizes the place of occurrence for violent crimes among strangers for the 1973–1975, 1980–1982, and 1987–1989 time periods.

As shown in Table 6.2, public streets are the most dangerous location for each type of violent crime involving strangers, and the particular location for violent crime has changed very little over time. For example, about 33 percent of the physical assaults in 1980–1982 and 27 percent of the physical assaults in 1987–1989 were committed on a street not adjacent to the home of the victim or his or her friends and relatives. There is no comparable figure that can be derived for 1973–1975 due to differences in the coding of the location of crime for this time period. About 7 percent of the robberies occurred in the victim's home in 1973–1975 compared to about 5 percent for the 1980–1982 and 1987–1989 time periods. A sizeable minority of rapes by strangers (17 percent to 19 percent) occurred within the victim's home, and these rates were also similar across time periods. Among the other locations, parking lots and public garages were relatively frequent locales for violent crime, whereas rapes were slightly more likely than other crimes to take place in open spaces (e.g., parks, fields, playgrounds). Robberies were more apt than assaults to occur on public transit or inside a transit station. However, assaults were more likely than other violent acts to take place in entertainment establishments (e.g., restaurants, bars, nightclubs) and other commercial buildings.

Variation in victimization risks by place of occurrence takes on a different meaning when one considers the amount of time people actually spend at particular locales. Time-utilization data are not available for each of these particular locations (or for the same time periods), but rough

Table 6.2 Places of Occurrence for Violent Crimes by Strangers for 1973–75, 1980–82, and 1987–89 Time Periods Based on NCS Data

Place of Occurrence	RAPE			ROBBERY			ASSAULT		
	73–75	80–82	87–89	73–75	80–82	87–89	73–75	80–82	87–89
At/In Own Home	16.7	19.2	17.6	6.6	4.9	5.3	5.1	3.8	3.0
Near Own Home	14.9	11.7	7.8	9.3	8.6	9.1	9.6	9.3	9.9
Inside Commercial Places/Buildings	9.2	3.3	5.9	8.0	10.5	11.4	18.5	16.9	17.8
a. Bar/Restaurant	[na]	[1.7]	[2.0]	[na]	[3.9]	[3.1]	[na]	[9.7]	[8.3]
b. Store/Bank/Office	[na]	[1.6]	[3.9]	[na]	[6.6]	[8.3]	[na]	[7.2]	[9.5]
Inside School	3.2	0.8	0.0	2.6	1.4	1.2	5.3	2.3	3.3
Public Transit	na	0.8	5.9	na	6.9	5.3	na	1.6	1.1
Open Public Places	44.2	47.4	47.1	68.7	61.2	57.4	50.2	50.6	50.0
a. Street*	[na]	[30.0]	[29.4]	[na]	[47.5]	[43.3]	[na]	[32.8]	[26.7]
b. Parking Place/Lot	[na]	[8.3]	[9.8]	[na]	[9.1]	[9.6]	[na]	[10.6]	[14.8]
c. Parks/Field	[na]	[5.8]	[5.9]	[na]	[2.9]	[3.3]	[na]	[4.5]	[5.0]
d. On School Property	[na]	[3.3]	[2.0]	[na]	[1.7]	[1.2]	[na]	[2.7]	[3.5]
Other Locations	11.8	16.8	15.7	4.8	6.5	10.3	11.3	15.5	14.9

Note:

*Street refers to crimes that occur on a street that is not immediately adjacent to the victim's home or the dwelling of a friend, relative, or neighbor.

adjustments can be made for the relative exposure of persons to some of these places. For example, time-budget studies (see Robinson 1977) report that the average United States citizen spends far less time at restaurants and bars (three hours per week) than at home (at least twelve hours per day). However, stranger assaults are only about one and one half times more likely to occur in or near the home (12.9 percent) than inside restaurants and bars (8.3 percent). Similarly, people spend a trivial amount of their daily life on public transit or inside a station, however about 6 percent of the rapes in 1987–1989, 5 percent of robberies and 1 percent of the stranger assaults occurred in such locations. A parking lot or garage represents the physical location for about 13 percent of all violent crimes among strangers, even though average citizens spend little of their daily time in these places.

The results in Table 6.2, and estimates of the relative level of activity by place, have direct implications for theories of victimization by highlighting the greater risks of non-household activity, and especially activities which take place in particular public places (e.g., eating/drinking establishments, public transit, parking lots). Given the relatively large amount of time people spend in other public locations (e.g., commercial buildings for work, inside schools) or at home, time-adjusted victimization rates for these places indicate their relative safety from violent crime.

The Location of Property Crime

According to various macro-level theories of criminality, rates of residential burglary and motor vehicle theft should be higher in geographical areas with high levels of residential mobility, ethnic heterogeneity, family disruption, and low levels of economic opportunity. Rates of property crime for "low," "medium," and "high" categories of these basic demographic attributes are presented in Table 6.3.

Police reports of property crime yield several patterns that are largely consistent with social disorganization and other theories of criminality. First, rates of burglary and motor vehicle theft are generally higher in areas with greater ethnic heterogeneity, more residential mobility, lower economic status (i.e., lower family income, higher unemployment), and lower rates of children living with both parents (see Table 6.3). Second, differences in rates of property offending, by these demographic attributes, are most pronounced when the census tract is used as the unit of analysis. Differences across cities are also noteworthy, but the results are far less dramatic and less theoretically consistent for analyses based on the SMSA.

Characteristics of the physical environment are also associated with

Table 6.3 Property Crime Rates per 100,000 by Categories of Theoretically Relevant Variables and Aggregate Units

Predictor Variable	BURGLARY			MOTOR VEHICLE THEFT		
	Tract	City	SMSA	Tract	City	SMSA
Overall Mean Rate	2089	2131	1210	827.1	625.6	477.2
Ethnic Heterogeneity						
Low	1855	1588	1088	431.7	528.8	411.8
Medium	2402	2092	1224	652.9	592.0	503.4
High	4613	2715	1315	1396.9	756.6	515.7
Population Mobility						
Low	2089	1783	—	474.2	662.6	—
Medium	2899	2284	—	743.5	597.3	—
High	3883	2318	—	1263.8	617.8	—
Median Family Income						
Low	4412	2525	1231	1401.8	728.2	390.6
Medium	2634	2054	1127	733.9	560.5	436.9
High	1824	1812	1272	345.8	587.9	604.9
Unemployment Rate						
Low	1817	1931	1181	381.9	561.3	478.1
Medium	2523	2143	1084	710.1	631.3	516.8
High	4531	2318	1378	1389.4	684.1	432.5
Children in Two–Parent Homes						
Low	3625	2784	1399	1080.8	832.8	491.0
Medium	2774	2158	1286	774.1	558.3	534.6
High	2501	1453	947	638.2	486.7	408.4

increased risks of burglary and motor vehicle theft. For example, persons who live near areas with higher levels of public activity have greater risks of both types of property crime. These persons are also more vulnerable to having property stolen from around their dwelling (property theft) than persons who live in less busy areas. Similarly, residents of areas with higher levels of neighborhood deterioration are more susceptible to property victimization. About 26 percent of the residents of deteriorated areas have been burglarized in the last two years, compared to only 14 percent in low "decay" areas. Persons' risks of property theft and auto theft are more than twice as high for residents of these socially disorganized areas (13 percent versus 6 percent for property theft, 37 percent versus 18 percent for auto theft). As one would expect, due to the amount of time spent in this location, the most common place for car theft (41 percent) is near the victim's home. Thus, as with violent crime, particular aspects of the immediate environment predispose residents differentially to the risks of property victimization.

TIME OF OCCURRENCE OF CRIME

Predatory crime not only varies by physical location but also by the time of day. The timing of crime is important because it indicates when particular types of non-household activity are most dangerous in increasing individuals' risks of victimization and the exposure of their property to crime.

An analysis of NCS data for 1987–1989 reveals that a majority of rapes by strangers (74 percent), assaults (59 percent) and robberies (54 percent) occurred at nighttime (6 p.m. to 6 a.m.). For each type of violent crime, the modal time is from 6 p.m. to midnight. Excluding the sizeable minority of cases in which the time is unknown, burglaries are equally likely during both daytime (51 percent) and nighttime (49 percent) hours. A clear majority of motor vehicle thefts (74 percent) are committed during evening hours. The period from midnight to 6 A.M. is the modal interval for motor vehicle theft, whereas the modal category for burglary is from noon to 6 P.M.

From the perspective of criminological theory, these results are important because they suggest that frequent nighttime activity increases the risks of both violent and property crime. Only in the case of residential burglary are the risks of victimization similar for daytime and nighttime hours. When these findings are combined with data on the location of crime, they suggest that frequent public activity at night is especially hazardous to individuals' risks of predatory crime.

SOCIAL CHARACTERISTICS OF OFFENDERS AND VICTIMS

In addition to accounting for the social distribution of crime over particular times of the day and at particular locales, a sound theory of criminality or victimization must also explain the relative risks of crime for various groups of people. Are rates of predatory offending and victimization higher among males, non-whites, young persons, the unemployed and poor, single persons, and those with lower education than their respective counterparts? What accounts for these differences? Below, we review available data on the demographic characteristics of offenders, and analyze survey data on the social attributes of crime victims.

Self-reports of offending and UCR data yield profiles of predatory crime offenders that vary primarily in terms of degree rather than type. In other words, groups with the highest rates of offending are similar for both sources, but the differences between groups are far more dramatic in UCR data. For example, official crime data for 1988 indicate that males account for about 88 percent of the arrestees for homicide, 92 percent for robbery, 87 percent for assault, 92 percent for burglary, and 90 percent for motor vehicle theft (FBI 1988). The percentage of predatory crimes involving the arrest of suspects under 18 years old ranged from 11 percent for homicide, 15 percent for rape, 22 percent for robbery, 13 percent for assault, 33 percent for burglary and 65 percent for motor vehicle theft. Given that about 8.5 percent of the United States population in 1988 was between the ages of 13 and 18 years, teenagers are clearly overrepresented in official data for each type of predatory crime. Furthermore, UCR data reveal major racial differences in arrests for these crimes. Although African Americans make up about 13 percent of the United States population, they account for 54 percent of the arrested murderers, 46 percent of the rapists, 63 percent of the robbers, 41 percent of the assaulters, 31 percent of the burglars, and 40 percent of the arrested motor vehicle thieves (FBI 1988).

National rates of offending, based on responses to self-report items, highlight several trends. For example, when respondents are asked whether they had ever been picked up or arrested by the police, gender and age differences follow the same general pattern as UCR data, but the magnitude of differences within social categories is less dramatic. Specifically, men in 1984 were about four times more likely than women (22 percent versus 6 percent) to report contact with the police, whereas 33 percent of the 18–20 year olds reported having contact with the police, compared with only 8 percent of the persons over 50 years old (see

Sourcebook for Criminal Justice Statistics, 1985). There were no differences in self-reported offending by race (13 percent for both blacks and whites). Overall, both self-report and UCR arrest data demonstrate that particular groups of persons have greater contact with the police and are more likely to be officially designated as criminals.

The NCS data and the Seattle victimization survey can be used to develop a rather detailed profile of the demographic attributes of various kinds of crime victims. It is this demographic profile of victims that forms the basis for current theories of victimization. Tables 6.4 and 6.5 provide summaries of victimization rates by select characteristics of residents for these two data sources.

As shown in Table 6.4, victimization rates in the NCS data vary widely according to the personal characteristics of the residents. Based on the NCS data for 1989, risks of violent crime are generally higher for persons who are under 30 years old, male, non-white, have lower family income, never married, less than high school educated, more transient, live in multi-unit dwellings, and are renters (see Table 6.4). Risks of property victimization are generally higher among persons who are 30–59 years old, female, black, have lower family income, are separated or divorced, college educated, frequent movers, apartment dwellers, renters and live alone. Regarding specific offenses, rates of stranger assault are over fourteen times higher for persons under 30 than for those over 60 years old, but vary little by family income, educational attainment, and household size. Rates of both assault and robbery are about twice as high for males, the never married, apartment dwellers, and renters than their respective counterparts. Burglary risks are about twice as high for persons in particular categories of ethnicity, family income, marital status, and household size. Only three demographic variables (age, marital status, and type of housing unit) exhibit differences in risks of motor vehicle theft that are at least twice as large across categories, whereas none of the comparisons for property theft from around the dwelling are of this magnitude.

Analysis of the Seattle victimization survey reveals similar patterns to the NCS data. As shown in Table 6.5, risks of violent crime are generally highest among persons who are younger, non-white, have lower family income, unemployed, have lower formal education, are frequent movers, apartment dwellers, renters, and live alone. Differences by gender and marital status vary by type of violent crime. Men are more than twice as likely as women to be assault victims, but are less likely to be victims of personal robbery.[4] Widowers have the highest risk of robbery among the different marital groupings, and persons who have never married have the highest risk of assault victimization. Demographic differ-

Table 6.4 Victimization Rates per 1,000 by Select Characteristics of the Resident (NCS 1989 Data, N = 16,855)

Predictor Variable	Total Violent*	Stranger Robbery	Stranger Assault	Burglary	H'hold Theft	Vehicle Theft
Overall Mean Rate	46.0	14.0	31.7	77.9	134.1	27.2
Age Category						
16–29 yrs. old	70.8	16.6	53.6	67.5	129.5	27.3
30–59 yrs. old	37.4	13.3	24.0	87.2	149.3	32.2
60 and older	13.8	10.1	3.6	75.3	101.4	13.0
Gender						
Female	28.6	10.1	17.3	86.5	149.0	27.7
Male	65.1	18.3	47.4	68.5	117.7	26.8
Ethnicity						
White	44.8	11.7	32.5	75.1	133.3	25.8
Black	53.8	31.6	23.8	105.9	146.3	39.4
Other	54.0	17.3	36.7	58.3	110.2	25.9
Median Family Income						
Low (<$10k)	55.4	20.9	34.5	120.5	152.7	19.8
Medium ($10–$30k)	44.5	12.2	31.8	74.9	145.1	30.1
High (>$30k)	41.9	11.0	30.8	64.1	116.6	26.8
Marital Status						
Married	28.6	9.0	19.5	67.7	139.7	24.6
Widowed	15.1	14.1	1.0	111.0	130.2	22.2
Separated/Divorced	56.0	18.2	36.3	143.2	172.2	48.8
Never Married	76.4	20.7	55.5	63.9	112.4	24.9

Educational Attainment						
<High School Grad.	17.4	102.6	67.3	37.7	16.9	54.2
High School Grad.	25.7	143.0	78.6	28.5	12.7	41.7
Some College or More	34.6	147.7	83.8	30.9	13.3	44.8
No. of Moves in Last 5 yrs.						
0 moves	21.6	110.8	63.0	19.0	10.0	28.9
1 move	30.6	134.7	80.0	36.9	18.1	55.6
2 or more moves	34.5	172.6	101.7	49.7	17.5	68.0
Housing Unit						
Single–unit Dwelling	21.2	127.9	72.9	28.0	10.1	38.1
Multi–unit Dwelling	43.6	149.0	90.9	40.2	24.5	65.7
Home Tenure						
Renter	37.4	161.8	99.4	45.1	22.1	67.7
Owner/Buying	21.4	118.3	65.7	24.0	9.4	33.6
Household Size						
Live Alone	39.1	163.2	142.9	27.2	18.0	46.4
2 People	25.7	141.6	75.8	30.6	10.6	41.2
3 or more People	24.3	113.9	54.6	34.7	16.4	51.4

Note:

*Total Violent includes rape, robbery, and assault. There are not enough cases (n = 19) to do a separate analysis of rape.

Table 6.5 Victimization Rates per 1,000 by Select Characteristics of the Resident (Seattle Victimization Survey, N = 5,302)*

Predictor Variable	Total Violent	Stranger Robbery	Stranger Assault	Burglary	H'hold Theft	Vehicle Theft
Overall Mean Rate	68.1	23.8	50.5	167.5	77.1	227.3
Age Category						
16–29 yrs. old	121.3	34.1	92.6	170.3	73.6	328.3
30–59 yrs. old	67.9	18.4	56.7	191.9	98.0	281.3
60 and older	44.7	28.8	20.8	123.1	41.6	85.1
Gender						
Female	55.7	25.8	33.4	165.3	79.2	200.2
Male	80.3	21.8	67.6	169.7	75.1	254.1
Ethnicity						
White	67.9	23.8	50.6	169.4	76.9	230.8
Black	53.1	23.6	32.4	156.3	61.9	147.5
Other**	86.5	24.4	68.7	170.7	90.9	255.0
Median Family Income						
Low (<$10k)	111.8	48.2	83.3	142.5	68.0	144.7
Medium ($10–$30k)	77.6	28.1	55.4	164.5	75.4	196.5
High (>$30k)	51.2	15.2	40.0	174.8	80.4	271.2
Marital Status						
Married	48.2	16.4	34.2	153.0	85.6	255.4
Widowed	60.0	41.8	25.5	143.6	54.5	54.5
Separated/Divorced	80.3	36.8	56.9	202.3	68.6	215.7
Never Married	114.7	27.5	98.5	197.1	71.9	255.4
Major Daytime Activity						
Unemployed	152.8	41.7	125.0	194.4	27.8	222.2
Homemaker	58.7	31.2	31.2	117.4	91.7	187.2

Retired	43.6	28.8	20.1	114.2	37.5	79.3
Student	108.4	19.7	98.5	128.1	98.5	320.2
Working	74.0	20.8	60.2	193.3	88.8	285.1
Other**	70.2	20.1	53.5	220.7	93.6	250.8
Educational Attainment						
< High School Grad.	91.5	39.6	61.0	137.2	67.1	122.0
High School Grad.	61.6	23.8	42.7	143.7	80.5	191.3
Some College or More	68.7	22.5	52.6	178.6	77.3	248.4
No. of Moves in Last 5 yrs.						
0 moves	49.0	21.1	31.6	155.9	69.4	173.7
1 move	79.2	25.0	60.4	179.2	97.9	271.9
2 or more moves	103.7	29.4	86.7	185.8	80.5	320.4
Housing Unit						
Single–unit Dwelling	53.5	19.8	37.8	165.4	83.4	220.1
Multi–unit Dwelling	122.0	37.9	98.5	177.1	53.3	252.9
Home Tenure						
Renter	115.6	37.3	90.8	176.7	74.0	263.1
Owner/Buying	42.5	16.6	28.8	163.5	78.7	208.0
Household Size						
Live Alone	93.4	39.5	67.5	181.3	59.3	175.2
2 "adults"***	54.2	17.2	40.2	165.6	72.9	248.2
3 or more "adults"	69.3	16.1	57.2	154.6	114.5	250.0

Notes:

* The reference period for each crime is "over the last two years". All violent crimes are restricted to acts committed by strangers. Total Violence refers to whether a person was victimized by an assault or robbery; property theft involves stealing property from the outside of the dwelling; and vehicle theft includes having a car stolen or broken into.

** "Other" ethnicity includes Asian, Hispanic, and Native American. "Other" major daytime activity include armed services, vacationing, and disabled. "Adults" for household size refer to persons over 16 years old.

ences in risks of stranger assault are usually of a larger magnitude (exceeding a between-group factor of two in most cases) than demographic differences in robbery victimization.

Social differences in the risks of property crime in the Seattle survey vary widely by type of property offense. Only in the case of ethnicity and family income did the same category (i.e., "other" ethnicity, "high" income) have the highest risks for each property crime. The odds of burglary are higher for persons who are middle-aged, wealthier, more educated, more transient (i.e., frequent mover, apartment dweller, renter), and live alone. Risks of property theft from around the dwelling are greater for persons who are middle-aged, wealthier, moved at least once in the last five years, and live with other adults. The likelihood of motor vehicle theft is greater for persons who are under 30 years old, male, have higher incomes, more educated, more transient, and live with other adults.

The results from Tables 6.4 and 6.5 clearly indicate that some demographic variables are associated with greater variation in risk of predatory crime than others. For both surveys, differences in victimization risks by age, gender, income, and marital status are large in magnitude, and are generally consistent within different types of violent and property crime. Regardless of the survey, persons who are young, male, single, and have lower income have higher risks of stranger assault than persons who are older, female, married, and have higher income. Except for a gender difference (i.e., females had a higher risk of robbery in the Seattle data), the profile for robbery victims is similar to that of assault victims across surveys. However, the demographic characteristics of property victims vary for different types of property crime within a particular survey, and differ widely, in many cases, across surveys. The best example of this is that high-income persons have the highest risks of each type of property crime in the Seattle survey, but low-income persons generally have the highest risks of property victimization in the NCS data. The relationship between gender and risks of burglary and motor vehicle theft also differs across surveys. There are several possible explanations for these differences: differences in sample composition (e.g., the Seattle respondents are older, less mobile, and have higher levels of home ownership) and measures of crime (e.g., auto theft in the Seattle survey includes attempted entry into the vehicle). These variations make bivariate comparisons across surveys somewhat problematic.

Differential risks of predatory crime are also apparent when one considers the joint distribution of many of these demographic variables. For example, men are more susceptible to assault than women across studies, but gender differences in this type of victimization progressively decrease as age increases. In other words, gender differences in assault victimization are most pronounced among persons less than 30 years old. Similarly, gender differences in assault victimization are larger, in both samples, among persons who are single (i.e., never married or separated/divorced) than among married persons. Low income persons have greater exposure to robbery, but income differences in robbery victimization are largest among middle-aged persons. In contrast, income differences in risks of burglary, in both samples, are largest for persons under 30 years old. Each of these supplemental findings identifies an interactive effect among demographic variables. However, these interactions, in most cases, are fairly small in magnitude, suggesting that the "main" effects of the demographic variables reported in Tables 6.4 and 6.5 give an adequate representation of their observed relationships.

In summary, the analysis of social characteristics of offenders and victims of predatory crime reveal several general trends. First, neither offending nor victimization is randomly distributed across social groups. Persons who are young, black, or male are disproportionately represented in UCR data on predatory crime, and it is reasonable to assume that persons who possess each of these characteristics (i.e., young, black males) are especially vulnerable to official designation as offenders. Self-report studies validate the higher rates of offending among young persons and males. Risks of victimization by a violent crime are higher among persons who are younger, males (especially for assault, less so for robbery), low income, unmarried, and more transient (i.e., frequent movers, apartment dwellers, renters). Victims of property crime are also more transient, but they tend to be older (30-59 years old), wealthier, and have higher educational attainment than victims of violence. Second, the results for violent crime provide some support for the argument that there is a homogeneous pool of victims and offenders (see Singer 1981; Sampson and Lauritsen 1990), in that both groups are disproportionately young, male, and poor. Victims and offenders of property crime, however, do not share similar characteristics. Third, coupled with the results for the location and timing of predatory crime, persons who partake in greater levels of non-household activity at night, and come into greater contact with young males, should be especially vulnerable to violent crime. Whether or not lifestyle differences account for demographic differences in risks of both violent and property victimization will be addressed in chapter 8.

SUMMARY AND CONCLUSIONS

The primary goal of this chapter has been to describe the empirical distribution of crime and victimization over time, space, and social groups.

Nighttime activity is associated with higher risks of violent crime and the majority of property offending (except burglary). Geographical areas (especially census tracts and cities) with higher levels of ethnic heterogeneity, greater population mobility, lower economic resources, and greater family disruption have higher rates of predatory crime than their respective counterparts. Living in proximity to areas with high levels of public activity, or more signs of neighborhood decay and disintegration, are also associated with increased risks of victimization. The analysis of NCS data reveals that a majority of violent crimes are committed by strangers, and these rates have remained fairly stable over time. When adjustments are made for the amount of time people spend in various locations, violent crimes by strangers are disproportionately more likely to occur on streets, inside bars and restaurants, on public transit, and in parking lots/garages than in the home or at school.

Social groups have differential risks of predatory offending and victimization. UCR data supports the characterization that predatory crime is disproportionately committed by persons who are male, young, black, and poor. Self-report data on offending yields a similar profile in most cases. Higher rates of victimization by stranger violence are found among persons who are male, young, non-white, low SES (i.e., low income, unemployed, low education), live alone, and more transient (i.e., frequent movers, renters, apartment dwellers). In contrast, the social profile of property victims varies widely by type of crime and across victimization surveys. Burglary victims in each sample are more likely to be middle-aged, separated or divorced, college educated, more transient, and live alone. Gender and income differences in risks of burglary vary across surveys.

The social ecology of predatory crime represents the basic empirical observations to be explained by current theories of criminality and victimization. The success of current theories in explaining the social ecology of predatory crime is described in the next chapters.

Predicting Crime Rates

It is virtually axiomatic among sociologists that crime is associated with high levels of population heterogeneity, residential mobility, low socio-economic status, and family disruption. These correlates of criminal motivation are found in sociological theories that attribute them to lower levels of internal social control and supervision of youth in communities, weakened bonds to mainstream society, greater opportunities for learning criminal norms, and fewer social and economic resources to develop and achieve collective goals.[1] In contrast, theories of victimization identify the causes of criminal behavior in those aspects of individuals' routine activities and lifestyles that produce criminal opportunities by enhancing their attractiveness as crime targets, increasing their exposure to risky situations, and reducing their guardianship.

In the next three chapters, we evaluate research hypotheses about these factors that are derived from theories of criminality and victimization. We begin, in this chapter, by examining how measures of theoretical concepts influence rates of predatory crime for three different aggregate units: SMSAs, cities, and census tracts. Subsequent chapters use responses from the Seattle telephone survey to evaluate how measures of the key components underlying criminal opportunity theories (i.e., proximity, exposure, target attractiveness, and guardianship) affect individuals' risks of victimization, and whether these factors have context-specific effects on these risks.

CRIME RATES AND THEORETICALLY DERIVED VARIABLES

Each theoretical perspective identifies major variables that ought to account for the level of crime in geographical areas and changes in crime rates over time. Three types of analysis are performed to assess how strongly these theoretically relevant variables are associated with crime rates. First, we examine the bivariate correlations between each variable and different types of predatory crime rates for samples of (1) 148 United States SMSAs in 1970, (2) 584 U.S. cities for the years 1960, 1970, and 1980, and (3) 114 census tracts in Seattle for 1960, 1970, and 1980. These correlations are presented in Table 7.1. Second, offense-specific models of crime rates are estimated for each sample. These regression models are presented in Table 7.2, and include measures derived both from theories of criminality and criminal opportunity theories of victimization. Third, data from the U.S. cities and census tracts in Seattle are used to examine how changes in the conditions that foster criminal motivation and criminal opportunities are associated with changes in crime rates over the 1960–1970 and 1970–1980 decades. These models with change scores and lagged variables are presented in Table 7.3. The performance of each major theoretical variable in these analyses is summarized below.

Socio-Economic Status (SES)

We hypothesized that *the lower the socio-economic status of a geographic area, the higher its crime rate.* This hypothesis is derived from a long tradition of criminological research, although research has not yielded a consistent relationship between SES and criminality (see Tittle and Meier, 1990, 1991). An inverse relationship between socio-economic status and crime rates is compatible with virtually all major theories of criminality. Shaw and McKay's theory of community social disorganization, for example, attributes the crime-enhancing influence of low socio-economic status to its impact on reducing communal resources and supervision of youth. Anomie and relative deprivation theories emphasize how the general oppressiveness of lower income and living in an impoverished environment create despair and frustration by not allowing the equal achievement of culturally shared goals. Social bond theory recognizes how lower socio-economic status is reflective of social marginality and weak bonds to conventional society. Thus, while the explanation for the association is theory-specific, the expectation of an inverse relationship between indicators of socio-economic status and crime rates is firmly rooted in traditional theories of criminality.

In our data, the direction and magnitude of the correlation between socio-economic status and crime rates varies across indicators of the concept. As shown in Table 7.1, higher unemployment rates are strongly associated with higher rates of predatory crime for both violent and property offenses.[2] When median family income is used as a measure of SES, however, this expected negative correlation is observed across the majority of comparisons for only murder and assault rates.

Table 7.2 shows several trends regarding the impact of socio-economic condition on crime rates once controls are introduced for other elements of criminal motivation and criminal opportunities. First, contrary to expectations, the unemployment rate has little net influence on crime rates across comparisons. Second, the only strong support for this component in theories of criminal motivation is found in the net effect of family income on crime rates in census tracts, where higher income is associated with significantly lower crime rates for five of the six offenses.

As shown in Table 7.3, the net impact of changes in socio-economic status on changing crime rates varies widely by indicator of the concept, type of crime, and unit of analysis. For example, higher initial levels and increases in unemployment have a significant net impact on increasing rates of both murder and rape in U.S. cities, but such a pattern of support for theories of criminality is not found for other crimes, or when the census tract is the unit of analysis. Increases in family income are not associated with significant net decreases in crime rates. In the majority of all possible comparisons across indicators, crimes, and units, the expected negative relationship between socio-economic condition and crime rates is not found in the longitudinal analysis.

Residential Mobility

The criminogenic impact of population mobility has been widely investigated in previous research. Based on traditional theories of criminality, we hypothesized that *the greater the population mobility, the greater the crime rate*. As pointed out earlier, population changes are associated with greater opportunity for acquiring criminal norms, decreases in informal social control, and, perhaps, increases in the physical opportunity for crime. Population change can also be an indicator of social heterogeneity, itself a correlate of crime. Here, we use residential mobility as an indicator of population change.

The correlations in Table 7.1 indicate that census tracts with higher proportions of their population that have moved in the last five years have significantly higher crime rates for each type of predatory offense. This expected relationship also holds true once controls are introduced for

Table 7.1 Bivariate Correlations between Theoretically Relevant Variables and Crime Rates for Various Aggregate Units

	HOMICIDE			RAPE		
	SMSA	City	Tract	SMSA	City	Tract
CRIMINAL MOTIVATION						
Ethnic Heterogeneity	.731***	.636***	.371***	.336***	.415***	.406***
Residential Mobility	—	.009	.308***	—	.040	.397***
Median Family Income	-.306***	-.206***	-.361***	-.057	.020	-.328***
Unemployment Rate	-.227***	.321***	.662***	.105	.435***	.400***
"Intact" Families	-.680***	-.680***	-.359***	-.434***	-.713***	-.402***
CRIMINAL OPPORTUNITY						
Female Labor Force	—	.375***	-.405***	—	.500***	-.104
Public Transit	.132*	.115*	.361***	.034	-.016	.354***
Food/Drink Sales	-.198***	.140**	—	.048	.301***	—
Family Income	-.306***	-.206**	-.361***	-.057	.020	-.328***
Household Size	.006	-.225***	-.315***	-.024	-.442***	-.325***

	ROBBERY			ASSAULT		
	SMSA	City	Tract	SMSA	City	Tract
CRIMINAL MOTIVATION						
Ethnic Heterogeneity	.432***	.461***	.338***	.495***	.481***	.356***
Residential Mobility	—	-.047	.341***	—	-.021	.306***
Median Family Income	.261***	.003	-.317***	-.235***	-.072	-.302***
Unemployment Rate	-.074	.365***	.567***	-.098	.399***	.493***
"Intact" Families	-.262***	-.681***	-.289***	-.524***	-.702***	-.368***

	BURGLARY			CAR THEFT		
	SMSA	City	Tract	SMSA	City	Tract
CRIMINAL OPPORTUNITY						
Female Labor Force	—	.421***	-.325***	—	.487***	-.235***
Public Transit	.556***	.233***	.348***	.059	-.020	.313***
Food/Drink Sales	.323***	.227***	—	-.106	.227***	—
Family Income	.261***	.003	-.317***	-.235***	-.072	-.302***
Household Size	-.177**	-.340***	-.306***	.058	-.344***	-.278***
CRIMINAL MOTIVATION						
Ethnic Heterogeneity	.200**	.402***	.374***	.144	.258***	.208**
Residential Mobility	—	-.009	.350***	—	-.115	.407***
Median Family Income	.126	.106	-.254***	.314***	.094	-.346***
Unemployment Rate	.244***	.392***	.551***	-.037	.237***	.567***
"Intact" Families	-.356***	-.752***	-.419***	-.076	-.499***	-.382***
CRIMINAL OPPORTUNITY						
Female Labor Force	—	.608***	-.086	—	.371***	-.158
Public Transit	.021	-.071	.305***	.455***	.244***	.343***
Food/Drink Sales	.157*	.408***	—	.328***	.234***	—
Family Income	.126*	.106*	-.254***	.314***	.094	-.346***
Household Size	-.111	-.552***	-.410***	-.157*	-.355***	-.465***

Notes:

* $p < .10$
** $p < .05$
*** $p < .01$

Table 7.2 Unstandardized Regression Coefficients for Models of Crime Rates that Include All Theoretically Relevant Variables

	HOMICIDE			RAPE		
	SMSA	City	Tract	SMSA	City	Tract
Ethnic Heterogeneity	.480***	25.3***	26.5	.050	-5.45	295.5***
Resident Mobility	—	.005	25.3*	—	.367***	270.1***
Family Income	.103	.00008*	-.0003	.367***	.0009***	-.007***
Unemployment Rate	-.159***	.002	12.1	.073	.88***	-520.3***
"Intact" Families	-.262**	-.51***	-7.45	-.565***	-2.03***	64.9
Female Labor	—	-.28***	-130.5***	—	-1.27***	-518.7***
Public Transit	-.125**	.023	63.1***	-.178*	.085	252.0***
Food/Drink Sales	-.074	-.0001	—	.030	.004	—
Household Size	-.286***	-.805	-.60	-.161*	-1.94	55.76***
Household Crowding	.300**	.248***	77.1	.156	.076	-499.2**
OLS R-square Total	.659	.546	.539	.288	.583	.355
OLS R^2 Crime Motiv.	.590	.519	.463	.253	.574	.309
OLS R^2 Crime Opport.	.335	.275	.423	.098	.305	.202

	ROBBERY			ASSAULT		
	SMSA	City	Tract	SMSA	City	Tract
Ethnic Heterogeneity	.474***	-276.1***	2780.77***	.214	257.35***	995.2
Resident Mobility	—	.532	1722.3***	—	.95*	1450.7***
Family Income	.298***	.011***	-.056***	.112	.0013	-.047***
Unemployment Rate	.100	-.41	-1337.7	-.094	3.79*	-380.4
"Intact" Families	-.004	-22.66***	1109.5**	-.358**	-14.74***	143.1
Female Labor	—	-11.03***	-5471.9***	—	-7.57***	-3087.9***
Public Transit	.261***	4.78***	3262.5***	-.117	.073	1605.0**

Food/Drink Sales	.159**	-.060**	—		-.070	.031	—
Household Size	-.207***	-45.2**	389.3**		-.131	63.5***	601.0***
Household Crowding	.158*	8.94***	-5500.0**		.189*	-.69	4591.7***
OLS R-square Total	.526	.570	.451		.329	.513	.358
OLS R² Crime Motiv.	.363	.496	.370		.303	.508	.299
OLS R² Crime Opport.	.387	.306	.314		.163	.270	.218

	BURGLARY			CAR THEFT		
	SMSA	City	Tract	SMSA	City	Tract
Ethnic Heterogeneity	-.162	546.2*	4183.8**	.016	-720.0***	-1044.8
Resident Mobility	—	9.88***	2931.8***	—	1.10	755.2*
Family Income	.734***	.024***	-.075***	.434***	.014***	-.026**
Unemployment Rate	.176**	4.30	2475.2	.040	.332	643.2
"Intact" Families	-.741***	-56.0***	508.56	-.086	-24.0***	-549.7*
Female Labor	—	-38.0***	-3332.3*	—	-10.4***	-1343.8*
Public Transit	-.222***	-1.40	4446.8***	.288***	10.94***	1295.1*
Food/Drink Sales	-.064	.34***	—	.0007	-.08	-28.54
Household Size	-.311***	-285.6***	713.01***	-.239***	-225.1***	19.30
Household Crowding	.370***	13.4***	-5496.1	.397***	21.1***	
OLS R-square Total	.486	.683	.430	.371	.388	.415
OLS R² Crime Motiv.	.378	.662	.406	.193	.301	.373
OLS R² Crime Opport.	.250	.463	.250	.364	.275	.352

Notes:

* p< .10
** p< .05
*** p< .01

"OLS R-square Total" refers to the proportion of variation in offense-specific crime rates that is explained by both criminal motivation and criminal opportunity factors. "OLS R-square Crime Motiv." is that variation explained when only criminal motivation variables are included in the models. "OLS R-square Crime Opport." is the variation explained when only measures from criminal opportunity theories are included.

Table 7.3   Models of Change in Crime Rates over Time

	HOMICIDE			
	584 Cities		114 Tracts	
	X1–X2	X1	X1–X2	X1
Ethnic Heterogeneity	17.38**	40.54***	−13.31	85.13***
Residential Mobility	.025	.048*	7.16	16.91
Median Family Income	.0002*	.00008	.0004	.0008**
Unemployment Rate	.282***	.263*	35.92	178.84***
"Intact" Families	−.197***	−.215***	12.02	−.156
Female Labor Force	.00027	−.194**	−29.17	−198.72***
Use Public Transit	−.0006	.081**	1.74	46.72*
Food/Drink Sales	.0012	−.0013	—	—
Household Size	−2.98**	−4.57***	−4.18	−15.1***
Household Crowding	.754***	.718***	78.50	98.41
Lag Crime Rate		−.75***		−.832***
Y-Intercept		30.98***		70.39**
R-square Total		.637		.831
R-square Crime Motivation		.598		.785
R-square Crime Opportunity		.569		.804

	RAPE			
	584 Cities		114 Tracts	
	X1–X2	X1	X1–X2	X1
Ethnic Heterogeneity	−7.31	48.58***	480.03***	−29.14
Residential Mobility	.256**	.537***	90.39*	191.16***
Median Family Income	.0013***	.0002	−.0033**	.001
Unemployment Rate	1.198***	1.239***	−392.5**	158.99
"Intact" Families	−1.35***	−1.10***	124.9***	25.23
Female Labor Force	.021	−.891***	−145.3	−510.3***
Use Public Transit	−.021	−.00097	66.9	285.6***
Food/Drink Sales	.0012	.0022	—	—
Household Size	−6.90	−6.79**	51.5**	2.59
Household Crowding	1.457***	.309	−109.71	178.1
Lag Crime Rate		−.394***		.182
Y-Intercept		114.4***		34.86
R-square Total		.630		.840
R-square Crime Motivation		.621		.806
R-square Crime Opportunity		.549		.775

	ROBBERY			
	584 Cities		114 Tracts	
	X1–X2	X1	X1–X2	X1
Ethnic Heterogeneity	647.6***	441.05***	4768.6***	2891.2***
Residential Mobility	.775	1.683	267.9	1945.7***
Median Family Income	−.0025	.0037**	−.0067	.047**

ROBBERY

	584 Cities		114 Tracts	
	X1–X2	X1	X1–X2	X1
Unemployment Rate	−3.25	3.27	−11.90	8246.9***
"Intact" Families	−8.38***	−6.998***	1448.09***	820.43
Female Labor Force	−1.37	−6.95***	−1798.11*	−6888.05***
Use Public Transit	4.16***	5.59***	1894.8**	5372.8***
Food/Drink Sales	−.027	.111***	—	—
Household Size	−35.62	−52.94*	236.8	−322.2
Household Crowding	21.55***	9.698***	−3253.6	−1381.01
Lag Crime Rate		−.307***		−.88***
Y-Intercept		791.1***		−296.09
R-square Total		.745		.838
R-square Crime Motivation		.694		.797
R-square Crime Opportunity		.703		.786

ASSAULT

	584 Cities		114 Tracts	
	X1–X2	X1	X1–X2	X1
Ethnic Heterogeneity	44.94	170.38	2487.6***	1166.01**
Residential Mobility	.215	.817	−77.72	772.99**
Median Family Income	.006	−.001	−.0095	.0100
Unemployment Rate	5.75*	5.72	−854.7	3220.9***
"Intact" Families	−9.20***	11.00***	654.5***	234.2
Female Labor Force	4.51	−2.37	−1375.5***	−4185.1***
Use Public Transit	.065	−1.052	554.99	1978.5***
Food/Drink Sales	−.019	−.014	—	—
Household Size	42.26	46.13	249.05**	−101.3
Household Crowding	9.698***	2.55	−115.5	915.4
Lag Crime Rate		−.417***		−.210***
Y-Intercept		924.81		765.98
R-square Total		.546		.920
R-square Crime Motivation		.537		.898
R-square Crime Opportunity		.500		.886

BURGLARY

	584 Cities		114 Tracts	
	X1–X2	X1	X1–X2	X1
Ethnic Heterogeneity	2687.7***	1715.8***	1505.4	2052.0
Residential Mobility	10.21***	10.51***	1028.8	1847.3
Median Family Income	.020*	.012	.029	.080**
Unemployment Rate	14.59	5.12	410.8	10195.5**
"Intact" Families	−31.01***	−33.62***	1295.8*	2355.2**
Female Labor Force	−14.38	−27.46***	660.1	−6389.8***

Table 7.3   *Continued*

| | BURGLARY | | | |
| | 584 Cities | | 114 Tracts | |
	X1–X2	X1	X1–X2	X1
Use Public Transit	−5.31	−3.37	4963.6***	8020.8***
Food/Drink Sales	.163	.478***	—	—
Household Size	−252.50*	−306.27***	−134.6	−1057.97***
Household Crowding	42.86***	22.63***	11658.2***	24063.0***
Lag Crime Rate		−.658***		−.666***
Y-Intercept		4719.08***		−438.9
R-square Total		.660		.806
R-square Crime Motivation		.648		.777
R-square Crime Opportunity		.602		.789

| | CAR THEFT | | | |
| | 584 Cities | | 114 Tracts | |
	X1–X2	X1	X1–X2	X1
Ethnic Heterogeneity	731.43*	−65.79	−1135.2	−989.14
Residential Mobility	4.63**	1.33	83.72	368.06
Median Family Income	−.0076	.0039	.029**	.014
Unemployment Rate	5.98	10.58	1308.8	2469.8
"Intact" Families	−9.09***	−5.85	−770.2**	−769.4
Female Labor Force	−1.45	−16.30***	143.6	−3965.4***
Use Public Transit	−1.37	18.78***	482.35	3212.14***
Food/Drink Sales	.096	.36***	—	—
Household Size	−265.4***	−240.6***	−335.7	−578.8***
Household Crowding	33.27***	30.58***	2082.7	7716.8***
Lag Crime Rate		−.885***		−.787***
Y-Intercept		1615.4***		2633.83**
R-square Total		.542		.788
R-square Crime Motivation		.448		.763
R-square Crime Opportunity		.525		.775

Notes:

Because there are two 10-year intervals from 1960 to 1980, the actual sample size for cities and census tracts in Seattle is 1168 and 228, respectively.

   * $p < .10$
  ** $p < .05$
*** $p < .01$

other variables in the multivariate analysis (see Table 7.2). When the city is the unit of analysis, crime rates are not strongly correlated with the level of residential mobility. However, for three offenses (rape, assault, and burglary), higher residential mobility in cities is associated with significantly higher net crime rates. For the analysis of change in crime rates over time (see Table 7.3), both the initial level and increases in residential mobility are associated with net increases in rape rates for each aggregate unit. The impact of residential mobility on changing crime rates over time is in the expected theoretical direction for the other predatory crimes, however only about one third of these comparisons are statistically significant. Contrary to the cross-sectional results, population mobility performed equally well in accounting for crime rates over time in both census tracts and cities.

Ethnic Heterogeneity

There is another dimension of heterogeneity pertaining to the ethnic composition of the population. We hypothesized that *the greater the ethnic heterogeneity, the greater the crime rate*. Ethnic heterogeneity may reflect value differences in a community and the extent to which common values are lacking. This is the argument made by Shaw and McKay (1942) in their classic work on social disorganization. In those areas where common values might be found, ethnic heterogeneity may inhibit their effective realization. Heterogeneity has been linked with objective measures of social inequality and measures of perceived inequity, which might also be associated with increased criminal motivation. We use the product of the proportion of the population that is black and non-black as an indicator of ethnic heterogeneity.

    Our data show that, across each aggregate unit (i.e., SMSAs, cities, census tracts) and type of offense, higher levels of ethnic heterogeneity are strongly correlated with higher crime rates. This expected relationship persists in a majority of the comparisons for homicide, robbery, and burglary after controls are introduced for other measures of criminality and the opportunity variables. When examining changes in crime rates over time, Table 7.3 reveals that for all predatory offenses either higher initial levels of ethnic heterogeneity or increases in it over time are associated with net increases in crime rates. This is especially true for robbery and homicide. There are no major differences in how this variable influences changes in crime rates over time by type of aggregate unit.

Single-Parent Families

We hypothesized that *the greater the level of "intact" (two-parent) households, the lower the crime rate*. As we argued in chapter 2, single-parent households are often identified as a major causal factor in theories of criminality because they tend to be associated with fewer economic resources and lack an additional adult to help socialize children into conventional norms or effectively supervise youthful family members. From a criminal opportunity perspective, this expected positive relationship between single-parent households and crime also may be attributed to lower levels of guardianship of persons and property in such households. At the community level, high rates of one-parent households in a geographical area would therefore be associated with low levels of community social control, and fewer collective resources to supervise and socialize youth to engage in conventional behavior.

Our data shows a strong negative correlation between the rate of children living with both parents and the crime rate in a geographical area across aggregate units. This hypothesized relationship holds for all types of predatory crime, and persists in a clear majority of the possible comparisons (11 of 18) after statistical controls are introduced for other variables (see Table 7.2). For the models of change over time, two-parent households influence changes in crime rates for cities in the expected manner, but this was not the case for analyses based on the census tract (see Table 7.3). Specifically, for predicting between-city differences, both higher initial levels and increases over time in the proportion of two-parent households are associated with significantly lower net increases in rates of homicide, rape, robbery, and burglary. Increases in two-parent households (but not the initial level) are also linked to lower net increases in assault and car theft rates in U.S. cities. In contrast, higher initial levels or increases in two-parent households, in nearly all comparisons, did not significantly reduce crime rates in census tracts over time.

Exposure to Motivated Offenders

One of the major components underlying criminal opportunity theories of victimization is exposure to risky and vulnerable situations. From this perspective, we hypothesized that *the higher the level of exposure to motivated offenders, the higher the crime rate.* Given the social ecology of predatory crimes (see chapter 6), we consider the rate of female labor force participation, the rate of public transportation among workers, and the amount of retail sales from eating and drinking establishments to be good aggregate-level measures of exposure.

Our analysis for these variables reveals several trends. First, for each measure of exposure, at least one-half of the correlations are statistically significant and in the expected theoretical direction. These correlations are generally more consistent with expectations when the city is the unit of analysis, and for the specific crimes of homicide, robbery, and car theft. Second, the regression analysis indicates that public transportation is the only measure of exposure associated with significantly higher net crime rates across the majority of our comparisons. Higher levels of female labor force participation or retail sales from eating and drinking establishments are rarely associated with higher net crime rates. In fact, geographical areas with higher levels of female labor force participation actually have *lower* net crime rates for each offense and aggregate unit. Third, similar trends are observed for the analysis of change in crime rates over time. Either the initial level or increases in public transportation are linked to greater increases in crime rates in one-half of the comparisons by crime and sampling unit. The impact of changes in female labor force participation is largely opposite to theoretical expectations, whereas retail sales generally has a null impact on changes in crime rates over time.

Target Attractiveness

From a criminal opportunity theory, offenders select targets for victimization that have material or symbolic value. Accordingly, we hypothesized that *the greater the attractiveness of targets in a geographical area, the greater its crime rate.* Our aggregate measure of target attractiveness is the median family income of the geographical area. This variable was used previously to represent low socio-economic status in theories of criminality.

An examination of the bivariate correlations reveals little support for this expected positive association between target attractiveness and crime rates. In fact, a significant *negative* correlation best represents the relationship between family income and crime rates. As predicted from an opportunity perspective, however, family income has a significant net positive effect in the majority of comparisons for all crimes except murder and assault (see Table 7.2). The fact that this measure of target attractiveness does not exhibit its expected net impact on these violent crimes is understandable given that such offenses are not usually motivated by economic concerns. Furthermore, either higher initial levels or increases in family income have a significant crime-enhancing effect on increasing rates of homicide, robbery, and burglary for both aggregate units (see Table 7.3). The expected crime-enhancing impact of family income on changing crime rates over time is not generally observed for the other predatory offenses.

Guardianship

The level of protection or guardianship of potential crime targets is widely assumed to reduce criminal opportunities. We hypothesized that *the greater the level of guardianship in a community, the lower its crime rate.* Our aggregate measure of guardianship is the average household size.

Geographical areas with larger households have significantly lower crime rates across different types of offenses and most aggregate units (except the SMSA). The regression analysis indicates that this expected inverse relationship between guardianship and crime rates persists in nearly one-half of the possible comparisons by offense and sampling unit. Either higher initial levels or increases in the average household size over time are significantly related to decreasing rates of homicide, burglary, and car theft. Changes in crime rates over time are largely independent of the level and change in household size for the other predatory offenses (see Table 7.3).

VARIATION IN THE PREDICTORS OF CRIME RATES

A major purpose for examining the correlates of crime rates for different types of predatory offenses and aggregate units utilizing cross-sectional and longitudinal data is to assess the robustness of our findings. Under these conditions, each sub-analysis can be considered a replication of the expected theoretical relationships. Given the variability in findings in Tables 7.1 to 7.3, we now summarize these results according to which elements of the two theories are most strongly supported, and what particular crimes, aggregate units, and temporal designs are best explained by each theoretical perspective.

Variation by Theoretical Component

Of the variables underlying theories of criminal motivation, ethnic heterogeneity, residential mobility, and family structure had the strongest and most consistent effects on crime rates across analyses. Each of these variables continued to influence both the level of crime in geographical areas and changes in crime rates over time, even after controlling for other motivational factors and criminal opportunity variables. In contrast, measures of low socio-economic status (i.e., average family income and the unemployment rate) achieved significant net relationships in the expected theoretical direction in less than one-third of our comparisons across crime types, sampling units, and temporal design.

Although multiple interpretations are possible, we think the most sound explanation for the impact of heterogeneity, residential mobility, and single-parent households on crime rates is that these factors are especially symptomatic of attenuated social control. Geographical areas with high levels of these factors are more transient and less socially integrated, lacking the social bonds necessary for a community to articulate or achieve common goals. This social disorganization does not appear to be economically-based (as reflected in our findings for income and unemployment on crime rates), but rather seems to derive from the unavailability of effective, informal mechanisms of social control in culturally diverse and transient communities. It is in this manner that our findings offer the most support for traditional theories of criminal motivation (e.g., social disorganization, differential association, social bond theories).

The guardianship component of criminal opportunity theories received the most empirical support across our analyses. Average household size was strongly correlated with crime rates for each offense, and the crime-reducing benefit of larger households persisted in nearly a majority of the multivariate analyses. Our best explanation for the impact of household size is that it serves to reduce crime rates in two ways: (1) it reduces criminal opportunities by increasing the guardianship over persons and property, and (2) it increases the monitoring or social control over other persons making them less able to express their criminal inclinations. The level of public transportation altered crime rates as expected in most cases, but the other measures of exposure did not. Finally, family income influenced crime rates more in line with criminal opportunity theory than theories of offender motivation. One-half of the cross-sectional models, and one-third of the longitudinal analyses, resulted in a significant, positive net effect of this measure of target attractiveness on crime rates.

Variation by Offense Type

The predictive ability of theories of criminal motivation and criminal opportunity theories of victimization varied greatly by type of crime. Theories of criminal motivation that highlight elements of attenuated social control (i.e., primarily ethnic heterogeneity, population mobility, and family disruption) were best able to predict rates of homicide, rape, and burglary, and least effective in predicting auto theft. Opportunity theories of victimization were best able to predict rates of robbery, burglary, and car theft, and least predictive of assault, rape, and homicide. These conclusions are based on the average explanatory power of the statistical models for each crime (as measured by R-square), and the number of comparisons that were statistically significant and in the expected theoretical direction.

Differences in the particular characteristics of these predatory offenses account for differences in the ability of current theories to explain their distribution across geographical areas. Specifically, violent crimes against the person such as murder, rape, and assault are usually spontaneous and expressive acts among intimates, whereas robbery and property offenses such as burglary and car theft tend to involve greater planning and instrumental concerns (e.g., economic rewards, impressing peers). When acts involve greater planning and rationality, would-be offenders are more likely to assess aspects of the immediate environment to determine the relative exposure, accessibility, attractiveness, and guardianship of different persons and property. Under these conditions, it is easy to understand why criminal opportunity theories perform better in accounting for robbery and property crime than most violent crimes. Similarly, traditional theories of criminal motivation may be less able to explain car theft than other predatory crimes because such acts are more indicative of frivolous group activities to gain acceptance by peers, rather than of motivational factors like cultural conflict, detached interpersonal relations, or attenuated social control.

Variation by Unit of Analysis

Based on the correlations and cross-sectional models, analyses based on the SMSA as the sampling unit were the least theoretically consistent. Theories of criminal motivation were better able to explain changes in the crime rates of cities over time, but generally the results were similar for both the city and census tract as units of analysis. This latter finding is contrary to our expectations that census tracts would be the preferred aggregate unit because they best maximize between-group and minimize within-group variation. We attribute the relatively poor performance of our theories in explaining crime rates in SMSAs to the fact that this aggregate unit is so amorphous that it actually reduces between-group variation and masks major variation that occurs within this geographical area.

Variation by Temporal Design

Based on our literature review, we assumed that macro-level theories of criminal motivation and criminal opportunity theories were able to explain both the social organization of crime across geographical units (e.g., why some cities have more crime than others) and changes in crime rates over time. However, our analyses revealed that these theories were best able to account for crime rates at one point in time rather than temporal changes in them. When we examined the determinants of changes in crime rates over time (see Table 7.3), most of the theoretically derived variables (except ethnic heterogeneity and public transportation) did not alter crime rates in the expected direction, in the majority of possible comparisons. The most plausible explanation for these findings involves the possibility of conflicting macro-dynamic forces that may counteract and nullify the causal significance of any particular variable. In other words, changes in one aspect of life may elicit simultaneous changes in another domain, which cancel out the crime-inhibiting or crime-enhancing effects of particular variables.

As an illustration of this perspective, the primarily null effects of changes in exposure and target attractiveness on changing crime rates may be attributed to such parallel and counteracting forces. Exposure to crime may increase over time without necessarily increasing crime rates, because such changes in female labor-force participation, public transportation, or non-household leisure activities may be met with contemporaneous increases in safety precautions and guardianship while persons are engaged in public activities. Similarly, the crime-enhancing effect of increases in median family income (i.e., through increases in the supply of portable consumer goods) may be easily offset by increases in guardianship activity to protect these attractive goods. The criminogenic effect of increasing rates of residential mobility may be cancelled by parallel increases in family income that reduce criminal motivation. Unfortunately, although such parallel changes are likely to occur in any dynamic system, there is no definitive way to evaluate or falsify this explanation with our data.

An interesting feature of our longitudinal results is that lagged values of the criminal opportunity and criminality factors often have such an effect on crime rates that they overwhelm the change coefficients. In the case of homicide, the lagged values for public transportation and female labor force participation are large enough to be statistically significant, but the influence of changes in these factors is trivial. Similarly, both the lagged and change coefficients for population mobility on rape rates are substantial, but the lagged effect is, relatively, much larger. Patterns of this type can be observed for several variables in the equations for each type of crime.

The pattern of these longitudinal results is clearly consistent with the model of gradual changes in ecological structure that underlies a social disorganization theory of criminality. From a criminal opportunity perspective, however, the results suggest that crime rates only slowly adjust to variations in the supply of opportunities over time. Cities and census tracts with opportunities favorable to crime at the beginning of a decade tend to suffer higher offense rates ten years later, regardless of how conditions have changed in the interim. Opportunity factors may create an environment conducive to crime, an environment that is then relatively resistant to alteration. Phrased another way, variation in criminal opportunities may often be more useful in explaining long-term trends in crime rates than in accounting for short-term fluctuations (see Miethe et al. 1991).

This interpretation of our results is highly speculative. In many cases, changes in the variables do have an appreciable influence on crime rates, and large lagged effects are not always paired with small change coefficients. Overall, the longitudinal models are complex, and they are not entirely consistent with current versions of either theories of victimization or macro-level theories of criminality.

THE VALUE OF THEORETICAL INTEGRATION

Theoretical integration is widely endorsed by contemporary criminologists. As long as the perspectives do not make incompatible assumptions, theoretical integration may substantially improve our understanding of crime beyond that which is gained from each perspective taken separately. Macro-level theories of criminality identify factors that promote criminal motivations and the decision to engage in crime, whereas opportunity theories of victimization highlight characteristics of persons and property that increase their likelihood of selection as crime targets. By covering both of the basic decisions underlying crime (i.e., the decision to engage in it and the selection of a victim), the consolidation of these theories should greatly improve our understanding of predatory crime.

One way to demonstrate the value of this particular theoretical integration is by examining the major determinants of crime rates. Our multivariate analyses of crime rates reveal that three variables derived from theories of criminality (ethnic heterogeneity, population mobility, and single-family households), and two variables underlying theories of victimization (public transportation and household size) are the most predictive of crime rates and changes in them over time. Consequently, particular elements from each theory are important for understanding the distribution of predatory crime within and across geographical areas.

The value of theoretical integration is also demonstrated by examining how well each set of variables improves the overall fit of the regression models. As derived from the rows labelled "R-square" in Table 7.2, criminality-related variables significantly improve our ability to predict crime over that accounted for by victimization-related variables, in all comparisons by type of crime and aggregate unit. Likewise, the victimization-related variables derived from criminal opportunity theories significantly improve our predictive power over criminality-related factors for all crimes and most aggregate units, except the SMSA. Each set of variables also significantly improves the fit of models of change in crime rates over time for all offenses (see Table 7.3). These findings clearly indicate the importance of each set of variables in explaining crime rates.

Finally, the integration of theories is important to properly specify the relationship between theoretical concepts and crime rates. The best example of this is the effect of female labor force participation on crime rates in cities. Consistent with previous research and opportunity theory, we observed a significant positive correlation between this measure of exposure and crime rates for each predatory crime. However, we found that higher levels of female labor force activity did not significantly increase crime rates once statistical controls were introduced for the fact that higher rates of this activity occurred in cities with more ethnically diverse populations. By controlling for the variation that this measure of exposure shares with an element of criminality, we are better able to isolate the unique impact of female labor force participation on crime rates that is attributed to this underlying dimension.[3] The integration of measures from both perspectives into models of crime rates has a great deal of merit for the proper specification of each type of theoretical relationship.

CONCLUSIONS AND IMPLICATIONS

Crime in a community is related to social structural features that help increase the extent of criminal motivation, lessen social restraints on behavior, and increase the physical opportunities for it. Theories of criminality and criminal opportunity theories of victimization have been used in this chapter to account for crime rates in geographical areas. The value of integrating these theories of crime commission and target selection is clearly reflected in the significant improvement in fit of our estimated models of crime rates once each set of theoretically relevant variables is included.

The observed relationships between crime and residential mobility, ethnic heterogeneity, and single-parent families will not surprise either criminologists or citizens. Criminologists have talked about such effects for a long time, although it is fair to say that there is not a distinct criminological theory that incorporates only these causal forces. Citizens will intuitively recognize these relationships, and no special training is needed to understand that (1) when people move a lot, they do not develop strong ties to an area and its people, (2) cultural diversity is not conducive to defining and achieving common cultural goals, and (3) adolescents with less supervision are more likely to get into trouble than those with greater supervision. Similarly, our findings on how criminal opportunity factors influence crime rates are also easily understandable. Everyone seems to know that geographical areas have higher crime rates when (1) more of the residents are exposed to risky and vulnerable situations, (2) there are more expensive goods to steal, and (3) there are fewer household members around to offer protection. It is comforting to have anticipated these findings; it suggests that our understanding of the process of crime is not idiosyncratic and has a familiar ring to it.

The theoretical and policy implications of these findings are relatively straight-forward. First, any adequate theory of predatory crime must account for its particular social ecology. Both violent crime and property crime are most prevalent in geographical areas with smaller household sizes, and higher levels of ethnic heterogeneity, population mobility, single-parent households, and public transportation. These factors should form the basis for any theory of crime. Second, based on these findings, public policy on crime control would benefit from directing attention to the social conditions which generate both criminal motivation and criminal opportunities. The social correlates examined in this chapter give some indication of the possible sources of criminal motivation (e.g., attenuated social control through weak bonds to conventional values and lack of supervision) and the factors that enhance criminal opportunities (e.g., exposure, target attractiveness, and guardianship). Unfortunately, the policy relevance of these findings is somewhat limited because our data do not include the information necessary to isolate the particular causal mechanisms by which these social correlates promote higher crime rates and increases in crime rates over time. Without measures that tap these underlying causal mechanisms, we are unable to determine which particular theory of offender motivation is most predictive of crime rates, or why public transportation and household size actually do affect crime rates. Nonetheless, our aggregate-level results are largely consistent with the basic tenets underlying most theories of criminal motivation and criminal opportunity theories of victimization.

Predicting Individuals' Risks of Victimization

The development of theories of victimization, during the past two decades, represents an important turning point in criminological theory. Disciplinary tradition held that the role of theory in sociological criminology was to explicate the social processes that led offenders to commit crimes. Victims were largely assumed to be irrelevant to the process, except in the most elementary, theoretically uninteresting, ways. Yet, the notion that victims might play some role in the development of their own victimization was sufficiently intriguing to make some traditional offender theories take it into account (e.g., Wolfgang, 1958; Amir, 1971). It was not until the idea that victims also act and live in a social context conducive to crime was identified that the role of the victim became systematic (see Gottfredson 1981).

EXPLAINING THE VICTIMIZATION EXPERIENCE

Just as theories of criminality choose to portray crime as the combination of a select group of causal factors, so, too, do theories of victimization. Theories of victimization depict the victimization process as one characterized by social risk. Some persons and groups are more likely to be victimized because of the social risk they run in their everyday lives. Social risks arise from demographic factors, status configurations, lifestyles, and proximity to offenders. Regardless of what else might be said about the lives of crime victims, some persons run a greater risk of crime due to these factors. The ability of criminal opportunity theories of victimization to predict crime rates in geographical areas was addressed in chapter 7. Here, we examine its predictive power in explaining individuals' risks of criminal victimization.

Demographic Factors

We hypothesized that *demographic differences (e.g., age, gender, race, income, marital status, education) in victimization risks should decrease in magnitude once controls are introduced for routine activities and lifestyles.* This hypothesis is based on the assumption that demographic differences in victimization risks are due to differences in routine activities and lifestyles (Hindelang et al. 1978; Miethe et al. 1987).

Analysis of the Seattle data on 5,302 residents reveals several trends consistent with this hypothesis. First, there are major differences in routine activities and lifestyles for different social groups. Persons with the following characteristics are far more likely, than their counterparts, to engage in dangerous public activities (e.g., going to bars) and spend more time in daytime and nighttime activities away from the household: young (under 30), male, white, high income (over $30,000), college educated, and never married. Second, victimization risks by these demographic attributes were generally altered once statistical adjustments were made for differences in the level and type of public activity. The exception to this pattern was gender. Differences in victimization risks remained fairly stable even after controlling for the higher level of public activity among men. Thus, this hypothesis receives empirical support in the vast majority of cases, suggesting that differences in routine activities and lifestyles do contribute to the demographic variation in individuals' risks of victimization.

Status Configurations: High-Risk Groups

We hypothesized that *persons with the configuration of status characteristics commonly recognized as having the most vulnerable lifestyles (e.g., young males, low-income young males) should have greater risks of victimization than any other status configuration. These differences in victimization risks should be explained by differences in non-household activities for each group.* The high risk of stranger assault and robbery for young men, in the NCS sample, is consistent with their high levels of public activity, but age-gender differences in public activity cannot explain why young women have the highest risks of property victimization. Similarly, low-income, young males have the highest risks of violent victimization and the highest rates of participation in "dangerous" public activities. The high risks of property victimization for high-income, young females, however, is not consistent with their relatively lower levels of public activity. Thus, our ability to endorse this hypothesis is mixed; the hypothesis receives the most support in predicting risks of violent victimization.

Status Characteristics over Time

We hypothesized that *differences in victimization risks by status characteristics should dissipate over time.* This hypothesis is based on the presumed greater social and economic opportunities available to the less advantaged over the past two decades. In contrast to this "liberation" hypothesis, comparisons of demographic differences in victimization risks for 1974–1975 and 1988–1989 reveal few changes over time. While age differences in stranger assault actually increased over time (i.e., younger people had even greater risks than older people in recent years), differences by gender, race, income, marital status, and education remained fairly stable for each crime. Structural changes in routine activities and lifestyles have occurred in the United States in the last two decades (e.g., there have been greater levels of non-household activity, a rise in single-person households), but these changes have not apparently altered the nature of social differences in victimization risks. Thus, no empirical support is found for this hypothesis. Differences in victimization risks across social groups are largely invariant over time.

Proximity to Offenders

We hypothesized that *the greater the proximity to motivated offenders, the higher the risks of victimization.* The Seattle survey data shows that each indicator of proximity was positively correlated with individuals' victimization risks for each crime (see Table 8.1). After controlling for other elements in criminal opportunity theories, however, the victimization rate of the neighborhood is the only measure of proximity that has a significant net impact on individuals' risks of victimization for a majority of offenses. The perceived safety of one's neighborhood is associated with significantly higher net risks of most property offenses, but this factor has no substantial net impact on the likelihood of violent victimization. The positive correlation between the level of socio-economic decay and victimization risks was reduced to insignificance for all crimes after statistical control for other aspects of criminal opportunity theory. Thus, this hypothesis receives mixed support. It is most strongly confirmed on the basis of the bivariate relationships and when examining risks of property crime.

Table 8.1 Predictors of Individuals' Risks of Victimization

	Violent Crimes	
	Stranger Assault	Personal Robbery
PROXIMITY TO CRIME		
Violent Victimization Rate		
r	.268***	.142***
b	8.72***	5.89***
Perceived Safety of Neighborhood		
r	.131***	.060**
b	-.114	-.029
Socio-Economic Decay in Area		
r	.144***	.056*
b	.151	-.077
EXPOSURE TO CRIME		
Nights Out per Week		
r	.107**	.006
b	.056	-.006
Night Walks in Neighborhood		
r	.079**	-.003
b	.007	-.058
Number of Dangerous Activities		
r	.141***	.035
b	.309***	.155
Busy Public Places Near Home		
r	.110**	.029
b	.070*	.005
Times in Dangerous Situation		
r	.184***	.070**
b	.402***	.257**
TARGET ATTRACTIVENESS		
Family Income		
r	-.049*	-.060*
b	.005	-.193**
Carrying Valuables in Public		
r	.008	.002
b	-.0004	.028
GUARDIANSHIP		
Number of Adult Housemates		
r	-.009	-.038
b	.089	-.129
Friends Live on Same Block		
r	-.018	-.006
b	-.092	-.050
Social Integration Scale		
r	-.015	-.022
b	.078	.005
Safety Precautions Index		
r	-.032	-.025
b	.142***	-.004
Defend Oneself from Attack		
r	.049	.020
b	.043	.418**

| | Property Crimes | | |
	Residential Burglary	Property Theft	Auto Theft
PROXIMITY TO CRIME			
Burglary Victimization Rate			
r	.291***	.082**	.056*
b	6.43***	1.38***	.285
Perceived Safety of Neighborhood			
r	.129***	.095**	.088*
b	.067	.762***	.763***
Socio-Economic Decay in Area			
r	.114***	.084**	.067*
b	.045	.111	.009
EXPOSURE TO CRIME			
Nights Per Week Home Vacant			
r	.064**	-.001	.092**
b	.044**	-.008	.042**
Busy Public Places Near Home			
r	.047*	.038	.059**
b	.009	.028	.018
TARGET ATTRACTIVENESS			
Family Income			
r	.035	.016	.122***
b	.105***	-.009	.122***
Owning Expensive Consumer Goods			
r	.055**	.064**	.158***
b	.108***	.157***	.150***
GUARDIANSHIP			
Number of Adult Housemates			
r	-.016	.069**	.051*
b	.003	.253***	.012
Friends Live on Same Block			
r	-.011	.005	-.037
b	-.030	-.134	-.105
Social Integration Scale			
r	.022	.050**	.047*
b	.133***	.174***	.078***
Safety Precautions Index			
r	-.053**	.007	.005
b	-.114***	-.011	.022

Notes:

"r" refers to the bivariate correlation whereas "b" represents the logit coefficients from the estimation of logistic regression models.

   * p< .10
  ** p< .05
 *** p< .01.

Exposure to Risky Situations

We hypothesized that *the greater the exposure to risky and vulnerable situations, the higher the risks of victimization.* Using the Seattle survey data, we find that measures of exposure vary widely in their association with individuals' risks of victimization. Individuals' risks of stranger assault are strongly influenced by the level of exposure to risky and vulnerable situation. Higher levels of participation in dangerous public activities (e.g., visiting bars, places where teenagers congregate, taking public transit), living near busy public places that attract strangers, and visiting places where the person felt in danger are associated with significantly higher net risks of stranger assault. Risks of personal robbery, however, are largely unrelated to exposure.[1] Both risks of burglary and car theft are higher for persons whose homes were more frequently unoccupied at night, but living near places that attract strangers has no significant net impact on the likelihood of any type of property victimization. Thus, this hypothesis is supported in the majority of comparisons involving (1) the correlations between measures of exposure and victimization risks and (2) the net impact of indicators of exposure on individuals' risks of stranger assault, burglary, and car theft. In the aggregate analysis of crime rates (see chapter 7), the level of public transportation was the only measure of exposure that significantly altered crime rates across various analyses.

Target Attractiveness

We hypothesized that *the greater the attractiveness of the crime target, the higher the risks of victimization.* When predicting individuals' experiences with predatory crime, measures of target attractiveness vary widely in their association with victimization risks. Individuals' risks of violent crime are largely independent of family income and the frequency of carrying valuable property in public (see Table 8.1). After controlling for other variables, both measures of target attractiveness for property crime (i.e., family income and the level of ownership of valuable consumer goods) have a significant net impact on increasing risks of burglary and car theft. Risks of property theft from around the dwelling are also significantly higher for persons with more valuable consumer goods, but this offense was unaffected by family income. Thus, this hypothesis is clearly supported only for predicting individuals' risks of property victimization. As noted in chapter 7, aggregate measures of target attractiveness (average family income) also performed better in explaining the level and changes in property crimes than violent crime.

Guardianship

We hypothesized that *the greater the level of guardianship, the lower the risks of victimization*. As shown in Table 8.1, however, we find little evidence for the deterrent effect of physical or social guardianship on individuals' risks of predatory crime. The only exception to this pattern is that persons who take greater safety precautions have significantly lower risks of residential burglary. Unexpectedly, higher levels of social integration are associated with significantly higher risks of victimization for each property crime, whereas other measures of guardianship (i.e., household size, having friends live nearby, taking safety precautions, defending oneself) are largely unrelated to victimization risks. Our aggregate-level measure of guardianship (average household size) did strongly influence the level of crime in geographical areas and changes in them over time in nearly one-half of all comparisons (see Chapter 7). Thus, the hypothesis receives some support for predicting crime rates for geographical areas, but it is not supported in analyses of individuals' risks of criminal victimization.

CONCLUSIONS AND IMPLICATIONS

Predatory crime is related to both the social characteristics of victims and situational factors which place victims and offenders in time and social space. To say that victim characteristics are associated with crime is not, of course, to say that victims chose or were otherwise responsible for their victimization. Yet, there are some features of victims, their lifestyles, and social and economic circumstances, that increase their risk of criminal victimization.

The findings reported here will not surprise either criminologists interested in the development of victimization theory or citizens who have experienced criminal victimization. Criminologists will find comfort in the association between lifestyle variables and higher risks of victimization, and potential crime victims will find comfort in the knowledge that there are certain behaviors that will reduce risks. For both criminologists and citizens, there is something that can be done about crime. We can understand and manipulate criminal risks independent of changing the conditions that increase criminal motivation. This, after all, is the basic task of current theories of victimization and social policies aimed at reducing the opportunity structure for crime.

Our results point to several general trends. First, major demographic differences in individuals' risks of victimization (by age, income, and marital status) are reduced substantially once controls are introduced for differences in lifestyles and routine activities for each group. These findings support the basic tenet of criminal opportunity theories: that variation in victimization risks across social groups is explained by differences in their routine activities and lifestyles. Second, proximity and exposure to crime strongly influence individuals' risks of stranger assault, residential burglary, and auto theft. Third, measures of target attractiveness are linked with significantly higher net risks of victimization for most property crimes, but have no consistent impact on the likelihood of violent crime. Fourth, regardless of how they are measured, individuals' risks of victimization are largely unaffected by the amount or type of guardianship.

The predictive utility of criminal opportunity theories of victimization differs by the type of predatory offense. In the case of stranger assault, for example, lifestyle factors that enhance one's proximity and exposure to high-crime locales differentiate victims from non-victims, but elements which should enhance one's selection as a crime victim (e.g., the person's economic attractiveness, level of protection) are unrelated to these victimization risks. In contrast, at least one indicator of each theoretical concept significantly altered individuals' risks of residential burglary in the expected direction. For this crime, social factors that predispose a dwelling to higher risks (e.g., being located in a high-crime area) and increase its target-selection value (e.g., its perceived attractiveness, level of vacancy at night) are associated with a higher likelihood of victimization. Living in proximity to high-crime environments and having more frequent contact with dangerous situations are lifestyle factors that alter the risks of both stranger assault and personal robbery. However, neither of these violent crimes are adversely affected by individuals' economic attractiveness or level of guardianship.

While our analyses, to this point, have identified some of the factors associated with offenders and with victims as they are linked to predatory crime, additional questions pertain to the wider social context in which these factors combine to produce crime. That is, how do elements of the wider geographical context influence individuals' risks of victimization, and do individuals' routine activities and lifestyles have a similar impact on these risks across social contexts? Such context-specific models of victimization are described and evaluated in the next chapter.

Crime and Context

There is little debate that some social contexts are more conducive to crime than others, and that the presence of particular factors either facilitate or constrain the occurrence of crime. Our study follows a long tradition of sociological research that has examined the ecological structure and characteristics of dangerous places and "hot spots" for criminal activity (see Roncek 1981; Stark 1987; Sherman et al. 1989). Differences in routine activities and lifestyles have also been widely associated with differences in individuals' risks of victimization in this study and others (see, for review, chapters 3 and 8). Nonetheless, little is actually known about the net impact of the wider geographical context on individuals' risks of victimization, and whether measures of individuals' routine activities and lifestyles have similar effects across these contexts. The scarce use of contextual analysis in studies of crime and victimization is surprising, given that multi-level modeling and contextual analysis has been widely endorsed as a research tool to bridge the macro-micro gap in other studies of social phenomena (see, for review, Hauser 1974; Blalock 1984; Liska 1990).

TYPES OF CONTEXTUAL EFFECTS

A fundamental assumption underlying a contextual analysis of predatory crime is that individuals' risks of victimization are determined, to some extent, by forces in the wider environment. Macro-level theories of criminality (like social disorganization theory) provide a basis for identifying criminogenic conditions in geographical areas, whereas micro-level theories of victimization (like criminal opportunity theories) establish a set of necessary elements for predatory crime (proximity to offenders, exposure to crime, target attractiveness, absence of guardianship). When we integrate these traditions in a multi-level analysis, several types of contextual effects are possible in models of criminal victimization.

The most basic type of contextual effect involves the situation in which aggregate-level measures of theoretical concepts exhibit a significant net impact on individuals' risks of victimization. Such an effect would be observed if, for example, the levels of economic resources, public activity, or protective actions in the neighborhood altered residents' victimization risks regardless of their own personal characteristics. From a social disorganization perspective, these aggregate-level variables should overwhelm the impact of their individual-level counterparts (e.g., average income in the neighborhood versus a resident's income) because observed individual-level effects are considered spurious and primarily reflective of wider community-level dynamics (see Smith and Jarjoura 1989). Aggregate-level measures of the routine activities and lifestyles of residents in a geographical area should also exhibit a significant "main effect"[1] on victimization risks as these factors offer cues to offenders about the general accessibility and relative attractiveness of persons and property in that area.

Another type of contextual effect involves statistical interaction between aggregate- and individual-level variables. The presence of interaction implies that the impact of individual-level variables is not uniform across different geographical areas. For example, living in a highly disorganized area may be so oppressive that victimization risks for each resident are largely unaffected by differences in their particular lifestyles and routine activity patterns. In contrast, the greater internal supervision and protection provided in affluent neighborhoods may force offenders in these geographical areas to more selectively evaluate the personal characteristics of their potential victims. This hypothesis, that victimization risks for residents of low-income neighborhoods are independent of their personal characteristics, is also consistent with the image of lower social class as a "master status" (Becker 1963), and suggests that only residents of more affluent areas have some personal control over predatory crime. Statistical interaction would also be observed if individuals' routine activities and lifestyles were important in explaining victimization risks across different contexts, but the magnitude of their effects are stronger in one geographical area than another. Regardless of the particular type of contextual effect, our major point is that risks of criminal victimization should be influenced by the routine activities of residents and the composition and structure of the wider geographical area.

THE IMPORTANCE OF CONTEXTUAL EFFECTS

The importance of including both measures of individuals' lifestyles and contextual variables in studies of predatory crime can be justified on several grounds. First, most sociological theories assume that the community context has a direct impact on victimization risks independent of the characteristics of the individual. Consequently, studies which exclude this community context would suffer from serious problems with model misspecification. Second, it is possible that many of the presumed individual-level effects are actually social accompaniments of community dynamics. As mentioned previously (see chapter 3), the strong impact of being unmarried or young on victimization risks is commonly attributed to the lifestyles of such persons (see Hindelang et al. 1978; Miethe et al. 1987). Yet, the influence of these variables may stem from the fact that both single persons and young adults are more likely to live in transitional neighborhoods with more potential offenders, lower internal social control, and higher rates of public activity (see also Smith and Jarjoura 1989). Under these conditions, failure to include the community context would also misspecify the true relationship between individuals' characteristics and victimization risks. Thus, measures of contextual variables are important because they may directly influence victimization risks and explain the effects of individual-level variables.

Although previous research has examined multi-level models (see, for review, chapter 3), most studies have used small numbers of aggregate units that are also vague in terms of their physical geography (e.g., census tracts, electoral wards). Except for the study in Great Britain by Sampson and Wooldredge (1987), previous work has also not included detailed measures of routine activity at the aggregate level (e.g., rates of public activity, ownership of valuable consumer goods, safety precautions). Furthermore, none of the past studies have examined whether particular factors are more important in some geographical areas than others, nor have they looked at smaller contextual units (e.g., city blocks rather than entire cities). Rectifying these problems is important because it allows for further specification of how the social context influences individuals' risks of victimization.

Using survey responses from 5,098 Seattle residents on 300 pairs of city blocks, multi-level models of victimization risks are estimated to address the following research questions. First, does including aggregate-level measures of criminogenic forces (e.g., economic conditions, ethnic heterogeneity, population mobility) and other elements of the community context (e.g., level of guardianship in the area) improve our ability to predict victimization risks over models which include only individual-level characteristics? Second, do models of victimization risks, with and without controls for contextual factors, yield similar substantive conclusions about the importance of personal characteristics and lifestyles? Third, are individuals' routine activities and lifestyles more important in explaining victimization risks in some types of geographical contexts than others? The descriptive statistics and coding of the particular variables underlying these analyses are presented in Table 9.1.[2] Each research question is examined below.

MAIN AND MEDIATIONAL EFFECTS
OF CONTEXTUAL FACTORS

Aggregate-level measures of the major concepts underlying theories of criminality and victimization are included with the individual-level variables in order to assess both the main and mediational effects of the contextual variables. These aggregate ratings are developed by computing average rates across all individual respondents on each city block.[3] The results from these analyses are presented in Table 9.2.

The estimation of logistic regression models of victimization, which includes both aggregate- and individual-level measures of the theoretical concepts, reveals several trends. First, including the contextual variables significantly improves the fit over a baseline model of control variables [age, gender, race] and the individual-level attributes, regardless of the type of crime. For each crime, the contextual factor that is most important in explaining individuals' risks of victimization is the socio-economic status of the neighborhood. Residents of areas with more signs of economic decay and fewer indications of community supervision have higher risks of both violent and property victimization. Second, the socio-economic status of the neighborhood is the only contextual variable that exhibits a significant net impact on risks of mugging, residential burglary, and theft of property from the home. Risks of stranger assault are also significantly lower for residents of areas with higher population mobility (i.e., higher percentage of residents moving in the last three years), greater rates of public activity at night, and higher rates of protective actions.[4] Third, only for stranger assault did contextual variables mediate the impact of the individual-level attributes. A comparison of models in Table 9.2 with and without the contextual variables (i.e., Model 1 versus Model 2) reveals that differences in risks of assault by income and living alone are eliminated once controls are introduced for the contextual variables. Thus, the socio-economic condition of the wider neighborhood exhibits a strong net effect on victimization risks, but only in the case of stranger assault do contextual variables alter the impact of some of the individual-level attributes.

INTERACTIONS BETWEEN CONTEXTUAL AND INDIVIDUAL FACTORS

The models estimated in Table 9.2 are specified in terms of *main* effects, such that the impact of any particular individual-level factor is assumed to be constant across levels of other personal and contextual variables. This model specification presumes that the crime-inhibiting effect of safety precautions or living with other adults, for example, is identical within both high and low income areas. Similarly, under this specification, the net impact of owning valuable possessions on risks of burglary is assumed to be identical across different geographical areas.

Although main-effect models are widely used in previous research, there are strong reasons for challenging the appropriateness of this specification. For example, a person's routine activities and lifestyle may not alter victimization risks within economically depressed areas because living in such an area, in and of itself, may be sufficient to increase one's vulnerability to crime. In high income areas where there are higher levels of community supervision and control, however, personal characteristics may be more important in distinguishing victims from non-victims, because the social context forces would-be offenders to be more selective in their choice of targets. Individuals' activities and lifestyles may also be less important for persons who live in areas with a high density of public activity because the greater anonymity and weaker community supervision in these areas increases all residents' vulnerability to crime. Under these conditions, failure to consider that the impact of individual-level factors depends on the wider social context is a form of specification error that could dramatically alter substantive conclusions about the importance of criminal opportunity factors in explaining risks of victimization.

To examine whether the impact of individual-level variables is invariant over different contexts, we dichotomized several of the contextual variables at their median levels and performed separate analyses within each group. These context-specific models included the control variables and the individual-level attributes. Contrasts between "low" and "high" groups were made on the basis of the following contextual variables: family income, low SES status, busy public places, safety precautions, and living alone. These results are presented in Table 9.3.[5]

When predicting individuals' risks of stranger assault and burglary,

Table 9.1 Variables, Coding, and Descriptive Statistics*

VARIABLES	[Coding]	DESCRIPTIVE STATISTICS		
		Mean	St.Dev	Range
DEPENDENT VARIABLES				
Stranger Assault Victim?	[0 = no; 1 = yes]	.025	.16	0–1
Mugging Victim?	[0 = no; 1 = yes]	.006	.08	0–1
Burglary Victim?	[0 = no; 1 = yes]	.170	.38	0–1
Household Theft Victim?	[0 = no; 1 = yes]	.078	.27	0–1
Automobile Theft Victim?	[0 = no; 1 = yes]	.177	.38	0–1
INDEPENDENT VARIABLES				
a. Individual-Level Attributes:				
Nights Out	[nights per week]	2.43	1.99	0–7
Home Unoccupied	[days/nights per wk]	1.79	1.97	0–7
Dangerous Activities	[No. of activities]	.88	.81	0–3
Family Income	[1 = <$10k ...7 = >$100k]	3.37	1.37	1–7
Carried Valuables	[No. times per month]	3.26	2.63	0–8
Expensive Goods	[No. items owned]	2.54	1.41	0–5
Safety Precautions	[No. of precautions]	3.89	1.46	1–8
Live Alone?	[0 = no; 1 = yes]	.28	.45	0–1
b. Contextual Variables: **				
Residential Mobility	[% moved last 3 yrs]	.318	.17	0 – .83
Busy Places	[No. of public places nearby]	2.52	1.32	.06 – 6.24
Ethnic Heterogeneity	[%nonwhite x %white]	.09	.08	0 – .25
Low SES Status	[No. signs of deterioration]	1.33	.71	0 – 3.44

Mean Nights Out	2.43	.60	1.00 – 4.33
Mean Home Unoccupied	1.78	.62	.35 – 3.83
Mean Dangerous Activity	.88	.33	.22 – 1.94
Mean Family Income	3.36	.65	1.33 – 5.31
Mean Carried Valuables	3.24	.73	1.50 – 5.20
Mean Expensive Goods	2.53	.46	1.29 – 3.65
Mean Safety Precautions	3.90	.70	2.22 – 5.61
Mean Live Alone?	.28	.17	0 – .94

CONTROL VARIABLES

Age	[1 = 10–19 … 7 = 70 and older]	4.37	1.72	1–7
Gender	[0 = female 1 = male]	.50	.50	0–1
Race	[0 = white 1 = nonwhite]	.15	.36	0–1

Notes:

* See text for a description of the variables.

** Descriptive statistics for contextual variables are based on the city block as the contextual unit. The slight discrepancy between the mean values for the individual–level variables and their aggregate counterpart (e.g., family income and mean family income) is due to differences in sample size. When the aggregate rates were computed, all residents who did not have missing data on that variable were used, whereas only cases with no missing data on any variable (n = 5098) were used for the individual–level variables.

Table 9.2 Logistic Regression Estimates for Models of Individuals' Risks of Violent and Property Victimization*

Independent Variables	STRANGER ASSAULT		ROBBERY/MUGGING	
	Model 1	Model 2	Model 1	Model 2
Intercept	-3.06***	-1.93	-4.82***	-4.70***
Age	-.14**	-.14**	.14	.10
Gender	.32*	.30	.03	.06
Race	-.19	-.63**	-.22	-.97*
Nights Out/ Home Unoccupied	.06	.06	-.03	-.01
Dangerous Activity	.44***	.28**	.53**	.50*
Family Income	-.23***	-.05	-.62***	-.46**
Carry Valuables/Expensive Goods	.01	-.02	.03	.004
Safety Precautions	-.10	.09	-.12	-.10
Live Alone	.56***	.08	1.10**	.92**
Residential Mobility		-1.25*		-1.23
Busy Places		.03		.01
Ethnic Heterogeneity		-.52		3.06
Low SES Status		1.02***		1.02***
Mean Nights Out/Mean Home Unoccupied		-.39**		-.67
Mean Dangerous Activity		.08		.47
Mean Family Income		-.32		-.02
Mean Carried Valuables/Mean Expensive Goods		.19		.07
Mean Safety Precautions		-.61**		-.09
Mean Live Alone		1.13		1.06

	BURGLARY		HOUSEHOLD THEFT		AUTO THEFT	
Model Chi-Square =	79.6	112.9		42.7		23.7
Degrees of Freedom	9	10		9		10
Probability:	<.01	<.01		<.01		<.01
N	5098	5098		5098		5098
	Model 1	**Model 2**	**Model 1**	**Model 2**	**Model 1**	**Model 2**
Independent Variables						
Intercept	-1.48***	-2.48***	-1.94***	-3.92***	-1.20***	1.93***
Age	-.07***	-.05**	-.16***	-.12**	-.29***	-.27***
Gender	-.03	-.05	-.10	-.12	.17**	.16**
Race	.01	-.21*	-.02	-.23	-.32***	-.45***
Nights Out/Home Unoccupied	.04**	.05**	-.03	-.04	.002	.0003
Dangerous Activity						
Family Income	.06*	.10***	-.05	.01	.08***	.09***
Carry Valuables/Expensive Goods	.08***	.10***	.14***	.14***	.13***	.17***
Safety Precautions	-.09***	-.10***	.02	.00001	.04	.07**
Live Alone	.20**	.17*	-.18	-.18	-.14	-.25**
Residential Mobility		-.02		.71		.01
Busy Places		-.0003		-.07		-.09**
Ethnic Heterogeneity		.29		.26		.38
Low SES Status		.48***		.56***		.45***
Mean Nights Out/Mean Home Unoccupied		.07		.08		-.06
Mean Dangerous Activity						
Mean Family Income		.01		-.08		.25**
Mean Carried Valuables/Mean Expensive Goods		-.10		.12		-.14
Mean Safety Precautions		.12		.19		-.11
Mean Live Alone		-.12		-.37		.59

Table 9.2 *Continued*

Independent Variables	BURGLARY		HOUSEHOLD THEFT		AUTO THEFT	
	Model 1	Model 2	Model 1	Model 2	Model 1	Model 2
Model Chi-Square =	60.8	74.6	47.8	56.2	264.0	62.9
Degrees of Freedom	9	10	9	10	9	10
Probability:	<.01	<.01	<.01	<.01	<.01	<.01
N	5098	5098	5098	5098	5098	5098

Notes:

The logit coefficients in the table represent the change in the log of the odds of each type of victimization for a unit change in the independent variable. The Model Chi-Square for Model 1 represents the improvement in fit in the likelihood ratio chi-square when the individual-level variables are added to a model containing the intercept only. However, the value of the model chi-square for the equations with contextual variables (Model 2) represents the improvement in fit when the contextual variables are added to the model containing an intercept and the individual-level predictor variables (i.e., the improvement over Model 1).

* p< .10
** p< .05
*** p< .01

Table 9.3 Context-Specific Models of Individuals' Risks of Violent and Property Victimization

Independent Variables	Family Income		Socio-Econ. Decay		Busy Places		Precautions		Live Alone	
	Low	High	Low	High	Low	High	Low	High	Low	High
Assault										
Intercept	-3.07***	-5.34***	-2.15*	-3.40***	-4.30***	-2.99***	-3.76***	-1.98*	-2.82**	-3.20***
Age	-.18**	-.10***	-.32**	-.07	-.14	-.12	-.09	-.23*	-.41**	-.08@@
Gender	.48**	-.58@@@	-.09	.42**	.33	.31	.28	.35	.68	.23
Race	-.47	.58	.29	-.48	.31	-.32	-.24	-.12	.006	-.26
Nights Out	.04	.07	-.01	.06	.07	.05	.10*	.09	-.20	.10@@
Danger Activity	.37***	.72***	.56**	.34***	.72***	.33***	.36***	.53***	.63***	.35**
Family Income	-.11	.02	-.56***	-.07@@	-.34**	-.12@	-.05	-.61***@@@	-.38**	-.13
Carry Valuables	-.01	.05	.007	.004	.04	-.005	-.04	.12@	.12	-.02
S. Precautions	-.006	-.33**@@	.02	-.09	.01	-.06	.007	-.07	.02	-.06
Live Alone	.53**	.37**@	-.24	.60***	.20	.55***	.71***	-.43@	-.43	.43**
Burglary										
Intercept	-1.71***	-1.43***	-1.82***	-1.55***	-1.72***	-1.46***	-1.54***	-1.42***	-1.12***	-1.72***
Age	-.04	-.10***	-.06	-.05	-.08**	-.05	-.06*	-.08**	-.10**	-.06*
Gender	.01	-.09	-.11	.03	.02	-.06	-.02	-.01	-.07	.003
Race	-.002	-.10	-.02	-.17	.27*	-.21@@	-.02	.05	-.09	.07
Home Unoccupied	.05*	.04	.05*	.04	.08**	.02	.02	.08**@	.08**	.02@
Family Income	.05	.11**	.12**	.07	.08	.06	.01	.11*@	.06	.06
Expensive Goods	.05	.12**	.11**	.07*	.12**	.05	.07*	.08	.07	.08**
S. Precautions	-.001	-.17***@@@	-.17***	-.02@@@	-.14***	-.02@@	-.0001	-.17***@@@	-.17***	.01@@
Live Alone	.07	.37**@	.24	.11	.45***	-.001@@	.08	.39***@	.26	.14
N of Cases:	2550	2548	2530	2568	2536	2562	2471	2627	2404	2694
LRX² Assault:	40.6		44.4		29.2		29.2		36.5	
p (9 df) =	<.01		<.01		<.01		<.01		<.01	
LRX² Burglary:	23.7		58.0		34.1		20.4		16.8	
p (8 df) =	<.01		<.01		<.01		<.03		<.03	

Table 9.3 Continued

Independent Variables	Family Income Low	High	Socio-Econ. Decay Low	High	Busy Places Low	High	Precautions Low	High	Live Alone Low	High
Household Theft										
Intercept	-2.25***	-1.96***	-1.59**	-2.37***	-1.38***	-2.55***	-2.58***	-1.27**	-1.70***	-2.11***
Age	-.16***	-.13**	-.16***	-.13***	-.17***	-.14***	-.09*	-.23***	-.14***	-.18***
Gender	.14	-.41**@@	-.27	.02	-.25	.04	.02	-.20	-.32**	.13@@
Race	-.11	.06	-.27	-.09	.03	-.04	-.11	.08	-.12	.06
Nights Out	-.03	-.05	-.06	-.03	-.03	-.04	-.04	-.02	.03	-.09**@@
Family Income	-.01	-.01	-.13*	.06@	-.11**	.04	-.01	-.09	-.03	-.06
Expensive Goods	.13**	.15**	.18**	.12**	.15**	.13**	.11*	.16**	.14**	.12**
S. Precautions	.08	-.05	-.06	.07	-.06	.10*	.12**	-.05	-.07	.10*@@
Live Alone	-.22	-.15	-.23	-.21	-.31	-.10	-.13	-.32	-.14	.16
Auto Theft										
Intercept	-.89***	-1.78***	-1.57***	-1.22***	-1.14***	-1.48***	-1.68***	-.94***	-.82***	-1.56***
Age	-.31***	-.25***	-.29***	-.26***	-.28***	-.29***	-.24***	-.32***	-.35***	-.24***
Gender	.24**	.08	.02	.28***@	-.01	.31***@@	.13	.20*	.12	.20*
Race	-.25*	-.54***	-.27	-.46***	-.28*	-.35***	-.10	-.54***	-.35***	-.29*
Home Unoccupied	-.01	.02	-.02	.02	.0003	.003	.04	-.04	-.03	.02
Family Income	.07	.11**	.12***	.09**	.11**	.09**	.11**	.07	.09**	.08*
Expensive Goods	.06	.22**@	.17***	.12***	.10**	.17***	.13***	.15***	.11**	.16***
S. Precautions	.05	.05	.05	.05	.02	.08**	.12***	.02	.02	.07**
Live Alone	-.16	-.13	-.29*	-.13	-.33*	-.04	-.17	-.15	-.15	-.19

N of Cases:	2550	2548	2530	2568	2536	2562	2471	2627	2404	2694
LRX^2 H'hold Theft:	16.1		34.5		11.5		10.7		15.1	
p (8 df) =	<.05		<.01		>.05 (ns)		>.05 (ns)		>.05 (ns)	
LRX^2 Auto Theft:	8.8		36.8		16.2		14.4		8.3	
p (8 df) =	>.05 (ns)		<.01		<.01		>.05 (ns)		>.05 (ns)	

See text for description of variables.

   *   significant main effect at p<.10

   **   = p<.05

 ***   = p<.01.

   @   significant interactions at p<.10

  @@   = p<.05

@@@   = p<.01.

LRX^2 is the likelihood ratio chi-square test for the improvement in fit of the interactive model over the main-effects model.

including the interaction between the aggregate- and individual-level variables significantly (p<.05) improved the fit over models incorporating only the main effects for each contextual variable.[6] In the majority of comparisons for household larceny and auto theft, however, the improvement in fit was not statistically significant. This result suggests that the individual-level attributes, in most cases, had similar effects on these crimes across different contexts. Several major differences in the predictors of victimization risks formed the bases for the context-specific models of stranger assault and burglary.

With regard to risks of stranger assault, measures of target attractiveness and guardianship have a significant impact within some contexts but not in others. The crime-inhibiting effect of higher income, for example, is especially true for residents of areas with low levels of socio-economic decay, low public activity, higher safety precautions, and low levels of living alone. For the other levels of these contextual variables, individuals' income has a minimal impact on risks of stranger assault in their neighborhood. Similarly, the risk-enhancing effect of living alone is most evident in areas with either higher levels of socio-economic decay, higher rates of public activity, lower safety precautions, or higher rates of single-person households. In less socially disorganized neighborhoods, risks of stranger assault are largely independent of one's living arrangements.

Burglary is the only property crime for which measures of target attractiveness and guardianship exhibit significant interactions across the majority of group comparisons. These context-specific effects for burglary also have a clear pattern. Specifically, regardless of the measure of this concept, lower guardianship is generally associated with significantly higher risks of burglary only for residents who live in areas with higher income, fewer signs of socio-economic deterioration, lower public activity, and greater safety precautions. Risks of burglary are unrelated to the level of guardianship for residents of more socially disorganized neighborhoods. A similar trend is found for measures of target attractiveness (i.e., both individuals' income and ownership of valuable goods have a stronger impact in more affluent areas), but these context-specific effects are smaller in magnitude. There is no discernable pattern in the small number of context-specific effects observed in models of household larceny and auto theft.

CONCLUSIONS AND IMPLICATIONS

When applied to the study of crime, a contextual analysis presumes that individuals' risks of victimization are, to some extent, determined by the routine activities and social control actions of others in their immediate environment. Data limitations in previous studies, however, have hampered the evaluation of whether contextual effects alter substantive conclusions about the impact of individual-level attributes on victimization risks. Several types of contextual effects were proposed and observed in this chapter. First, regardless of one's own lifestyle or routine activities, individuals who live in areas with high levels of socio-economic deterioration have higher risks of both violent and property victimization than residents of more affluent areas. No other contextual variable had a significant "main" effect on both types of crime. Second, the detrimental effects of lower income and living alone on increased risks of stranger assault were eliminated once controls were introduced for contextual variables, but contextual factors did not alter the main effect of individual attributes on risks of property victimization. Third, individual-level characteristics strongly influenced victimization risks within some contexts, but not in others. This was especially true for stranger assault and residential burglary. The magnitude of these contextual effects, and their implications for theories of criminality and victimization, are described below.

The socio-economic condition of the neighborhood was the contextual variable that had the strongest net impact on victimization risks for each type of crime. As a composite measure of social and economic elements in one's neighborhood (i.e., self-reports of groups of teenagers "hanging around" the street, litter and trash on street, abandoned houses and run-down buildings, poor street lighting, and vandalism), we think this variable is an adequate measure of proximity to the type of criminogenic conditions identified by macro-theories of criminality. Social disorganization theory, for example, would attribute this relationship to the adverse impact of low economic resources and low levels of supervision of youth on weakening internal social control, and the ability of residents to articulate and achieve community goals. From a criminal opportunity perspective, the greater risks of victimization for residents of lower socio-economic areas is attributed to their greater proximity to pools of motivated offenders. Regardless of the particular interpretation placed on this variable, our major point is that knowledge of victimization risks would be limited without considering how the socio-economic condition of the wider environment creates a climate for predatory crime.

The need for the integration of theories of criminality and victimization, however, is most evident when one considers the interaction between aggregate- and individual-level measures. The impact of individuals' routine activities and lifestyles is not invariant across different contexts. In fact, the context-specific effects observed here are large in magnitude and theoretically meaningful for burglary and assault. For example, measures of guardianship and, to a lesser extent, target attractiveness influenced risks of burglary only for residents of middle- and upper-class areas (i.e., neighborhoods with higher income, few signs of socio-economic decay, fewer public activities that attract strangers, and more safety precautions). In more disadvantaged areas, where there may also be a greater concentration of motivated offenders, none of these individual-level factors dramatically altered risks of residential burglary. These context-specific effects would have gone unnoticed in traditional analyses of victimization risks that fail to include measures of aspects of criminality. Context-specific models also significantly improved our ability to explain individuals' risks of stranger assault. However, the only clear pattern for this offense was that the crime-inhibiting effect of higher family income was stronger for residents of more affluent neighborhoods.

The context-specific effects for burglary have immediate theoretical and policy implications. From the perspective of crime control policy, these findings suggest that efforts to reduce one's vulnerability to property crime by increasing safety precautions and other forms of guardianship will only be effective in areas which have lower risks of burglary in the first place (i.e., higher social class areas). In more disadvantaged areas, residents have higher risks of burglary (at the bivariate level) and less personal control over its occurrence because victimization risks are less responsive to individual differences in routine activities and lifestyles. Theoretically, these findings suggest that victimization risks are largely independent of the target-selection factors identified by criminal opportunity theories for residents of neighborhoods with higher potential for criminal motivation. Two of the key elements underlying theories of victimization (i.e., target attractiveness and guardianship) differentiate victims from non-victims only in relatively affluent areas, where lower levels of criminal motivation are presumed. Thus, a full understanding of predatory crime must involve an integrative perspective that takes into account the criminal opportunities provided by crime victims and the overall level of offender motivation in the wider geographical context.

Summary and Implications

This final chapter summarizes the results of our study and directly addresses their implications for future research on the causes and social distribution of predatory crime. We pay particular attention to the implications of our findings for integrating general theories of criminality and victimization in an effort to account for the distribution and occurrence of crime.

SUMMARY OF RESULTS

Various types of data analysis were performed to assess the social distribution of predatory crime, the predictors of crime rates and changes in crime rates over time, and the predictors of individuals' risks of victimization. The results of these analyses are summarized below.

The Social Ecology of Predatory Crime

Regardless of the aggregate unit or type of crime, geographical areas with higher level of ethnic heterogeneity, lower income, higher unemployment, and greater rates of children living with only one parent have the highest rates of predatory crime. The exception to these specific bivariate relationships in each case involved using the SMSA as the unit of analysis. As part of the social context for crime, victimization data revealed that persons who live near busy public places, or in areas with greater signs of social and economic decay, are about four times more likely to be victimized by a stranger assault than persons who live in other geographical areas. After

165

adjusting for the amount of time spent in these locales, rates of violent crime by strangers are disproportionately higher at restaurants and bars, parking lots, and public transit stations. Risks of violent victimization are also higher among persons who are younger, lower income, frequent movers, reside in multi-unit dwellings, and live alone. Risks of property victimization are generally in the same direction, but the demographic differences are smaller in magnitude. Victimization rates for property crime, for example, are only about twice as high for residents of socially disorganized areas than they are for residents of more affluent areas.

Predicting Crime Rates

Several factors, derived from social disorganization theories of criminality and criminal opportunity theories of victimization, were found to have significant net effects on crime rates across offenses and aggregate units. Specifically, higher rates of population mobility, family disruption, public transportation, and family income were associated with significantly higher net crime rates in most cases. In nearly one-half of the possible comparisons, areas with higher rates of ethnic heterogeneity and smaller household sizes had significantly higher net crime rates (see Table 7.2). Many of these variables (i.e., residential mobility, family disruption, ethnic heterogeneity, public transportation, household size) were also linked to significantly higher increases in crime rates over time in at least a substantial minority (i.e., greater than 40 percent) of all comparisons (see Table 7.3).

Predictors of Individuals' Risks of Victimization

Individuals' risks of victimization by stranger assault were greatly enhanced for persons who participated in dangerous public activities, and for those who lived in neighborhoods with high rates of violence and more public places that attract strangers. Risks of burglary were higher for persons who had higher family income, greater ownership of expensive consumer goods, took fewer safety precautions, had more nights per week in which their home was unoccupied, and lived in neighborhoods with higher levels of property crime. Persons who lived in areas with higher rates of crime also had higher risks of personal robbery and theft of property from around their dwelling. When separate analyses were performed in different neighborhood contexts, higher levels of target attractiveness (i.e., family income, ownership of expensive goods) and reduced guardianship (i.e., fewer safety precautions, living alone) were significantly related to increased risks of burglary in more affluent areas, but these factors had little net impact in areas with higher levels of social disorganization and lower economic resources. The crime-reducing effects of higher income on risks of stranger assault were true only for residents of higher socio-economic areas and areas with fewer commercial establishments nearby. Individuals' risks of assault were unaffected by differences in economic attractiveness for residents of lower income areas.

IMPLICATIONS FOR MACRO-LEVEL THEORIES OF CRIMINALITY

The patterning of our results is generally consistent with expectations based on a social disorganization perspective. Social disorganization theory highlights the causal significance of ethnic heterogeneity, population mobility, low socio-economic status, and family disruption. These factors are said to affect crime rates by influencing the level of community supervision of youth, ties to conventional institutions of social control, and the ability to articulate and achieve communal goals. While we do not have direct measures of these intervening processes, our results are nonetheless consistent with this general theoretical orientation.

Our support for a social disorganization perspective, however, is not uniform across units of analysis or types of offenses. The results are most theoretically divergent when the SMSA is the unit of analysis. Social disorganization performs equally well in explaining differences in crime rates across census tracts and cities.

The poor performance of social disorganization in explaining crime rates in SMSAs is understandable when one considers the nature of crime and the level of aggregation. Specifically, crime is not equally distributed across an entire SMSA, but rather there are smaller, "natural areas" for crime within any geographical unit. However, these crime-prone areas will have a progressively smaller impact on the overall crime rate as the size of the aggregate unit increases. In the case of SMSAs, the impact of these high-crime areas is minuscule, resulting in less dramatic differences in crime rates across these aggregate units. By ignoring major variation within each geographical area, SMSAs become an especially problematic aggregate unit for evaluating expected theoretical relationships.

Concerning types of crime, our measures of concepts underlying social disorganization and other theories of criminality are most effective in explaining rates of burglary and least successful in predicting auto theft. Social disorganization theory does about equally well in predicting each of the violent crimes. These differences by type of crime are unexpected under most current theories of criminality. For example, social disorganization is silent on the question regarding the types of predatory crimes which should be explained by this theory. This theory only says that ethnic heterogeneity, population mobility, and low socio-economic status are characteristics of neighborhoods conducive to crime. Similarly, anomie and social bond theories recognize that crime is caused either by a disjunction between legitimate means and institutional goals or the weakening of bonds to mainstream society, but these theories also cannot easily account for differences by type of crime.

Our best explanation for the relatively poor performance of traditional macro-level theories of criminality in explaining auto theft has to do with the nature of these offenses. In contrast to most property offenses, which involve primarily an economic motive, auto theft is commonly an act of joyriding, which is less utilitarian and more situationally induced. There may also be relatively fewer cars to steal in neighborhoods or cities that have higher levels of social disorganization. These characteristics may contribute to the lower explanatory power of traditional theories of criminality in accounting for rates of motor vehicle theft.

IMPLICATIONS FOR THEORIES OF VICTIMIZATION

Routine activity and lifestyle theories of victimization emphasize daily life activities that increase victimization risks by increasing one's proximity to motivated offenders, exposure to high-risk situations, and target attractiveness and by decreasing the level of protection or guardianship. Measures of proximity and exposure are found to increase individuals' risks of stranger assault and robbery, but these violent crimes are largely unaffected by differences in the economic attractiveness of potential targets and the level of guardianship. However, each of the major components underlying criminal opportunity theories received empirical support when we examined individuals' risks of residential burglary. Context-specific analyses also indicated that criminal opportunity theories were better able to account for risks of burglary among residents of more affluent areas. Risks of burglary for residents of more socially disorganized areas were largely independent of differences in individuals' attractiveness and guardianship. Almost all of these components (except guardianship) also significantly influenced individuals' risks of auto theft in the expected direction.

When attention shifts to explaining crime rates, higher levels of guardianship (i.e., larger household size) were significantly related to lower crime rates in the majority of comparisons for robbery, burglary, and car theft. Temporal changes in rates of homicide, burglary, and car theft were also strongly related to the level and changes in household size over time. Higher target attractiveness (i.e., higher family income) was associated with higher net levels of robbery, burglary, and car theft, but significantly lower rates of murder and rape. Both robbery and auto theft were related to the level of public transportation for each aggregate unit, however this measure of exposure did not generally impact the other crimes as theoretically expected. Overall, criminal opportunity theories of victimization were best able to explain aggregate rates of robbery, car theft, and burglary. Individuals' risks of burglary and auto theft were also clearly explained by these theories.

The fact that criminal opportunity theories perform better in accounting for property crime than violent crime is attributable to several factors. First, property offenses have clear economic motives, whereas the motivations for violent crimes are more diffuse. The multitude of motives for violent crime (e.g., revenge, jealousy, power/control, mistaken identity, economic gain, "cheap thrills") make it difficult to develop an adequate measure of target attractiveness for these offenses. However, in similarity to property offenses, higher robbery rates are observed in areas with higher family income, suggesting that economic attractiveness may be important in understanding some violent crimes.

A second explanation for the crime-specific effects is based on our inability to disaggregate violent crime rates by the victim-offender relationship. Specifically, violent crimes involve a direct confrontation between parties and, in most cases (except robbery), these parties are non-strangers. For violent crimes involving non-strangers, the type and frequency of non-household activity, guardianship, or economic attractiveness should be unimportant when compared to one's proximity to an aggrieved relative, friend, or co-worker. The relative unimportance of routine activities in disputes among known parties, and the inability to disaggregate crime rates by the victim-offender relationship, would account for the poorer performance of criminal opportunity theories in explaining violent crimes. However, the fact that measures of target attractiveness and guardianship did not significantly influence individuals' risks of stranger assault also suggests that the inability to disaggregate violent crimes is only, at best, a partial explanation for these observed differences.

A third explanation for these differences involves the possibility that violent offenses are more situationally specific than property crimes. As crimes that involve a direct confrontation between victims and offenders, the specific actions of potential victims in a particular setting is what determines the victim-offender encounter and the subsequent victimization by a violent crime. Of course, particular actions of potential victims will also determine the risks of property offending (e.g., did they lock the front door? leave lights on?). However, the victim of property crimes plays a far less direct and active personal role in his or her victimization. From the offender's perspective, the possibility of self-defense from personal victims also creates greater uncertainty about the likely success of a violent act than is true for most property offenses. Under these conditions, general measures of routine activities and lifestyles may be less able to capture the complexity and situational nature of violent offenses, thereby resulting in lower explanatory power for criminal opportunity theories of violent crime.

The major implication of these findings is that criminal opportunity theories are not generally applicable to all predatory crimes. These theories are better able to account for property crimes than for violent offenses. They are also unable to account for the risks of burglary for residents of less affluent and more socially disorganized areas, but do explain the risks of burglary among residents of more affluent neighborhoods. Thus, any statement about the general applicability of routine activity and lifestyle theories of victimization would not be empirically supported in this study.

IMPLICATIONS FOR A GENERAL THEORY OF CRIME

While general theories of criminality offer elegance and parsimony to our explanations of crime, the empirical results of our study do not readily support such a general perspective. Across various units of analysis, we find that many of the variables underlying theories of criminality and victimization have act-specific effects. Nonetheless, there is enough commonality in our results to suggest some virtue in a general theory of crime.

Support for a general theory is provided by the fact that most of the variables underlying traditional macro-level theories of criminality (i.e., racial heterogeneity, population mobility, and family disruption) are strongly correlated and have significant net effects on crime rates in a majority of the comparisons by aggregate unit and type of offense. For other variables identified in traditional theories of criminality (e.g., family income, unemployment) and measures of key concepts in opportunity theories of victimization, however, the results are not consistent across crime categories. Both aggregate rates and individuals' risks of property crimes (burglary and auto theft) and robbery are adequately explained by theories of victimization, however the results for other violent crimes (i.e., assault, rape, homicide) are less consistent with theoretical expectations.

Recently, Gottfredson and Hirschi (1990) developed a general theory of crime which emphasizes the lack of self-control as the fundamental cause. This work follows a long tradition of criminological research that seeks to identify general correlates of criminal behavior. While Gottredson and Hirschi (1990) claim that their theory applies to any "act of force or fraud done in self-interest," it is also true that previous theoretical formulations (e.g., anomie, social disorganization, differential association, social bond) are equally indicative of general theories that apply to various forms of criminal behavior. As described below, we think the results of this study have direct bearing on future efforts in developing general theories of crime.

A general theory of crime must recognize that criminal acts vary widely in terms of their social ecology and motivation. As shown in our analysis (see chapter 6), burglaries are equally likely during the daytime or nighttime, whereas physical assaults occur disproportionately at night. Murders and assaults frequently involve disputes among known offenders, whereas robberies and burglaries are usually considered economically motivated acts against strangers. Similarly, premeditation and the calculation of relative costs and benefits is widely assumed for some crimes (e.g., burglary, robbery), but other acts are considered spontaneous or impulsive (e.g., assaults, murders). While these differences, at first glance, seem to impede the development of general theory, there are basic similarities across these offenses that offer insights for a general theoretical integration.

The diversity in the ecology of crimes is easily understandable from the perspective of a general theoretical integration. From this perspective, two fundamental decisions underlie crime: (1) the decision to engage in criminal conduct (crime commission) and (2) the selection of a particular source or target of this action (target selection). Under these conditions, a person may be predisposed to crime for a variety of reasons (e.g., they are impoverished, suffer anomie, have weak bonds or low self-control, they are exposed to an excess of pro-crime definitions), but whether these motivations become translated into criminal action depends on the nature of the social context and the opportunity structure for crime (i.e., whether there are suitable targets for victimization who are attractive, accessible, and lack guardianship). Only when there is a union of offender motivation and attractive criminal opportunities in time and space will crime be a likely event.

Contrary to the implicit claims of separate theories of criminality and victimization, it is impossible to explain the social ecology of crime, or variation across crime categories, without recognition of both aspects of offender motivation and criminal opportunities. For example, theories of criminality explain high rates of violence at nighttime by identifying such causal factors as the effects of alcohol consumption on reducing social inhibitions and self-control. Yet, such an explanation is incomplete without noting that criminal opportunities for violence may also be greater at nighttime because there are fewer capable guardians (e.g., police, bystanders), and potential victims are engaged in more risky and vulnerable activities. Although practical opportunities for crime are rarely the topic of detailed scientific inquiry in most theories of criminality, these factors are, nonetheless, crucial in a general theory of crime to understand the conditions under which criminal motivations are translated into action. The union of offender motivation and the availability of criminal opportunities are essential ingredients for a general theory of crime that explains both its etiology and epidemiology.

It is important to note that there is nothing particularly novel about our call for the integration of theories of offender motivation and criminal opportunities. In fact, such an integration is, at least, implicit in several current theoretical perspectives. The routine activity approach developed by Cohen and Felson (1979), and the work of Cornish and Clarke (1986) on the "reasoning criminal," are clear instances of such theoretical integration. However, neither of these previous efforts develops this integration. By addressing the onset of criminal involvement and the selection of particular crime targets, the integration of these perspectives provides an essential compliment for understanding criminality and criminal events. We hope that future work would more directly recognize the mutual dependence of crime on the supply of motivated offenders and criminal opportunities.

IMPLICATIONS OF DATA
LIMITATIONS FOR TESTING THEORIES

Our conclusions about the predictive value of macro-level theories of criminality (e.g., social disorganization) and criminal opportunity theories of victimization are based on survey responses and census data. Such quantitative data are commonly used to evaluate theories of criminality and victimization. However, there are several fundamental problems with extant data from victim surveys and census reports which severely hampers our ability to make definitive statements about the utility of current theories. Several of these problems are described below.

An initial problem with current data involves the basic fact that crime is a rare phenomena, even in "high-crime" areas. This rarity of crime has direct implications for testing theories in several respects. For example, the relative infrequency of criminal acts makes observational studies in natural areas an impractical mode of inquiry. Under these conditions, retrospective survey methods, with their particular problems of recall and the selective misperception of actions and events, become the primary form of data collection by which to evaluate theories. Large sample sizes are also required to gain a sufficient number of victims of particular crimes for reliable multivariate analyses of the determinants of victimization risks. Even when a two-year recall period was used in the current study, for example, only 126 of 5,302 Seattle residents were found to be victims of a mugging or robbery. This distribution of victimization has forced other researchers to rely on large-scale national surveys (e.g., NCS data) that have larger sample sizes, but fewer adequate measures of key concepts.

A second general problem with current data involves inadequate measures of the major concepts underlying theories of criminality and victimization. Tests of social disorganization theory using U.S. census data, for example, have been limited, because such data do not include measures of the major intervening variables that explain how social disorganization influences crime rates (e.g., through the level of supervision of youth, voluntary associations, friendship networks, communal resources). Without incorporating the direct and mediational effects of these variables in models of crime rates, predictions from social disorganization theory are empirically indistinguishable from other traditional theories of criminality (e.g., anomie, differential association, social bond). If science advances through the falsification of alternative theories, future analyses based on available census data will not advance this goal.

Similar measurement problems exist in testing criminal opportunity theories of victimization. Specifically, when predicting individuals' risks of victimization, general routine activities and lifestyles (e.g., the frequency of nighttime activity last week) are used as predictor variables, rather than the particular actions at the time of the victimization. While this approach allows us to determine how well general lifestyle differences distinguish victims from non-victims, it does not provide the information necessary to assess whether persons were engaged in routine or non-routine activities when they were victimized. In fact, it may be that novelty has more to do with victimization risks than one's *routine* activities, if people are victimized by crimes when they are in a strange place at a strange time. Unfortunately, current data is not available to evaluate this hypothesis.

Another measurement problem involves the failure to include indicators of each theoretical concept and its various dimensions. Target attractiveness, for example, is commonly measured by family income, but targets for victimization are also attractive for other than economic reasons (e.g., they're accessible, physically vulnerable, easily portable). Measures of these other dimensions of target attractiveness, however, are not generally available in victimization data. Furthermore, if proximity, exposure, attractiveness, and guardianship are necessary conditions for predatory crime, the absence of measures of any of these concepts in secondary data is a type of specification error that has dramatic implications on substantive inferences. Under these conditions, it is impossible to disentangle and isolate the unique contribution of the major theoretical components, or to evaluate the overall predictive power of the general theoretical approach.

The implications of these measurement problems for testing theories of criminality and victimization are relatively straight-forward. Specifically, we will be unable to validate existing theories and eliminate others without greater attention given to the measurement of key concepts underlying these theories. We do not believe that existing census data or secondary data on victimization is of sufficient breadth or depth to be useful for theory testing. Future evaluations of theories of criminality and victimization must develop alternative data sources and additional primary data. Unfortunately, because collecting primary data is labor intensive and economically prohibitive in most cases, the collection of better data will not be realized without strong financial backing from federal and state funding agencies.

An alternative source of data on predatory crimes is criminal complaints and incident reports filed by police departments. Socio-demographic profiles of the participants and descriptive accounts of the criminal episode are contained in these documents. For purposes of contextual analysis, these data may be the single-best source because they provide information about each element of the social context (e.g., the physical setting, the interpersonal relationship, the behavioral domain). By using this data source, and having the police expand their descriptions of the events surrounding the criminal episode, victimization researchers may gain a greater understanding of the predisposing and precipitating factors in criminal events. The work of Luckenbill (1977) clearly illustrates the utility of police reports for understanding the episodal and situational nature of crime.

IMPLICATIONS FOR CRIME CONTROL POLICY

Over the last three decades, rising crime rates and growing levels of fear of victimization have led to a dramatic increase in public and private crime control activities. Traditional theories of criminality and criminal opportunity theories of victimization offer different solutions to the crime problem in contemporary American society. The implications of our results for crime control policy are summarized below.

Crime Control Policy Based on Offender Motivation

By identifying the social forces associated with crime rates, macro-level theories of criminality also identify the factors which require correction for purposes of crime control. Specifically, the causal significance of such factors as ethnic heterogeneity, population mobility, low socio-economic status, and family disruption lies in their adverse impact on the level of community supervision of youth, ties to conventional institutions of social control (i.e, family, schools), and the ability of communities to achieve communal goals. Any attempt at crime control, based on macro-level theories of criminality, must be directed at these conditions that enhance criminal motivation.

Various types of social welfare programs have been initiated over time to counteract criminogenic conditions in the community. Programs as diverse as the Chicago area projects, mobilization of youth, Head Start, and school busing share a common concern with improving the plight of lower-class residents. By enhancing educational and employment opportunities for the disadvantaged, these programs are designed to improve the conventional alternatives to criminal solutions for personal problems.

While these social welfare programs have provided some benefits to the socially disadvantaged, there is no conclusive evidence that they have been successful at reducing offender motivation and crime rates. Their lack of success in eradicating crime is understandable given the limited scope of most of these programs and the fact that realistic alternatives to crime have not been developed. In fact, no matter how attractive these conventional alternatives are, crime will remain a primary choice for many persons because it offers immediate benefits with little effort. Furthermore, many violent crimes are spontaneous, impulsive acts that arise out of a particular situational context. Under these conditions, crime control policy that is directed solely at the sources of offender motivation and ignores the supply of criminal opportunities would be quite limited in its capacity to reduce crime.

Crime Control Policy Based on Reducing Criminal Opportunities

In response to rising crime rates, a number of public programs and target-hardening initiatives have been undertaken to reduce the opportunity for criminal victimization. Regardless of the particular nature of these activities (e.g., private security alarms, extra locks, Neighborhood/Block Watch programs), all situational crime prevention strategies are designed to reduce opportunities for victimization and increase the risks of detection for those committing specific kinds of offenses (see, for review,

Clarke 1980, 1983; Rosenbaum 1987; Miethe 1991). Many of the citizen-based crime control efforts enhance the level of informal social control in the community, and thereby provide more surveillance and guardianship over other residents.

From a criminal opportunity perspective, the solution to crime is to reduce the opportunity for its occurrence. This can be accomplished in several ways: (1) by increasing the offender's risks of detection, (2) increasing the level of resistance against attack, (3) decreasing exposure to risky and vulnerable situations, and (4) reducing the attractiveness of potential crime targets. Changes in the micro-environment for crime (e.g., the physical design of buildings, increased lighting, redirecting foot traffic) would also decrease criminal opportunities, from this perspective. Our results on predicting individuals' risks of victimization suggest that basic changes in individuals' routine activities and lifestyles may have some utility for crime control. However, the burglary-reduction benefits of changes in routine activities that decrease criminal opportunities would be greatest in more affluent geographical areas.

While target-hardening and other types of opportunity-reduction strategies are widely endorsed, it is important to note that these programs may not reduce crime but simply displace it to more vulnerable locales and residents. This presumed "displacement" effect is a common criticism of social control actions and has received some empirical support (see, for review, Gabor 1990; Miethe 1991). Under criminal displacement, the efficacy of current crime prevention efforts is called into question since there would be no overall reduction in crime rates following the implementation of crime control actions. However, Barr and Pease (1990) have argued that displacement may have some desirable consequences, even if there is no overall reduction in crime. One of the positive consequences is that displacement may lead to a more uniform distribution of crime across socio-economic areas so that the burden of crime does not rest entirely with one segment of the community.

Aside from the possibility of displacement, crime control policies based on a criminal opportunity perspective may be met with mixed success for other reasons. Specifically, it is virtually impossible to eliminate criminal opportunities by changes in individuals' routine activities and lifestyles, or by modifying the physical design of geographical areas. Some offenders will make their own opportunities for illegal behavior, while others may be motivated to crime simply because of the challenge it provides. Furthermore, criminal opportunities grow out of the routine activities of everyday life, so any restrictions on criminal opportunities will come at a personal cost of reduced freedom and liberty in public life. Opportunities for crime will continue to exist because most individuals will be unwilling or unable to make the enormous personal sacrifice necessary to be totally crime-free. Thus, while opportunity-reduction programs are widely employed in contemporary American society, and have yielded some private crime control benefits (see Miethe 1991), our results indicate that they may only be effective in more affluent areas. The possibility of criminal displacement also raises questions about the collective or public benefits of these crime control actions.

As was true of our explanations for the social ecology of predatory crime, any effort at crime control must recognize the pivotal distinction between crime commission and target-selection. Crime control policy directed at reducing offender motivation is more difficult to initiate and maintain than citizen-based crime control actions directed at reducing the availability of attractive crime targets. Nonetheless, any successful program of crime prevention must address both elements of criminal motivation and target selection.

CRIMINAL PROPENSITIES AND THE SOCIAL CONTEXT

Of the three basic structural features of criminal acts (i.e., offenders, victims, and situations), offenders have received the most attention in criminological research. This preoccupation with offenders is understandable, in that they are the ones who initiate, persist, and ultimately desist in criminal activity. Whether compelled to behave criminally by factors outside of their control, or by the rational weighing of the relative utility of alternative courses of action, theories of criminality should occupy a central position in the understanding of crime and its control. However, the likelihood that criminal propensities will be translated into criminal action depends, to a great degree, on the particular characteristics of the situational context. Similarly, whether an attractive social context (i.e., a physical setting that provides cover, anonymity, and low guardianship) becomes the location of a criminal act depends on the differential proclivities of motivated offenders.

The interplay between criminal propensities and the social context of criminal events is clearly reflected in previous studies of personal robbery and residential burglary. For example, most robbers report both instrumental (e.g., the need for money, peer approval) and expressive (e.g., thrill-seeking, venting frustration) motivations for their criminal activity (see Conklin 1972; Feeney 1986; Walsh 1986; Gabor et al. 1987), but the importance of particular aspects of the social context in thwarting these intentions varies by the offender's crime history. Novice robbers and burglars (i.e., opportunists with little experience) seem to be especially deterred by target-hardening activity thought to increase the risks of detection and apprehension (see Winchester and Jackson 1982; Mayhew 1984; Feeney 1986; Walsh 1986; Wright and Logie 1988). Professionals and chronic offenders, in contrast, have already figured out ways to overcome the obstacles for committing crime (Walsh 1986). In fact, Petersilia et al. (1977) found that over one-half of their habitual offenders said that nothing would delay or deter their actions. Thus, aspects of the social context may be given more weight in the decision-making processes of different types of offenders.

The context-specific models of victimization risks observed in this study may be explained by these differential propensities toward offending in various geographical areas. For example, the largely null impact of victim characteristics on risks of residential burglary in more socially disorganized areas may result from the greater concentration of chronic and habitual offenders in these neighborhoods.[1] The low levels of community-based social control in these areas may also strengthen offenders' feelings of invincibility, thereby enabling them to select any target they so desire. In more affluent neighborhoods, with greater levels of informal social control, however, there may be a greater concentration of novice and opportunistic burglars who select only particularly "attractive" dwellings (i.e., those with more to steal and less protection). Of course, these explanations are highly speculative. Nonetheless, they do illustrate the crucial interplay between aspects of criminality and the social context for criminal events.

Finally, of the elements underlying an integrated theory of crime, the social context has received the least attention. We think this neglect has hampered our understanding of crime in several respects. First, the social context is where characteristics of potential offenders and victims converge in time and space to create criminal events. Any theory of predatory crime will be inadequate if it cannot account for its particular context—that is, why particular types of crime occur at particular places, particular times, and involve particular types of offenders and victims. Second, while predatory crimes vary widely in their situational clustering (see LaFree and Birkbeck 1991), some violent crimes (e.g., personal robbery) are remarkably similar in their physical and interpersonal attributes (e.g., they involve strangers, the use of weapons, occur at night, and in deserted public places). The prevalence of these common social and physical attributes of predatory offenses is directly relevant to ongoing efforts at crime control through environmental design and target-hardening strategies. Third, as reflected in our results for burglary victimization, the social context determines whether individual-level attributes increase, decrease, or have no impact on individuals' risks of victimization. Under these conditions, both criminological theory and public policy on crime control would be advanced by greater attention to the social context of criminal events.

CONCLUSIONS

The major conclusion from our analysis of crime rates and individuals' risks of victimization is that crime occurs in a particular social context. Any adequate theory of crime must account for the convergence in time and space of motivated offenders and potential crime targets. The value of theories of victimization is in their recognition of how the routine activities of everyday life create the supply of criminal opportunities, whereas traditional theories of criminality identify the factors that trigger offender motivation. The particular situational context is where the union of motivated offenders and criminal opportunities takes place. From an integrated perspective, crime control may be obtained either by eliminating the social conditions that foster criminal intentions, or by reducing the opportunity for its occurrence and the presence of "high risk" situations. We hope the results of the current study spark future research on crime causation that recognizes this fundamental interplay between offenders, victims, and the social context for predatory crime.

NOTES

CHAPTER 1 INTRODUCTION TO THE STUDY OF CRIME

1. We consider routine activity and lifestyle theories to be theories of victimization because they highlight how the actions of potential crime victims increase the likelihood and rate of criminal activity. While acknowledging the causal relevance of offender motivation, these theories clearly place primary importance on the characteristics of personal victims and other crime targets.

CHAPTER 2 THEORIES OF CRIMINALITY

1. The argument developed in Sykes and Matza (1957) is consistent with a number of theories of delinquency, including differential association (delinquents learn these neutralizations) and control theory (the neutralizations, by definition perhaps, remove restraints from delinquent behavior).

2. The reason that criminologists have so little to say to criminal justice practitioners and lawyers reflects the ideological differences in the philosophies that dominate these arenas. The scholarly pursuit of crime sought its legitimacy in the deterministic world of natural scientific methods and assumptions, while the legal system dealt with freely choosing actors (otherwise they were excused from criminal responsibility and punishment).

3. The theory of differential association is actually both a micro- and macro-level theory. The statement of the theory in the form of nine propositions spells out a process by which individuals come to commit crimes, while Sutherland talks about the larger context of the theory as

comprising normative or cultural conflict within communities characterized by differential social organization. See Matsueda (1988) for an excellent summary of the theory.

4. Control theorists complain that virtually all theories of crime and
delinquency use some notion of learning and that so-called "learning theories" do not "own" the variable (see Hirschi and Gottfredson 1980).
This is undoubtedly correct, since the idea of some element of socialization is as central to anomie (persons must first learn the normative and
value structures) and control theory (persons must be socialized to conventional society's restraints) as it is to the theory of differential association. But if this is so, one must surely wonder about the extent to which
learning theories, such as differential association, are different from
anomie and control explanations. Kornhauser's (1978) arguments about
the logical incompatibility of these different perspectives may not provide
the final say in the matter.

5. We are sensitive to the fact that, in recent writings, Hirschi (Gottfredson and Hirschi 1990) has suggested that "control theory" is a theory of individual differences based on the classical notion of hedonism.
The more modern term for this conception is "rational choice." Never-
theless, the ideas in the most popular statement of control theory (Hirschi
1969) are essentially structural, since they relate to structural constraints
on behavior, and are so interpreted here.

6. Rather, these are what Cohen (1955) would call "facts a theory
must explain." As such, they are closely related to theoretical elements but
their meaning must be interpreted within a theoretical perspective.

CHAPTER 4   AN INTEGRATED PERSPECTIVE

1. Lofland (1969) makes a similar point when he notes that deviant
acts are not possible without facilitating places, hardware, and others.

2. The major exception here involves measures of target attractiveness (e.g., family income, unemployment rates). Most theories of criminality assume a negative relationship between measures of economic status and crime rates, whereas opportunity theories assume a positive
relationship. The fact that these theories predict relationships with opposite algebraic signs allows for an independent appraisal of the predictive
validity of each theory. Unfortunately, the counteracting effects of economic status on the two decisions underlying crime (e.g., high income
reduces offender motivation but increases the attractiveness of persons as

crime targets) may ultimately result in the empirical observation of a null relationship between economic conditions and crime rates.

3. Because of the limitations of existing data, we are not able to test this particular theoretical model in its totality. We use the terminology of path analysis for definition purposes only.

4. For a small proportion of criminal offenses, it is possible that none of these conditions need to be present for the occurrence of crime. Some examples of this would be an accidental drive-by shooting in an affluent neighborhood, a mistake of fact that results in a criminal act, and criminal acts committed by persons who suffer from mental disease or defect. However, even for these types of offenses, there is some element of either offender motivation, victim characteristics, or the social context which tend to promote crime events. For example, in accidental drive-by shootings of innocent citizens, the suspect had some criminal motivation (why else would they discharge a weapon?). Similarly, insane people may be unable to formulate criminal intent, but the particular source of their victimization may nonetheless be someone who is the most accessible or in close proximity to them. Thus, while possible, it is difficult to think of any criminal event that does not contain at least one of these three "necessary" conditions for crime.

CHAPTER 5   DATA SOURCES FOR EVALUATING CRIMINOLOGICAL THEORIES

1. The census tracts in Seattle involve only those that had not changed their physical boundaries since 1960.

2. Actually, only six of the completed interviews are available to public users of the NCS data. The first interview is a bounding interview that establishes a reference point for subsequent interviews about victimization.

3. All residents lived on the same block on 54 percent (322/600) of the streets in the sample. One cross-street separated sample respondents on another 34 percent of the streets. We use the term "city block" to describe these units, even though a large minority of them cover more than one block.

4. "Wrong addresses" occurred when persons had recently changes addresses, but retained their same phone number. These respondents (n = 940) were excluded because the sampling design in the original study was

restricted to immediate neighbors on the 300 pairs of adjoining city blocks.

5. Possible aggregate units in the NCS data are "address segments" (i.e., groups of up to four housing units per wave) and census enumeration districts. Segments are generally too small for most contextual analysis, and enumeration districts are of varying sizes and have unknown physical boundaries in most cases. Confidentiality requirements of the U.S. Census Bureau preclude disclosure of the exact characteristics of each enumeration district. In the British Crime Surveys (see Sampson and Wooldredge 1987; Miethe and Meier 1990), possible aggregate units are wards and polling districts. These units are comparable to precincts in the United States and have an average size of about 4,000 residents. These units are similar to census tracts in that they are artificially constructed for political or administrative reasons. However, census tracts usually have a more uniform population size and seem to have boundaries more physically defined (by transportation arteries) than the aggregate units in the British Crime Surveys.

6. The only possible exception to this statement is that persons who live in cities or SMSAs with high rates of mobility, heterogeneity, low socio-economic conditions, *and* high rates of family disruption may be said to have greater proximity to pools of motivated offenders than residents of other areas. Under these conditions, our measures of the major correlates of criminality also serve as gross indicators of proximity to crime for aggregate-level analyses. Other than the obvious fact that the presence of criminogenic conditions in a community increases residents' contact with crime, however, we do not consider treating proximity as an aspect of criminality to be a very useful exercise.

7. However, for persons who have moved within the last two years, we used their current precautions on the grounds that they would otherwise be reporting behavior that occurred at a different dwelling and environment.

8. We impose this restriction because lifestyle and routine activity theories of victimization are unable to easily account for crimes involving non-strangers (see Miethe et al. 1987). The only prediction about "domestic" crimes that would be consistent with these theories is if increases in public activity over time lead to lower rates of crimes involving non-strangers and higher rates of crimes against strangers. We discuss the limited applicability of these theories for explaining violence among non-strangers more fully in the next chapter.

CHAPTER 6   THE EMPIRICAL DISTRIBUTION OF
CRIME AND VICTIMIZATION

1. Because these offenses do not usually involve a direct confrontation between the victim and offender, data on the victim-offender relationship is not routinely collected in cases of property crime (e.g., residential burglary, auto theft). However, it is reasonable to assume that a majority of these offenses are committed by strangers. Criminal opportunity theories would therefore be applicable to these offenses.

2. The only possible way that these results would be consistent with current theories of victimization is to argue that higher public activity creates a general anxiety which displaces crime to spouses and friends at home. However, this type of crime displacement seems unlikely and has not been examined in previous research.

3. Our explanation for this trend is that the level of within-unit variation increases so dramatically with higher levels of aggregation that it diminishes the magnitude of between-unit variation. This would suggest that theories of criminality may have the best predictive power in explaining crime rates in census tracts and cities.

4. The gender differences in robbery, across surveys, may be due to differences in the definition of these offenses in each survey. Specifically, purse snatching is considered "robbery" in the Seattle survey, but is considered a larceny-theft in the NCS data. This may explain why women in the Seattle survey have a higher risk of robbery victimization than men.

CHAPTER 7   PREDICTING CRIME RATES

1. Such general statements seem too obvious to require documentation but see Merton, 1968; Sutherland and Cressey, 1978; Hirschi, 1969; Kornhauser, 1978.

2. This was true for all crimes when the city and census tract are the aggregate units. However, the correlation between unemployment and crime rates was usually insignificant for analyses based on the SMSA.

3. The strong trend for higher female labor force activity to be associated with significant net decreases in crime rates in both the cross-sectional and longitudinal analyses is not consistent with criminal opportunity theories. One possible explanation for this finding is that greater participation by women in public work activity has a "humanizing" effect on public life that reduces crime rates.

CHAPTER 8   PREDICTING INDIVIDUALS' RISKS
OF VICTIMIZATION

1. The only exception is the frequency of being in dangerous public places, which is significantly associated with higher net risks of personal robbery.

CHAPTER 9   CRIME AND CONTEXT

1. As mentioned in chapter 3, a "main effect" in the statistical literature refers to a situation in which the impact of one variable on another is assumed to be constant across levels of another variable. It is contrasted with "interaction effects," in which the impact of a variable is assumed to depend on the level of another variable. Models of individuals' risks of victimization incorporating main effects and interactions will be presented shortly.

2. Given that we are concerned with assessing how aspects of the wider environment influence crime, our measures of victimization by stranger assault, stranger robbery, and auto theft are restricted to those acts which occurred within three blocks of the current home. Obviously, the characteristics of a resident's neighborhood would be irrelevant for explaining crimes that occurred elsewhere.

3. Contrary to what is sometimes done in multi-level analysis (see Boyd and Iversen 1979; Simcha-Fagan and Schwartz 1986), we did not adjust the values for all neighborhood-level variables to remove the impact of each individual's score from the group average. Our primary reason for not making this adjustment is that each resident provides information to would-be offenders about the potential attractiveness of the neighborhood as a site for crime. In other words, each individual household contributes to the overall assessment of the neighborhood and, therefore, the average ratings should reflect this fact. However, this procedure will result in a slight positive correlation between aggregate- and individual-level measures of each concept because the same persons are used in each case. With an average of eighteen observations per unit, the amount of inflation in this correlation is minimal.

4. The algebraic sign of the effects for population mobility and public activity, however, are in a direction contrary to expectations based on criminal opportunity theories.

5. There are not enough victims of mugging (n = 29) to do a con-

text-specific analysis for this crime. It is informative to note, however, that only about 21 percent of those who were mugged within three blocks of their present home lived in a "high income" area or in an area with "low" levels of public activity. Even though there are not enough victims of this crime for a reliable multivariate analysis, these findings nonetheless support the general view that conditions of the wider environment enable and constrain the expression of this type of predatory crime.

6. This was determined by examining the improvement in fit of the likelihood ratio chi-square when we added each of the two-way interactions between the contextual variable and the individual-level variables to the baseline model that incorporated only main effects.

CHAPTER 10   SUMMARY AND IMPLICATIONS

1. It is well known that crime occurs in close proximity to the offender's residence (see Brantingham and Brantingham 1984; Gottfredson and Hirschi 1990). We assume that persons who live in more socially disorganized areas would be more susceptible to the social forces (e.g., low education, low earning potential, frustration) conducive to chronic predatory offending.

BIBLIOGRAPHY

Agnew, Robert. 1992. "Foundation for a General Strain Theory of Crime and Delinquency." *Criminology*, 30(1): 47–87.

Akers, Ronald L. 1987. *Deviant Behavior: A Social Learning Approach.* 3rd Edition. Belmont, CA: Wadsworth Publishing Company.

————. 1989. "A Social Behaviorist's Perspective on Integration of Theories of Crime and Deviance." In *Theoretical Integration in the Study of Deviance and Crime: Problems and Prospects*, edited by Steven F. Messner, Marvin D. Krohn, and Allen E. Liska (pp. 23–36). Albany, N.Y.: State University of New York Press.

Amir, Menachem. 1967. "Victim-Precipitated Forcible Rape." *Journal of Criminal Law, Criminology, and Police Science* 58: 493–502.

————. 1971. *Patterns in Forcible Rape.* Chicago: University of Chicago Press.

Barr, Robert, and Ken Pease. 1990. "Crime Placement, Displacement, and Deflection." In *Crime and Justice: A Review of Research, Vol. 12*, edited by Michael Tonry and Norval Morris (pp. 277–318). Chicago: University of Chicago Press.

Becker, Howard S. 1963. *Outsiders: Studies in the Sociology of Deviance.* New York: The Free Press of Glencoe.

Bennett, Trevor. 1986. "A Decision-Making Approach to Opioid Addiction." In *The Reasoning Criminal: Rational Choice Perspectives on Offending*, edited by Derek B. Cornish and Ronald V. Clarke (pp. 83–102). New York: Springer-Verlag.

Bennett, Trevor, and Richard Wright. 1984. *Burglars on Burglary: Prevention and the Offender.* Hampshire, England: Bower.

Blalock, Hubert M. 1984. "Contextual-Effects Models: Theoretical and Methodological Issues." *Annual Review of Sociology* 10: 353–372.

Blau, Judith, and Peter Blau. 1982. "The Costs of Inequality: Metropolitan Structure and Violent Crime." *American Sociological Review* 47: 114–29.

Blumstein, Alfred, Jacqueline Cohen, Jeffrey A. Roth, and Christy Visher. 1986. *Criminal Careers and "Career Criminals."* Vols. 1 and 2. Washington, D.C.: National Academy Press.

Bonger, Willem. 1916. *Criminality and Economic Conditions.* Abridged Edition, 1969. Bloomington: Indiana University Press.

Boyd, L., and G. Iversen. 1979. *Contextual Analysis: Concepts and Statistical Techniques.* Belmont, CA: Wadsworth.

Brantingham, Paul, and Patricia Brantingham. 1984. *Patterns in Crime.* New York: MacMillian.

Bureau of Justice Statistics. 1987. *Violent Crime by Strangers and Non-Strangers.* Washington, D.C.: U.S. Department of Justice.

———. 1989. *Criminal Victimization in the United States.* Washington, D.C.: U.S. Department of Justice.

Bursik, Robert J., Jr. 1988. "Social Disorganization and Theories of Crime and Delinquency: Problems and Prospects." *Criminology* 26: 529–51.

Cantor, David. 1989. "Substantive Implications of Longitudinal Design Features: The National Crime Survey as a Case Study." In *Panel Surveys,* edited by D. Kasprzyk, G. Duncan, G. Kalton, and M. P. Signh (pp. 25–51). New York: Wiley.

Carroll, John, and Frances Weaver. 1986. "Shoplifters' Perceptions of Criminal Opportunities: A Process-Tracing Study." In *The Reasoning Criminal: Rational Choice Perspectives on Offending,* edited by Derek B. Cornish and Ronald V. Clarke (pp. 19–38). New York: Springer-Verlag.

Clarke, Ronald V. 1980. "Situational Crime Prevention: Theory and Practice." *British Journal of Criminology* 20: 136–147.

———. 1983. "Situational Crime Prevention: Its Theoretical Basis and Practical Scope." In *Crime and Justice: An Annual Review of Research, Vol. 4,* edited by Michael Tonry and Norval Morris (pp. 225–256). Chicago: University of Chicago Press.

Clarke, Ronald, Paul Ekblow, Mike Hough, and Pat Mayhew. 1985. "Elderly Victims of Crime and Exposure to Risk." *Howard Journal of Criminal Justice* 24: 1–9.

Cloward, Richard A., and Lloyd E. Ohlin. 1960. *Delinquency and Opportunity.* New York: Free Press.

Cohen, Albert K. 1955. *Delinquent Boys.* New York: Free Press.

Cohen, Lawrence E. 1981. "Modeling Crime Trends: A Criminal Opportunity Perspective." *Journal of Research in Crime and Delinquency* 17: 140–59.

Cohen, Lawrence E., and David Cantor. 1980. "The Determinants of Larceny: An Empirical and Theoretical Study." *Journal of Research in Crime and Delinquency* 17: 140–59.

————. 1981. "Residential Burglary in the United States: Life-style and Demographic Factors Associated with the Probability of Victimization." *Journal of Research in Crime and Delinquency* 18: 113–27.

Cohen, Lawrence E., and Marcus Felson. 1979. "Social Change and Crime Rate Trends: A Routine Activity Approach." *American Sociological Review* 44: 588–608.

Cohen, Lawrence E., Marcus Felson, and Kenneth C. Land. 1980. "Property Crime Rates in the United States: A Macrodynamic Analysis 1947–77 with Ex Ante Forecasts for the Mid-1980's." *American Journal of Sociology* 86: 90–118.

Cohen, Lawrence E., James R. Kluegel, and Kenneth C. Land. 1981. "Social Inequality and Predatory Criminal Victimization: An Exposition and Test of a Formal Theory." *American Sociology Review* 46: 505–24.

Cohen, Lawrence E., and Kenneth C. Land. 1987. "Sociological Positivism and the Explanation of Criminality." In *Positive Criminology,* edited by Michael Gottfredson and Travis Hirschi (pp. 43–55). Beverly Hills: Sage.

Conklin, John. 1972. *Robbery and the Criminal Justice System.* Philadelphia: J.B. Lippincott.

Cook, Phillip J. 1986. "The Demand and Supply of Criminal Opportunities." In *Crime and Justice: An Annual Review of Research, Vol. 7,* edited by Michael Tonry and Norval Morris (pp. 1–27). Chicago: University of Chicago Press.

Cornish, Derek B., and Ronald V. Clarke. 1986. *The Reasoning Criminal: Rational Choice Perspectives on Offending*. New York: Springer-Verlag.

———. 1987. "Understanding Crime Displacement: An Application of Rational Choice Theory." *Criminology*. 25: 933–943.

Curtis, Lynn. 1974. "Victim-Precipitation and Violent Crimes." *Social Problems* 21: 594–605.

Davidson, R. N. 1989. "Micro-Environments of Violence." In *The Geography of Crime*, edited by David J. Evans and David T. Herbert (pp. 59–85). New York: Routledge.

Dielman, Terry E. 1989. *Pooled Cross-Sectional and Time-Series Analysis*. Marcel Bekker.

Dubow, Fred. 1979. *Reactions to Crime: A Critical Review of the Literature*. Washington, D.C.: Government Printing Office.

Ellenberger, H. 1955. "Psychological Relationships Between the Criminal and his Victim." *Archives of Criminal Psychology* 2: 257–90.

Elliott, Delbert. 1985. "The Assumption That Theories Can Be Combined With Increased Explanatory Power." In *Theoretical Methods in Criminology*, edited by Robert F. Meier (pp. 123–149). Beverly Hills, CA.: Sage.

Farrell, Ronald A. 1989. "Cognitive Consistency in Deviance Causation: A Psychological Elaboration of an Integrated Systems Model." In *Theoretical Integration in the Study of Deviance and Crime: Problems and Prospects*, edited by Steven F. Messner, Marvin D. Krohn, and Allen E. Liska (pp. 77–92). Albany, N.Y.: State University of New York Press.

Federal Bureau of Investigation. 1988. *Crime in the United States-1988*. Washington, D.C.: U.S. Government Printing Office.

Feeney, Floyd. 1986. "Robbers as Decision-Makers." In *The Reasoning Criminal: Rational Choice Perspectives on Offending*, edited by Derek B. Cornish and Ronald V. Clarke (pp. 53–71). New York: Springer-Verlag.

Felson, Marcus, and Lawrence Cohen. 1980. "Human Ecology and Crime: A Routine Activity Approach." *Human Ecology* 8: 389–406.

Freud, Sigmund. 1930. *Civilization and Its Discontents*. New York: Cape and Smith.

Fuller, W. A., and G. E. Battese. 1974. "Estimation of Linear Models with Crossed-Error Structure." *Journal of Econometrics* 2: 67–78.

Gabor, Thomas. 1981. "The Crime Displacement Hypothesis: An Empirical Examination." *Crime and Delinquency* 26: 390–404.

———. 1990. "Crime Displacement and Situational Prevention: Toward the Development of Some Principles." *Canadian Journal of Criminology* January: 41–73.

Gabor, Thomas, Micheline Baril, Maurice Cusson, Daniel Elie, Marc Leblanc, and Andre Normandeau. 1987. *Armed Robbery: Cops, Robbers, and Victims*. Springfield, Ill.: Charles C. Thomas.

Garofalo, B. R. 1914. *Criminology*. Boston: Little, Brown.

Garofalo, James. 1987. "Reassessing the Lifestyle Model of Criminal Victimization." In *Positive Criminology*, edited by Michael Gottfredson and Travis Hirschi. Newbury Park, California: Sage.

Geis, Gilbert. 1974. "Avocational Crime." In Daniel Glaser (ed), *Handbook of Criminology*. Chicago: Rand McNally.

Gibbs, Jack P. 1985. "The Methodology of Theory Construction in Criminology." In *Theoretical Methods in Criminology*, edited by Robert F. Meier (pp. 23–50). Beverly Hills, CA.: Sage.

———. 1989. *Control: Sociology's Central Notion*. Urbana, Ill.: University of Illinois Press.

Glaser, Daniel. 1971. *Social Deviance*. Chicago: Markham.

Glueck, Sheldon, and Eleanor Glueck. 1950. *Unraveling Juvenile Delinquency*. Cambridge, Massachusetts: Harvard University Press.

Gottfredson, Michael R. 1981. "On the Etiology of Criminal Victimization." *Journal of Criminal Law and Criminology* 72: 714–26.

Gottfredson, Michael R., and Travis Hirschi. 1990. *A General Theory of Crime*. Stanford, CA: Stanford University Press.

Gove, Walter R., Michael Hughes, and Michael R. Geerken. 1985. "Are Uniform Crime Reports a Valid Indicator of the Index Crimes? An Affirmative Answer with Minor Qualifications." *Criminology* 23: 451–410.

Hannan, Michael T., and Alice A. Young. 1977. "Estimation in Panel Models: Results on Pooling Cross-Sections and Time Series." In *Sociological Methodology*, edited by David R. Heise (pp. 52–83). San Francisco, CA.: Jossey-Bass.

Hauser, Robert M. 1974. "Contextual Analysis Revisited." *Sociological Methods and Research* 2: 365–75.

Hawley, Amos. 1950. *Human Ecology: A Theory of Community Structure.* New York: Ronald Press.

Hindelang, Michael S., Michael Gottfredson, and James Garofalo. 1978. *Victims of Personal Crime.* Cambridge, Massachusetts: Ballinger.

Hirschi, Travis. 1969. *The Causes of Delinquency.* Berkeley: University of California Press.

———. 1986. "On the Compatibility of Rational Choice and Social Control Theories of Crime." In *The Reasoning Criminal: Rational Choice Perspectives on Offending,* edited by Derek B. Cornish and Ronald V. Clarke (pp. 105–118). New York: Springer-Verlag.

Hirschi, Travis, and Michael Gottfredson. 1980. *Understanding Crime: Current Theory and Research.* Beverly, Hills, CA.: Sage.

———. 1986. "The Distinction Between Crime and Criminality." In *Critique and Explanation: Essays in Honor of Gwynne Nettler,* edited by Timothy F. Hartnagel and Robert A. Silverman (pp. 55–69). New Brunswick, N.J.: Transaction Books.

Hough, Michael. 1987. "Offenders' Choice of Targets: Findings from Victim Surveys." *Journal of Quantitative Criminology* 3: 355–369.

Kennedy, Leslie, and David Forde. 1990. "Routine Activity and Crime: An Analysis of Victimization in Canada." *Criminology* 28: 137–151.

Kornhauser, Ruth. 1978. *Social Sources of Delinquency.* Chicago: University of Chicago Press.

LaFree, Gary D. 1989. *Rape and Criminal Justice: The Social Construction of Sexual Assault.* Belmont, CA.: Wadsworth.

LaFree, Gary D., and Christopher Birkbeck. 1991. "The Neglected Situation: A Cross-National Study of the Situational Characteristics of Crime." *Criminology* 29(1): 73–98.

Land, Kenneth C., Patricia L. McCall, and Lawrence E. Cohen. 1990. "Structural Covariates of Homicide Rates: Are There Any Invariances Across Time and Social Space?" *American Journal of Sociology* 95: 922–63.

Lavrakas, P. J., J. Normoyle, W. G. Skogan, E. J. Herz, G. Salem, and D.

A. Lewis. 1981. *Factors Related to Citizen Involvement in Personal, Household, and Neighborhood Anti-Crime Measures.* Washington, D.C.: Government Printing Office.

Lemert, Edwin. 1951. *Social Pathology.* New York: McGraw-Hill.

Lemert, Edwin. 1982. "Issues in the Study of Deviance." In *The Sociology of Deviance*, edited by M. Michael Rosenberg, Robert A. Stebbins, and Allan Turowetz (pp. 233–257). New York: St. Martin's.

Lewis, Dan A., and Greta Salem. 1981. "Community Crime Prevention: An Analysis of a Developing Strategy. *Crime and Delinquency* 27: 405–421.

Liska, Allen E. 1987. *Perspectives on Deviance*, 2nd Edition. Englewood Cliffs, N.J.: Prentice Hall.

———. 1990. "The Significance of Aggregate Dependent Variables and Contextual Independent Variables for Linking Macro and Micro Theories." *Social Psychology Quarterly* 53: 292–301.

Liu, Ben-Chien. 1976. *Quality of Life Indicators in U.S. Metropolitan Areas.* New York: Praeger.

Lofland, John. 1969. *Deviance and Identity.* Englewood Cliffs, N.J.: Prentice-Hall.

Luckenbill, David. 1977. "Criminal Homicide as a Situated Transaction. *Social Problems* 25: 176–186.

Lynch, James P. 1987. "Routine Activity and Victimization at Work." *Journal of Quantitative Criminology* 3: 283–300.

MacDonald, J. C. 1939. *Crime is a Business.* Palo Alto, CA: Stanford University Press.

Maguire, M. 1982. *Burglary in a Dwelling: The Offence, the Offender and the Victim.* London: Heinemann.

Massey, James L., Marvin D. Krohn, and Lisa M. Bonati. 1989. "Property Crime and the Routine Activities of Individuals." *Journal of Research in Crime and Delinquency* 26: 378–400.

Matsueda, Ross L. 1982. "Testing Control Theory and Differential Association: A Causal Modeling Approach." *American Sociological Review* 47: 489–504.

———. 1988. "The Current State of Differential Association Theory." *Crime and Delinquency* 34: 277–306.

Matza, David. 1964. *Delinquency and Drift*. New York: Wiley.

Maxfield, Michael G. 1987. "Household Composition, Routine Activity, and Victimization: A Comparative Analysis." *Journal of Quantitative Criminology* 3: 301–20.

Mayhew, Pat. 1984. "Target-Hardening: How much of an Answer?" Pp. 29–44 in *Coping with Burglary*, edited by Ronald Clarke and Time Hope. Boston: Kluwer-Nijhoff.

Mendelsohn, B. 1956. The Victimology. Cited in S. Schafer, *The Victim and His Criminal: A Study of Functional Responsibility*. New York: Random House.

Merton, Robert K. 1938. "Social Structure and Anomie." *American Sociological Review* 3: 672–682.

———. 1968. "Social Structure and Anomie." In *Social Theory and Social Structure*, edited by Robert Merton (pp. 131–194). New York: The Free Press.

Messner, Steven. F. 1988. "Merton's Social Structure and Anomie: The Road not Taken." *Deviant Behavior* 9: 33–53.

Messner, Steven F., and Judith R. Blau. 1987. "Routine Leisure Activities and Rates of Crime: A Macro-Level Analysis." *Social Forces* 65(4): 1035–1052.

Messner, Steven F., Marvin D. Krohn, and Allen E. Liska. 1989. *Theoretical Integration in the Study of Deviance and Crime: Problems and Prospects*. Albany: State University of New York Press.

Messner, Steven F., and Kenneth Tardiff. 1985. "The Social Ecology of Urban Homicide: An Application of the 'Routine Activities' Approach." *Criminology* 23: 241–67.

Miethe, Terance D. 1985. "The Myth or Reality of Victim Involvement in Crime: A Review and Comment on Victim-Precipitation Research." *Sociological Focus* 18(3): 209–220.

———. 1991. "Citizen-Based Crime Control Activity and Victimization Risks: An Examination of Displacement and Free-Rider Effects." *Criminology* 29(3): 419–431.

Miethe, Terance D., Michael Hughes, and David McDowall. 1991. "Social Change and Crime Rates: An Evaluation of Alternative Theoretical Approaches." *Social Forces* 70(1): 165–185.

Miethe, Terance D., and David McDowall. 1991. "Contextual Effects in Models of Criminal Victimization." Paper Presented at the Annual Meeting of the American Society of Criminology, San Francisco, CA: Nov. 20–23, 1991.

Miethe, Terance D., and Robert F. Meier. 1990. "Opportunity, Choice, and Criminal Victimization Rates: A Theory of a Theoretical Model." *Journal of Research in Crime and Delinquency* 27(3): 243–266.

Miethe, Terance D., Mark C. Stafford, and J. Scott Long. 1987. "Social Differentiation in Criminal Victimization: A Test of Routine Activities/Lifestyle Theory. *American Sociological Review* 52: 184–194.

Miethe, Terance D., Mark C. Stafford, and Douglas Sloane. 1990. "Lifestyle Changes and Risks of Criminal Victimization." *Journal of Quantitative Criminology* 6(4): 357–376.

Miller, Walter. 1958. "Lower-class Culture as a Generating Milieu of Gang Delinquency." *Journal of Social Issues* 14: 5–19.

Normandeau, Andre. 1968. *Trends and Patterns in Crimes of Robbery.* Ph.D. dissertation. Philadelphia: University of Pennsylvania.

Petersilia, Joan, Peter W. Greenwood, and Marvin Lavin. 1977. *Criminal Careers of Habitual Felons.* Santa Monica, CA.: Rand.

Quinney, Richard. 1980. *Class, State, and Crime.* 2nd Ed. New York: Longman.

Reppetto, Thomas A. 1974. *Residential Crime.* Cambridge, Massachusetts: Ballinger.

Robinson, John P. 1977. *How Americans Use Time: A Social Psychological Analysis of Everyday Behavior.* New York: Praeger.

Roncek, Dennis. 1981. "Dangerous Places." *Social Forces* 60: 74–96.

Roncek, Dennis, and Pamela A. Maier. 1991. "Bars, Blocks and Crimes Revisited: Linking the Theory of Routine Activities to the Empiricism of 'Hot Spots'." *Criminology* 29(4): 725–753.

Rosenbaum, Dennis P. 1987. "The Theory and Research Behind Neighborhood Watch: Is It a Sound Fear and Crime Reduction Strategy?" *Crime and Delinquency* 33: 103–134.

Rosenbaum, Dennis P. 1990. "Community Crime Prevention: A Review and Synthesis of the Literature." *Justice Quarterly* 5(3): 323–395.

Sampson, Robert J. 1986. "Crime in Cities: The Effects of Formal and Informal Social Control." In *Crime and Justice: A Review of Research, Vol. 8*, edited by Albert J. Reiss, Jr. and Michael Tonry (pp. 271–311). Chicago: University of Chicago Press.

Sampson, Robert J., and W. Bryon Groves. 1989. "Community Structure and Crime: Testing Social-Disorganization Theory." *American Journal of Sociology* 94: 774–802.

Sampson, Robert J., and Janet L. Lauritsen. 1990. "Deviant Lifestyles, Proximity to Crime, and the Offender-Victim Link in Personal Violence." *Journal of Research in Crime and Delinquency* 27(2): 110–139.

Sampson, Robert J., and John D. Wooldredge. 1987. "Linking the Micro- and Macro-Level Dimensions of Lifestyle-Routine Activity and Opportunity Models of Predatory Victimization." *Journal of Quantitative Criminology* 3: 371–93.

Scarr, Harry A. 1973. *Patterns of Burglary*. Washington, D.C.: Government Printing Office.

Schafer, S. 1968. *The Victim and His Criminal: A Study in Functional Responsibility. New York: Random House.*

Schuerman, Leo, and Solomon Kobrin. 1986. "Community Careers in Crime." In *Crime and Justice: A Review of Research, Vol. 8*, edited by Albert J. Reiss, Jr. and Michael Tonry (pp. 67–100). Chicago: University of Chicago Press.

Schultz, Leroy. 1968. "The Victim-Offender Relationship." *Crime and Delinquency* 14: 135–41.

Sellin, Thorsten. 1938. *Culture Conflict and Crime*. New York: Social Science Research Council.

Shaw, Clifford, and Henry McKay. 1942. *Juvenile Delinquency and Urban Areas*. Chicago: University of Chicago Press.

Sherman, Lawrence W., P. R. Gartin, and M. E. Buerger. 1989. "Hot Spots of Predatory Crime: Routine Activities and the Criminology of Place." *Criminology* 27(1): 24–55

Simcha-Fagan, Ora, and Joseph E. Schwartz. 1986. "Neighborhood and Delinquency: An Assessment of Contextual Effects." *Criminology* 24: 667–699.

Singer, Simon. 1981. "Homogeneous Victim-Offender Populations: A

Review and Some Research Implications." *Journal of Criminal Law and Criminology* 72(2): 779–788.

Skogan, Wesley G., and Michael G. Maxfield. 1981. *Coping with Crime: Individual and Neighborhood Reactions.* Beverly Hills, California: Sage.

Smith, Douglas A., and G. Roger Jarjoura. 1989. "Household Characteristics, Neighborhood Composition, and Victimization Risk." *Social Forces* 68: 621–640.

Sourcebook of Criminal Justice Statistics. 1985. Edited by Timothy J. Flanagan. U.S. Department of Justice, Bureau of Justice Statistics. Washington, D.C.: U.S. Government Printing Office.

Stahura, John M., and John J. Sloan III. 1988. "Urban Stratification of Places, Routine Activities, and Suburban Crime Rates." *Social Forces* 66: 1102–1118.

Stark, Rodney. 1987. "Deviant Places." *Criminology* 25: 893–908.

Stimson, James A. 1985. "Regression in Space and Time: A Statistical Essay." *American Journal of Political Science* 29: 914–47.

Sutherland, Edwin H. 1947. *Principles of Criminology.* 4th Edition. Philadelphia: Lippincott.

———. 1973. *On Analyzing Crime.* Chicago: University of Chicago Press.

Sutherland, Edwin H., and Donald R. Cressey. 1978. *Principles of Criminology.* 10th Edition. Philadelphia: Lippincott.

Sutherland, Edwin H., Donald R. Cressey, and David Luckenbill. 1992. *Principles of Criminology.* 11th Edition. Dix Hills, N.Y.: General Hall.

Sykes, Gresham, and David Matza. 1957. "Techniques of Neutralization: A Theory of Delinquency." *American Journal of Sociology* 22: 664–70.

Thrasher, Frederic M. 1927. *The Gang: A Study of 1313 Gangs.* Chicago: University of Chicago Press.

Thornberry, Terence P. 1989. "Reflections on the Advantages and Disadvantages of Theoretical Integration." In *Theoretical Integration in the Study of Deviance and Crime: Problems and Prospects,* edited by Steven F. Messner, Marvin D. Krohn, and Allen E. Liska (pp. 51–60). Albany, N.Y.: State University of New York Press.

Tittle, Charles R., and Robert F. Meier. 1990. "Specifying the SES/Delinquency Relationship." *Criminology* 28(2): 251–299.

Tittle, Charles R., and Robert F. Meier. 1991. "Specifying the SES/Delinquency Relationship by Social Characteristics of Contexts." *Journal of Research in Crime and Delinquency* 28: 430–455.

Tittle, Charles R., and Raymond Paternoster. 1988. "Geographic Mobility and Criminal Behavior." *Criminology* 25: 301–343.

Traub, Stuart H., and Craig Little. 1985. *Theories of Deviance*. Philadelphia: Peacock.

Tuma, Nancy Brandon, and Michael T. Hannan. 1984. *Social Dynamics: Models and Methods*. Academic Press.

van Dijk, Jan J. M., and Carl H. D. Steinmetz. 1984. "The Burden of Crime in Dutch Society, 1973–1979." In *Victimization and Fear of Crime: World Perspectives*, edited by Richard Block (pp. 29–43). Washington, D.C.: Government Printing Office.

Von Hentig, H. 1940. "Remarks on the Interaction of Perpetrator and Victim." *Journal of Criminal Law, Criminology, and Police Science* 31: 303–9.

———. 1948. *The Criminal and His Victim*. New Haven: Yale University Press.

Waller, Irvin, and Norman Okihiro. 1978. *Burglary: The Victim and the Public*. Toronto: University of Toronto Press.

Walsh, Dermot. 1980. *Break-in: Burglary from Private Houses*. London: Constable.

———. 1986. "Victim Selection Procedures Among Economic Criminals: The Rational Choice Perspective." In *The Reasoning Criminal: Rational Choice Perspectives on Offending*, edited by Derek Cornish and Ronald Clarke (pp. 39–52). New York: Springer-Verlag.

Warr, Mark. 1990. "Dangerous Situations: Social Context and Fear of Victimization." *Social Forces* 68(3): 891–907.

Wilson, James Q., and Richard Herrnstein. 1986. *Crime and Human Nature*. New York: Simon and Schuster.

Winchester, S., and H. Jackson. 1982. *Residential Burglary: The Limits of Prevention. Home Office Research Study No. 74*. London: Her Majesty's Stationery Office.

Wolfgang, Marvin. 1957. "Victim-Precipitated Criminal Homicide." *Journal of Criminal Law, Criminology, and Police Science* 48: 1–11.

———. 1958. *Patterns of Criminal Homicide*. Philadelphia: University of Pennsylvania Press.

Wright, Richard, and Robert H. Logie. 1988. "How Young House Burglars Choose Targets." *The Howard Journal* 27(2): 92–104.

Yin, Robert K. 1986. "Community Crime Prevention: A Synthesis of Eleven Evaluations." In *Community Crime Prevention: Does It Work?*, edited by Dennis Rosenbaum. Beverly Hills, CA: Sage.

AUTHOR INDEX

SUBJECT INDEX